Critical Issues in Software

Critical Issues in Software

A Guide to Software Economics,
Strategy, and Profitability

WERNER L. FRANK

A Wiley-Interscience Publication

JOHN WILEY & SONS
New York   Chichester   Brisbane   Toronto   Singapore

Library of Congress Cataloging in Publication Data:

Frank, Werner L.
   Critical issues in software.

   "A Wiley-Interscience publication."
   Bibliography: p.
   Includes index.
1.   Computer programming management.   I. Title.

QA76.6.F723   1983   001.64′25′068   82-15922
ISBN 0-471-87293-8

Printed in the United States of America
10 9 8 7 6 5 4 3 2 1

To Dori, Judith, and Daniel

Preface

Software has become the most critical issue of data processing for both suppliers and users. Because of the absence of a clear-cut discipline for developing software, as well as a methodology for evaluating it, frustrations are nurtured and a good number of myths have emerged. This book has been written to bring into focus these issues as well as to dispel misunderstandings. These reflections and positions result from twenty years of software experience and interactions with the clients and professional colleagues of Informatics General Corporation.

These writings were primarily motivated by my wife, Phoebe, who urged me to express on paper my many views and experiences. I owe gratitude to my talented secretary, Jeanne Laguzza, for her devoted and helpful editorial assistance.

WERNER L. FRANK

Calabasas, California
December 1982

Contents

Introduction: Common Perceptions About Software

Today's data processing world is still a world of hardware. While we all might agree that a computer is only as good as its software—and that a computer without software is useless—nevertheless, the focus of action and attention seems to be on the iron. This machine fixation can be observed in the attention accorded to new devices. Hardware performance, perhaps because it is easier to measure, is constantly reported upon in trade journals. How seldom, by contrast, are newly developed computer programs heralded for increased scope of application or improved efficiency of operation!

In the American Federation of Information Processing Societies' 1977 publication, "Information Processing in the United States: A Qualitative Summary," no mention of software is made in Chapter II, discussing industry suppliers. The price/performance ratio for computer hardware, value of the installed base, and value of new shipments are all portrayed to account for the industry's health, but there is no mention of software's impact.

Does a user ever seek software first and incidentally select the associated hardware? More often than not the hardware is selected while software becomes a secondary concern. Even the computer industry professional society, founded in 1947, is called the Association for Computing Machinery.

The general perception with respect to data processing today can be summed up in two statements:

Hardware advances continue, with more cost-effective components and systems constantly becoming available. These improvements are tangible and beneficial to the user.

Software remains on the critical path in developing and maintaining all information processing systems. Because software productivity and reliability are

1

intangible and are not quantifiable, software is perceived as out of control and viewed with apprehension.

These perceptions are founded upon some generalizations about software which continually reappear in the literature and cumulatively contribute to the general mystery about software. Examples of these statements are:

There exists worldwide more than $200 billion worth of developed software which is more than twice the value of the installed hardware base.

The software/hardware cost ratio has moved from 20/80 to 80/20 in the last 25 years.

There are around 500,000 programmer/analysts in the United States, approximately 40 percent of the data processing work force.

Only 15 percent of the total data processing labor is available for new application development.

Software maintenance occupies 60 percent of an installation's manpower efforts.

Personnel costs, often equated to software costs, are about 50 percent of an installation's total data processing expenditure.

Software purchased by the data processing installation is 5 percent of its total annual budget.

System software costs as a percent of hardware costs for new computer offerings are increasing by a factor of three over similar predecessor systems.

Software product sales are increasing at more than 30 percent per annum, representing the fastest growing segment of the computer services industry.

Software productivity improvement appears to be at a near standstill.

Average time to develop a new application is two years.

Average number of lines of code produced per unit of time is invariant for the different implementation languages.

The application programmer produces 10 to 15 debugged lines of program per day; the systems programmer generates about one third as much.

Individual programmer differences in rate of program statement generation and in end program efficiency can easily differ by an order of magnitude.

The use of structured programming techniques will double the productivity of the data processing effort.

The number of errors/defects in 1000 lines of code are on the order of 1 to 5 percent, depending upon use of structured techniques or conventional methods, respectively.

Only one-sixth of the total effort in developing an application should be devoted to programming; the balance of activity is involved in design and testing.

User's average backlog of number of pending applications awaiting development stands at more than 10 and would require over two years to accomplish with current staffs.

The invisible backlog of pending applications may well equal the size of the explicit backlog.

It is neither clear nor certain that all of the foregoing assertions are necessarily true. Many achieve credibility chiefly through constant repetition. In some cases it is difficult for an observer to reach conclusions about these statements because of the unavailability of the underlying facts. We even differ on definitions. For example, what do we mean by productivity? Is it code generation per unit time? Is it a performance measure based on some nominal standard? Or is it quality of code or quality of satisfying a user's needs?

Nevertheless, these perceptions (or even misperceptions) reflect the continued frustration experienced by users of data processing with the problems of developing, operating, and maintaining software. In spite of this frustration, there continues to be an underlying expectation that software should be more predictable, maintainable, operable, and certainly less expensive. In a world where continually decreasing prices of unit hardware accompany increasingly effective performance, why can't software cost effectiveness keep pace?

Software, indeed, has been the whipping boy of data processing. Software is blamed for project cost overruns as well as for schedule slippages. Software is perceived as treacherous because it sometimes produces results that do not conform to the end user's expectation. Added to this is the unpleasant fact that, because of the long lead time needed for developing an application, the program, by the time it is operational, may already be obsolete. Critics decry the seemingly low productivity in software development, even by practitioners with many years of experience, and are displeased that software needs so much tender care, an activity which we label "maintenance."

Since software is a human creation, it is as solid or as frail as those who are its authors. The creative relationship between software and the people who devise it makes software development more like a craft than a disciplined engineering task. Hence, opinions on any aspect of it may vary. Approaches to issues and their resolution are often widely divergent. In such an individualized climate, where can data processing management and end users turn for advice and for a balanced perspective on software? This book has been written to provide answers to this question.

Software is described and positioned from an economic and evolutionary point of view. Chapter 1 develops an understanding of the cost factors relating to software as well as the substantial economic benefits that can be derived. Chapter 2 concerns the life cycle process for developing, operating, and maintaining software.

In Chapter 3, software is described from a historical perspective, and its major components identified. Also described are major influences on software directions, including the impact of hardware advances and new environments (e.g., office automation).

Chapters 4 and 5 take up the economic issues of productivity as they relate to both construction and operation of software. The importance of managing the software process is described.

Next, in Chapter 6, the importance of software implementation systems is presented, with examples of application generators as well as more conventional systems. Chapter 7 presents in more detail the important implementation facility provided by the data management system.

The incredible impact of the microcomputer on all of data processing is treated specifically with respect to software in Chapter 8. Especially significant is the effect these small systems are having in schools and the professions as low-priced "personal" computers and/or electronic toys.

This discussion of software shifts in Chapter 9 to study the issues of acquiring software—either via in-house production or commercial purchase. Sources of software compendia are identified.

Chapter 10 discusses the commercial software industry and its economic impact on users and their needs. The economics of commercial software construction and its distribution are portrayed.

An editorial view of software is presented in Chapter 11 where various past, present and future endeavors are evaluated. Finally, in Chapter 12, the interactions of longer software life cycles and more cost-effective hardware lead to the exposition of the new software economics.

This introduction concludes with the observation that software is the result of an intellectual process. Its construction encompasses all the difficulties associated with controlling and predicting human understanding and behavior. Software is also an end product that can be measured and observed against preset requirements. This combination of attributes has led to problems in software productivity and responsiveness. In all its aspects, software presents problems in design, implementation, and operation. There are also problems in planning and managing the development process itself.

Software is a highly labor-intensive activity and, therefore, is an essentially 100 percent value-added activity. Possibly it is a unique commercial phenomenon. Sharing some economic characteristics with works of art, novels, movies, and music, software is set apart from them by its unique problems. Unlike these other creative endeavors, software, during its life cycle of repetitive utilization, exhibits a severe demand for maintenance and a continual need for enhancement. Nowhere in the marketplace does there seem to be another product with such characteristics. This suggests that software is a unique commercial phenomenon that must be better understood by those who create it and those who use it.

ONE

Software from
a Cost Perspective

In exploiting the capabilities of the computer, software is considered the major limitation. Combined with the rapidly declining cost of hardware, this leads observers to the false conclusion that software is costly.

To understand software from a cost perspective, it is first necessary to identify what is included under this item of expenditure. This we discuss in Section 1.1, while in Section 1.2 we review the differences between hardware and software cost components. Section 1.3 looks at the potential economic leverage that can be achieved in data processing as a result of the software contribution.

1.1. DEFINING SOFTWARE FROM A COST PERSPECTIVE

Data Processing (DP) professionals and users may well consider it unnecessary to define software. After all, is software not the program which provides the "intelligence" to make the computer do useful work?

To define software from a cost perspective will prove a little less elementary. For instance, is software that which is left over out of the total DP expenditure "pie" after the hardware, communications, and supply costs have been sliced away? Or again, is software the totality of DP personnel costs, plus the expenditure for purchased or leased computer programs? And finally, does not software also include that amount of the computer dollar reflecting the operating system component which the manufacturer typically bundles into the price of the hardware?

The definition of cost becomes even more difficult when one recognizes the extended reach of today's DP environment. The end user is often remotely coupled into the centralized computer operation and may, therefore, escape a census of software costs. Becoming even more elusive, the same end user may operate a local microcomputer with software acquired or developed outside the control of the centralized electronic data processing (EDP) department.

Defining software is useful and necessary—both for users and vendors. A definition will identify for users associated costs so that good business decisions can be made when software development and operations alternatives are being considered. The proper perspective on software will also reconcile accounting issues which face both user and developer.

The software effort includes the design and development of computer programs as well as their maintenance, but does not include cost expenditures associated with operations, such as data entry or production runs to achieve results for an end user. Therefore, end users' costs should typically not be included in assessing total software costs.

Unfortunately, the economics of software are most often observed from the perspective of hardware. This leads to some confusion. To eliminate this confusion and to clarify software costs as distinct from hardware costs, it is necessary to examine the hardware and software product cycle—the period from conception through service—which embodies the following phases:

specification
design
development
manufacturing
marketing, sales, and support
installation and training
maintenance

The order suggests the standard process for manufacturing and distributing almost anything. It certainly reflects the hardware vendor's scope of effort.

The steps also represent the software manufacturer's activities. Even software created on an in-house and customized basis follows this process. In the latter case, however, there is an interesting inversion with "marketing" usually coming first—that is to say, the particular software requirement is identified and "sold" to some user/sponsor at the outset and then the other phases are initiated.

Figure 1.1 compares the product cycle for vendor-provided hardware and software, assigning relative weights to each phase by setting cost levels as a percent of sales. The relative cost of the individual factors reflects the absorption in the ultimate product price of the amortized investment over an assumed production run. In keeping with our definition of software costs, the figure reflects only the developer's costs and not the user's conversion and ultimate operating expenditures.

In the case of hardware, no single cost element is deemed to be a "high" contributor. Design and development are spread over a large production run, as well as among a number of associated model families. Maintenance is

VENDOR HARDWARE/SOFTWARE
PRODUCT CYCLE RELATIVE COSTS

PHASES	HARDWARE	SOFTWARE
Design	Low	Medium
Development	Low	Medium
Manufacturing	Medium	None
Marketing	Medium	Very High
Implementation	Low	Low
Product Support	Medium	High

Figure 1.1. Hardware/software comparisons.

controlled either by the stability of the electronics or by simply charging a sufficient price to cover cost. The figure is representative of cost distribution for a typical hardware vendor, but not IBM. For IBM, manufacturing costs are believed to be relatively lower and product support costs relatively higher.

Software is quite different. The medium to high components of cost reflect the labor intensiveness of the process. In the software product cycle there is no element corresponding to what is called "manufacturing" in the hardware product cycle. This leads to a good bit of misunderstanding. For example, in a *Computerworld* article of January 16, 1978, a financial analyst asserted that "software is unique in that its incremental production cost is virtually zero. . . . Volume sales of software will provide even greater cost and flexibility advantages to suppliers than do volume sales of hardware." This statement ignored the unusually high cost of marketing and maintenance that overshadow the "incremental production cost" of software.

Development is most demanding of the proprietary software product supplier. The quality of product specification, reliability of code and detailed documentation is often more expensive by a factor of five or more compared with custom production for a single user. Marketing costs are significantly higher as a percent of revenue than is the case with hardware. The product support requirements for the user and the maintenance are also a somewhat higher percentage of revenue. These differences between hardware and software vendor economics have been misunderstood, and this is a major reason why the software vendor underprices goods and the user evaluates these prices from a hardware buyer's point of view.

Figure 1.2 summarizes the user's perceptions about hardware and software. Hardware is purchased as a commodity, whereas software is considered a specialty item. The impact of this psychology affects the sales cycle as well as the service demands placed on the vendor; it therefore affects the product's cost and its price to the user. It is much less difficult for a buyer to purchase a commodity than a specialty item since, typically, commodities are offered in a competitive marketplace where it is much easier to evaluate alternative offerings.

The purchaser of hardware often does not expect to receive a discount when buying multiple units; at the very most, a nominal reduction is available on a well-published sliding scale. On the other hand, users who buy

ITEM	HARDWARE	SOFTWARE
Product View	Commodity	Specialty
Multiple Sales	No Discount or Very Small	Expected Discount, Steep Drops
Maintenance	Accepted; 8% to 12% of Purchase Price	Not Universal; 5% to 10% of Purchase Price
Performance	Accepted As Is	Constant Request for Improvements
Upgrades	Clearly for Fee	Expected as Part of Product
Support	Limited; for Fee	Expected; Bundled
Life Cycle	Five to Seven Years	Almost 'Forever'
Design Details	Not Requested	Often Demanded

Figure 1.2.   Hardware/software perceptions.

multiple copies of software almost always expect to obtain them at substantially discounted values. The author is reminded of the early days of selling software products to the U.S. government.

In the late 1960s, the General Service Administration (GSA) energetically sought to persuade offerers of software products to give universal duplication and usage rights to all elements of the federal government after one copy was acquired. Fortunately, this effort did not succeed.

Maintenance is either built into the hardware lease price or sold separately, but each user understands that it is a necessary cost element when operating a computer. Annual fees for maintenance depend on the type of device being maintained. They can range from a low of 3 percent of list price for solid-state devices to a high of 20 percent of the product value for certain electromechanical equipment. Typically, however, for a mixed computer configuration, the hardware maintenance charge has been on the order of 8 percent per annum.

This generally accepted maintenance policy of the hardware vendor should be contrasted with that of the software product vendor. There is usually no obligation felt by the user to agree to software maintenance. Some users of software products feel they can get by without maintenance. Others, perhaps feeling that they have already paid for the software, resist the additional fee.

Nevertheless, software is a complex product needing constant attention and evolution, not only to correct defects in the product itself, but also to provide the changes necessary to keep up with evolving hardware and operating systems software. Maintenance fees charged by software product vendors typically have been in the 5 to 10 percent range and, at that level, appear to be inadequate to keep the product properly up to date and to supply the quality of enhancement expected. Users should remember that their own internal maintenance efforts for existing application software are substantial and, therefore, they should not expect to receive this type of service from the outside without being appropriately charged.

The performance of hardware is, for the most part, accepted "as is." Once a device is selected, users expect to incur incremental costs if they wish to improve capacity or features. With software, on the other hand, users somehow expect continuous improvement in performance and often feel that such a commitment was implicitly made at the time of purchase. While users are conditioned to expect limited, if any, support from hardware vendors once the equipment has been accepted and installed, the same users expect continuous and swift ongoing support from their software vendors. Now users even expect an around-the-clock, toll-free "hot line" to their software vendors if questions arise with respect to the purchased software.

At this time, hardware users recognize a five- to seven-year life cycle for their devices and establish appropriate amortization schedules based on tax considerations. Any useful life for the equipment beyond this depreciation period is looked upon as a bonus. On the other hand, users seem to expect software to live forever, especially in today's world of evolving compatible computers. In evaluating software prices, however, users think of its cost as though the software had a very short life.

Users do not expect to receive from a hardware vendor the logical design of the equipment, but they do expect to receive source code from their software product vendor. This is true even though that code is considered proprietary and can do very little for the user. In fact, it is counterproductive for a user to change commercial code, since changes invalidate some of the key economic benefits that led to software procurement in the first place. The user is urged, therefore, to use the software in its delivered form and limit customization to the setting of external parameters.

By contrasting these differences between hardware and software, we see that the general view of software is less enlightened than that of hardware. As a consequence, the software producer faces a difficult marketing and support climate. Cost and price structure are adversely affected, to the detriment of the vendor as well as the user. Economic issues identified in Figure 1.2 are the heart of the problem faced by the software product industry in its quest for recognition in the scheme of the overall DP user environment and in terms of its growth potential.

1.2. SOFTWARE VERSUS HARDWARE COSTS

The year to year improvement in hardware cost-effectiveness and the gradual reduction in unit price has led to a widely held belief that we are approaching a time when software costs will dominate the data processing scene. While hardware costs go down, software costs continually increase. This often leads to the conclusion that software costs are destined to become 80 to 90 percent of total DP expenditure. A vivid example of such forecasts was given in a June 30, 1980, article in *Computer Business News* quoting an industry analyst who predicted "an eventual 1000-to-one ratio of software costs to hardware costs." The graphics of this doom often appear in the trade press and are shown in Figure 1.3.

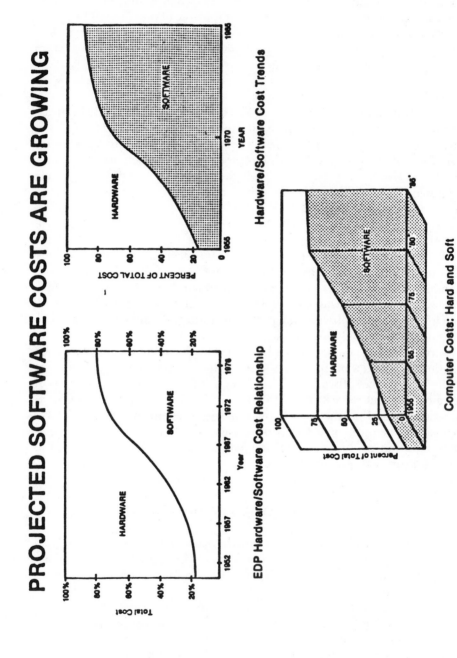

Figure 1.3.   Hardware/software cost relations.

10

Contradicting these predictions was another article asserting that a number of technological improvements, such as application languages, will stabilize the currently insatiable need for programmers and will lead to a tenfold improvement in productivity during the 1980s.

Presented with such conflicting points of view, how can we identify a reasonable expectation for software costs? What should we measure when counting the software and hardware expenditure dollar? The authoritative annual International Data Corp. (IDC 1981) budget analysis for U.S. DP installations provides one answer. A recent result of this annual study (Figure 1.4) gives a history and forecast of DP budget distribution for the period 1971–1981.

There is a remarkably steady state of staff and hardware costs as a percentage of total costs, even as the total expenditure increases significantly from year to year. This trend seems to be continuing.

Upon recognizing the influence of inflation during the decade, several conclusions can be reached from these data:

1. Level hardware expenditure, in a period when hardware cost-effectiveness was quadrupling, implies an enormous increase in number of installations, computing gear, and computing power.

2. Level people expenditure in a period of significant inflation implies a steady, if not decreasing, ratio of people to hardware.

But what are the pressures on hardware and software expenditures? Hardware costs are going down—that is to say, hardware unit costs are decreasing.

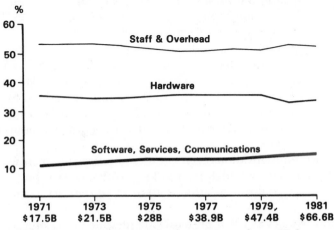

Figure 1.4.   EDP user budgets. (Data from IDC.)

As unit price drops, demand increases, as when visual display devices became available for less than $1000, and the demand for them jumped immensely. Similarly, as storage becomes cheaper, we can expect data-rich applications to become more brazen in their consumption of disk space.

Low-cost hardware, therefore, breeds two phenomena:

1. More hardware is purchased because the entry price makes it possible and economical.
2. Applications become more complex and resource-consuming.

Consequently, as these appetites are filled, the total hardware expenditure tends to stay level.

This brings us to software expenditures, which include internal personnel costs, outside labor and off-the-shelf software products. Three observations are made:

1. Budgets have a year-to-year inherent limit on expansion; organizations are prone to limit increases to the 10 to 20 percent range at the outside.
2. Because of the presence of inflationary wages, there is a limit to real growth in the range of 5 to 10 percent.
3. There is a limit on the availability of trained DP personnel.

The result is that DP staffs, at best, grow in pace with the growth of the business and sometimes even reduce proportionally. This natural limit on personnel growth, coupled with more demand on the staff for evolving more complex software, is somewhat lessened by more purchases of off-the-shelf commercial software and data services. In total, however, the software demand is not satisfied and, rather than increasing the spending for software, we are simply building up bigger backlogs and stretching out the delivery schedules. This phenomenon is graphically depicted in Figure 1.5 showing the increasing gap in available software, both from the expressed backlog and the "hidden" backlog of users. Today the hidden backlog seems to be equal to the identified backlog, a result reported in the Sloan School of Management, "User Managers' System Needs" (Alloway 1980). The slope of the curves of Figure 1.5 reflects a rather pessimistic outlook for the future. This is supported by the conclusions of the Sloan School report when it states that, "Users must recognize that DP cannot provide enough systems to meet all their needs."

There are some insidious second-order effects on the hardware/software expenditure equation which tend to keep both elements proportionally in balance as they continue to grow at 10 to 15 percent per annum:

1. More money is spent on hardware (despite decreasing unit costs) because more complex configurations are necessary to support the increasingly

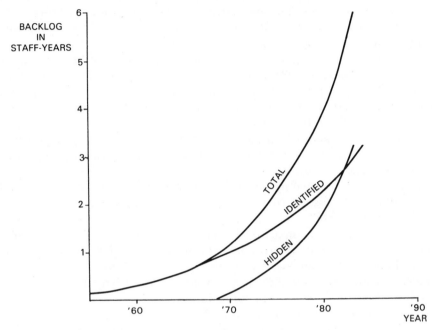

Figure 1.5. The true software gap.

complex requirements. The demand for remote processing gives rise to greater hardware needs in the form of terminals, multiplexers, concentrators, and communications lines.

2. Increasing complexity of operating systems results in an ever smaller fraction of machine resources being available for "useful" processing—requiring even more hardware capability per unit of application software operation.

3. More complex applications are being implemented, so that the software production task is more costly. Additional hardware supports software efforts as a productivity aid in on-line programming and in the form of minicomputers for more ready access.

4. More software (people) effort is devoted to ongoing maintenance because operational applications are increasing in number and complexity.

Measuring hardware and software cost has, however, been complicated in recent years by the trend to distributed and decentralized processing. The distribution of computing power and the assignment of technical staff to user organizations has relinquished some budget control and caused an exodus of people from the centralized DP organization. Because classical expenditure analysis for data processing has in the past been equated to the budget of the DP installations only, a change is now in order.

There would be a great deal of trouble if we were to measure the greater community of DP usage and associated costs. How does one perform the DP audit and what is included? Does one differentiate the developers and facility supporters from the operators of terminals and consumers of information?

One organization, Ingersoll-Rand, made such a study and published the results in the March 9, 1981, issue of *Information Systems News*. This study showed that the central DP expenditures for systems and processing were within the anticipated bounds of 1 to 2 percent of sales. The data communications costs add another 1 percent of sales. Further analysis disclosed that an additional cost of about 16 percent of sales was expended by the company's "knowledge workers" who perform both manual and automated information processing.

It stands to reason that if a broad definition of DP costs were to include all categories of cost associated with handling information then, indeed, it is likely that "software" costs will accelerate and dominate hardware costs.

At this point the comparison of hardware and software costs becomes meaningless. In fact, the ratio of hardware to software expenditures is hardly a useful quantity. What does become important in making any investment is the cost justification for the basic expenditure regardless of what is purchased. This can be seen in the following example.

An article in the *Harvard Business Review* (McFadden and Suver 1978) provided a scenario of a medium-size manufacturer moving from a conventional batch file processing environment to an upgraded data base management system (DBMS) operating in an on-line mode. Incremental hardware and software costs, over a five-year period, were judged to be:

Software		Hardware	
DBMS	$ 100,000	Central Processing	
Teleprocessing		Unit upgrade	$ 150,000
monitor	15,000	Memory expansion	125,000
Training	20,000	Storage devices	100,000
		Terminals	30,000
Total	$ 135,000	Total	$ 405,000

The indicated hardware increases include a step-up in the CPU itself, immediately doubling main memory to 512K bytes, the addition of several disk storage units and an associated controller, and the addition of six video terminals.

The model description was completed by recognizing a conversion cost of $115,000 and personnel additions to the current staff (i.e., DBMS administrators) at an annual cost of about $80,000. The article also estimated the five-year expected benefits to the total business as a result of this incremental expenditure and improvement in the DP activity.

The example provided an excellent microcosm of a financial decision resting with management. The total five-year additional cost in introducing

DBMS technology was put at more than $1 million, with an expected cumulative benefit value of over $2 million. The study concluded that the investment was worthwhile because it promised an attractive return on investment. The total additional investment breakdown was:

Software	12%
Hardware	38%
Operational support	50%

showing a three-to-one incremental expenditure of hardware to software.

Off-the-shelf software, of course, was purchased. Equivalent in-house development of a DBMS and teleprocessing monitor would have required two to three years and a cost of more than $1 million. Even if the organization had the investment capital and time to undertake such a project, it would not have had the manpower capacity or quality to staff such a highly technologically oriented activity.

Needless to say, in-house development of this nature, even if possible, would fail to yield a sufficient return on investment for the entity. A home-grown DBMS would not be a realizable option.

The model allows us to make these points:

Off-the-shelf software gives technological leverage to organizations, with leap-frogging increases in performance.

Purchased software, when applicable, is incredibly inexpensive compared to in-house development.

Software for sale has typically cost a fraction of the hardware necessary for its operation.

The article also observed that the economic benefit sought by the user was achieved by an incremental increase in the base hardware expenditure of 30 percent, with only an additional data base administrator added to the staff for a modest increase in head count of 4 percent. It was the software that prompted the investment decision, and it was the software that was expected to provide the major economic benefit. This leveraging aspect of software is further explored in Section 1.3.

1.3. ECONOMIC BENEFITS FROM SOFTWARE

The gloomy forecasts about cost growth of software relative to hardware suggest that hardware is the clear-cut winner in the cost-effectiveness race. This unfairly discounts the enormous economic leverage available from software. Let's explore a number of examples and situations that show how software can tremendously affect the economic balance with hardware. In so doing, we prepare the case for arguing that software is severely undervalued by the marketplace and its suppliers.

Consider the following example. A user evaluates the benefit of providing on-line programming support facilities to the DP staff. It is determined that 84 programmers can substantially enhance their productivity in sharing 21 on-line terminals by employing software products such as Applied Data Research, Inc.'s Roscoe and The Librarian.

The decision is made to proceed. The existing DP installation is augmented by the necessary hardware, including the terminals as well as communications controllers. The newly generated incremental costs per month are found to be $535 for software and $4908 for hardware—or almost a one-to-eight ratio in new obligation. In other words, to further exploit the computer, an expenditure of $1 in software required $8 more of hardware cost.

Consider now a different kind of example, evaluating in retrospect the benefits gained from extended usage of purchased software. The 10-year software purchase profiles of four typical large users of a single product are shown in Figure 1.6. The initial product value commitment is identified, together with subsequent purchases of optional features and educational services. The current maintenance charge, calculated as a function of the installed product value, ranges between 4 and 6 percent per annum. The cost of optional features is approximately two-thirds of the initial product value, and the education service is slightly more than 10 percent of the total expenditure. The user's average expenditure during the entire 10-year period is $60,000.

In all cases, the hardware expenditure level for these users was substantially greater than that of software. In fact, each of these users migrated through two CPU configurations during the decade, typically an IBM 360/30 or 40 to an IBM 370/145 or 158. The expenditure for software pales to insignificance beside the millions spent on hardware. It is a paradox that critical software commands a price that is but a fraction of the value of hardware.

One concludes from these cases the following:

1   *Software is very inexpensive relative to hardware.*
2   *Software creates a substantial hardware market.*

Percent Distribution

	USER A	USER B	USER C	USER D
BASE PRICE	50	51	76	49
OPTIONS	50	30	21	34
EDUCATION	0	19	3	17

Figure 1.6. Software product user spending profiles.

In this sense, software has an inherent leveraging capacity benefiting the hardware marketplace.

Consider the Informatics General Corporation software product SHRINK®, which automatically compresses data files for more economical recording of information on disk and tape storage devices. Compression can range from a conservative 50 percent to as high as 90 percent, depending on the specific file characteristics. For an initial product purchase commitment of $30,000, users have achieved typical savings of $5000 monthly in unneeded disk spindles or tapes. One user, with enormous files, displaced 40 spindles at an annual saving of more than $500,000, and a second user has achieved savings of more than $1 million per annum.

In other words, the cost of the software is paid back in a few months, with subsequent bottom-line benefit which staggers the return on investment calculations. Investment returns such as this are uncommon and suggest that the commercial software marketplace is due for a massive pricing correction. This brings into focus the third conclusion:

> *3 Commercial software is tremendously underpriced and can be a bargain.*

Benefits in this case do not stop here. In addition to disk storage savings, the user also has the potential for achieving better CPU utilization, faster throughput performance and lower cost in handling, management, and maintenance of the storage units themselves. In another reported case, such savings led to increased throughput performance of more than 35 percent for an annual decrease in resource consumption of $95,000.

This illustration is the inverse of the first example with respect to software's influence on hardware. Here, a little bit of software goes a long way in reducing the bill for hardware. This leads us to the fourth observation:

> *4 Software can substantially reduce hardware expenditures.*

There are, of course, a variety of commercially available software products that lead to more cost-effective use of a hardware system by:

Increasing the utilization of available hardware resources.
Reducing the need for memory and storage units.
Allowing more peripheral devices for given CPU power.
Performing more efficient processing; increasing throughput.

Any one or a combination of these can enhance performance, increase volume handled or delay acquiring additional hardware to meet current or expected loads. This leads to the fifth conclusion:

5   Software can substantially effect the more efficient use of hardware.

Good examples of software that fulfill these promises are performance monitors and tuning systems, improved sort packages, and better operating and administrative systems.

Let's now look at the inherent leveraging capability of software itself. Assume that a software product is purchased and used for a five-year period. Also assume that the purchase price is followed by a 15 percent annual maintenance charge. The total cost of this fully maintained software in a five-year period is therefore approximately 3.33 percent of the purchase price per month, or $1000 if the base product price is $30,000. This equates to less than one-fourth the total cost of a good programmer. But let's see how much further this product can be exploited.

First of all, the particular product can be used by many programmers. Also this software can be embedded in many applications. Unlike the hardware, software is comparable to the amoeba—it can split and be replicated over and over again with performance limited only by the available machine execution states. Thus, executing the same software in different partitions of a system bestows on the user considerable additional benefits for no additional cost. Software used in this way could have an effective cost which is only a small fraction of a DP professional's burdened compensation.

Software represents the world's greatest opportunity for cloning, leading us to the sixth principle:

6   Software is easily cloned and can be amortized over a substantial population of programmers and applications.

There is a seventh observation about the leveraging capacity of software. In a recent article, a user cited the purchase of a general ledger software package for $30,000. It was claimed that developing a similar system on an in-house basis would have cost this user at least $500,000. This better than 15-to-1 ratio of "make" over "buy" is impressive and so we observe:

7   Software can be manufactured and distributed as a product at substantial savings to the user.

This brings us to the eighth and final point on software leverageability. When compared with hardware, software has an exceedingly long life. A software investment can be amortized over a five- to ten-year period with no substantial risk—which is certainly not true for hardware as seen in the last decade.

Consider a typical user of a software product operating in dozens of installations. During a decade of utilization, this organization might spend about $500,000 for the use of the software, which would have consumed some 25 percent of ongoing computer resource capacity. The ratio of this software cost to its proportional use of the hardware cost during the decade has been less than 1:1000.

Further, based on the acknowledged manpower savings of 25 percent derived from this software, the user has gained a return on investment of 1000 percent in the 10-year period. Very few opportunities in business provide such a return with negligible risk. For example, two large users have asserted that for certain purchased software, the payback gained from manpower savings in software development alone is returned *each* month.

Software, as long as it is maintained and enhanced, will outlast the hardware. Indeed, this observation is confirmed by virtue of the many suppliers that have entered the market with IBM-compatible central processing units (CPUs), hoping to gain their foothold by exploiting existing IBM-oriented software. Semiconductor technology has now reached a point where it is cheaper to upgrade the existing hardware to a more cost-effective state to execute existing software rather than to reprogram an application to fit a new hardware logic. The conclusion is:

8 *Software has the potential for a long life cycle, so an investment can be thoroughly exploited with a large return.*

Software has been and will continue to be quite a bargain and can be utilized to achieve significant economic benefit in most DP operations. The overly modest pricing of software is totally out of proportion to its significance and its enormous leverage. These economics seem to dictate a market correction and it appears that software product prices must increase in order to reflect the appropriate business benefit provided.

Additional Readings

The material in this chapter can be further developed by referring to the following articles in the Bibliography at the end of the book: Bernstein, 1978; Boehm, 1973; Datamation, 1981; Datapro, 1976; Fisher, 1974; ICP, 1977; ICP, 1978; ICP, 1981; IDC, 1981a; McFadden and Suver, 1978; and Nyborg et al., 1977.

TWO

The Software
Life Cycle

The birth-to-death period of a computer program is known as the software life cycle. This period covers the initial conception stage, followed by the design and the development effort, and the ultimate operational phase. It is necessary to understand the component activities of this life cycle to cope with the challenge of software construction.

In the first of the four sections of this chapter, the life cycle elements are identified. Section 2.2 highlights critical factors that characterize the computer program, and Section 2.3 identifies critical factors of programmer productivity. From this vantage point, Section 2.4 orients the reader to the most difficult part of software, the ongoing maintenance.

2.1. THE LIFE CYCLE EXPLAINED

Software is a dynamic process that exists within the framework of a comprehensive life cycle. A definitive statement of this life cycle was given by B. Boehm in several publications (Boehm 1976a and 1981). This life cycle is illustrated in Figure 2.1 and consists of the following steps or activities:

System requirements
Software requirements
Preliminary design
Detailed design
Code and debug
Test and preoperation
Operation and maintenance

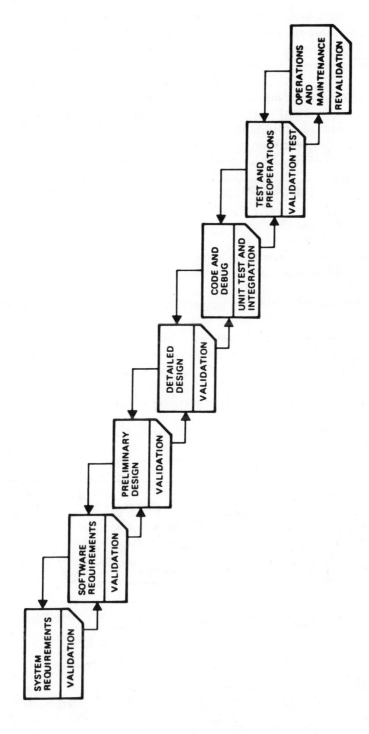

Figure 2.1. The software life cycle components. (From B. W. Boehm, "Software Engineering," IEEE Transaction, December 1976.)

Viewed in this broad sense, software becomes more than the computer program and more than the process of design and coding. Included are the additional activities listed above, as well as the ancillary but important tasks of documentation and training.

Cost and time are two important dimensions of the software life cycle. A software development effort can range from a few weeks to several years. The subsequent operational time frame can range from a one-time processing effort to a decade of utilization.

Figure 2.2 captures an important message (Zelkowitz 1978). The diagram clearly shows the impact of maintenance cost in the life cycle of software. Often, estimators of software cost forget this and concern themselves only with the left side of the "pie" chart of Figure 2.2 when making a software construction decision.

Maintenance represents the most misunderstood and underestimated aspect of software's entire life cycle. The maintenance of software includes two major activities—the removal of defects and the enhancement of operations.

Defects in the software are of two kinds:

1. Inconsistency with design or specifications which causes the program to do other than that which is desired by the user.
2. Errors in the program logic that cause the software to operate inconsistently with the written requirements or the intent of the programmer.

Enhancing the operational aspect of software has two objectives:

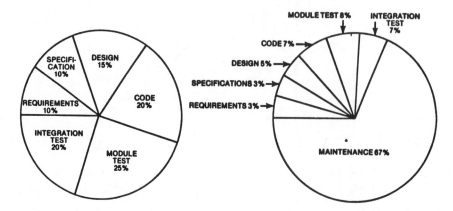

Figure 2.2. The software life cycle cost components. (From "Perspectives on Software Enginering," M. V. Zelkowitz, ACM Computing Surveys, June 1978.)

1. Changes must be made to keep pace with evolving hardware and operating system facilities.

2. Changes must be made to meet the evolving needs of the application itself.

While the industry does not now do so, the term *maintenance* should be restricted in scope. Rightfully, maintenance should refer to correcting and preserving the software's ability to operate in a selected hardware environment. Enhancements to the system should be identified separately and considered as new requirements for operating the system or the application.

Maintenance costs often surpass the original development effort by an impressive factor of three to five, assuming at least a five-year operating life for the software. The ratio of defect to enhancement may be in the neighborhood of one to four. It is not out of the ordinary for software developed in-house to grow in instruction size by 50 percent and have more than 50 percent of its original code replaced during the first three years of its operation! An insidious aspect of this problem is that in order to correct one line of code it is often necessary to generate five new lines of code. This process in itself causes the generation of new errors.

Another aspect of ongoing maintenance is the necessary experience factor. Maintenance is not one of the tasks relished by professionals; hence, there is a substantial turnover in this activity—an activity which is highly dependent on intimate knowledge of the system.

Personnel engaged in software are becoming increasingly more involved in maintaining it, as well as sustaining its environment. As an unpleasant consequence, less manpower is available for the development of new applications. Hence application backlogs are on the increase. Observers of the industry have reported that maintenance costs, as a percentage of the ongoing personnel budget, range from a low of 30 percent to as much as 60 percent. This is sufficiently large so that special attention given to its reduction could have real economic benefits.

The life cycle for software was once assumed to be rather short. It was, at most, identified with the life cycle of associated hardware, and that was perhaps six years. However, the software life cycle today transcends its target machine because of the growing impact of compatible computer families. In fact, target machines or their equivalent continue to operate long after they are depreciated.

As an example, software of the 1960s continues to operate in the 1980s. For instance, we can cite the life cycle history of the Informatics General Corporation, MARK IV® System. This software is still viable after more than a decade of service. This software has operated on the IBM 360 and 370 families of computers, and its capabilities are further extended today on the IBM series 30XX line of computers, as well as the IBM plug-compatible computers offered by many sources. A MARK IV source program written in 1968 can still operate today under its ninth and most recent release—and in a totally different hardware and operating system environment.

Users therefore have a variety of choices in extending their software's life cycle, including:

1. The emulation or simulation of old software on new computers.
2. The operation of existing software on used, cost-effective computers.
3. The preservation of existing software on life cycle kickers or compatible CPUs.

For the first time, this flexibility gives users a number of alternatives in preserving their investment in existing software or in making new commitments to off-the-shelf software.

2.2. IDENTIFYING CRITICAL FACTORS

To grasp problems associated with software, it is necessary to understand the nature and character of the computer program. There are empirical observations and findings that can help determine a strategy for improving the economics of software construction and operation. These items are critical factors of software structure.

First there is the issue of program size. Most problems occur with the larger software endeavors. In a study on program quality and programmer productivity, T. C. Jones of IBM (Jones 1978) cited the distribution of the world's population of programs and provided a breakdown of program size with respect to number of lines of source code, excluding comments. These results are shown in Figure 2.3. Note that 70 percent are essentially one-person tasks. These data, if generally true, suggest that major software problems really occur in only 4 percent of all programs that are developed.

PROGRAM POPULATION BY SIZE

NUMBER OF LINES OF CODE*	PROGRAM SIZE	PERCENT OF TOTAL PROGRAM POPULATION
Less Than 2K	Small	70
2K to 16K	Low-Medium	20
16K to 64K	Medium	6
64K to 512K	Large	3
Over 512K	Super Large	1

*Units of Assembly Code

Figure 2.3. Distribution of software by size. (Data from IBM Technical Report TR 02 764, January 1977.)

SOFTWARE ECONOMICS

Cumulative Percent of Program Population	A = Machine Operating Cost	B = Development Cost Plus 33% Maintenance	Ratio A/B
50%	$41,000	$7,992,000	.01
93%	$896,000	$14,823,000	.06
100%	$4,112,000	$15,894,000	.26

Figure 2.4. Software development versus operations cost. (Data from R. C. Kendall.)

Another issue concerns the life span and operating characteristics of a program. This subject was studied by Robert C. Kendall of IBM in his paper, "Management Perspectives in Programs, Programming and Productivity" (Kendall 1977). Kendall reviewed life cycle statistics for a population of 5328 application programs developed within several IBM organizations and found the average life span of a program to be about 16 months. Figure 2.4 summarizes some of his interesting findings. For example, the actual machine operating costs, over an assumed life cycle of 33 months, were unusually low in relation to the estimated development and maintenance costs. The data assumed that 33 percent of the staff provided maintenance for the resulting programs.

Figure 2.4 shows that the ratio of machine operating costs to development cost and maintenance was a surprisingly low 6 percent for up to 93 percent of the total number of programs in the population. The most time-consuming jobs, located at the upper end of the program count, showed a higher ratio, although the measure still remained low.

Kendall also concluded that 50 percent of all the programs in the study absorbed less than 2 percent of the machine's operating capacity devoted to that category of programming, and 2 percent of the programs occupy better than 50 percent of the machine's runtime for this latter category. The conclusion is that the cost of development and maintenance of many programs is substantially larger than their cost of operation. Based on these studies, ongoing software performance improvement, when it is an issue, can be relegated to a very small and identifiable set of applications. However, the author warned that the data reflect very specific studies at IBM. Users must, therefore, assess their own environments in order to establish conclusions relevant to each situation.

Perhaps the most useful data so far provided to aid in assessing programming expenses come from the previously cited landmark report of T. C. Jones. These results are shown in Figure 2.5. The author emphasized that those observations do not provide a panacea, but rather act as a roadmap to follow. Each data processing installation must analyze its own specific software environment.

PROGRAMMING EXPENSES BY PROGRAM SIZE
QUANTITY PER THOUSAND LINES OF CODE

Program Size In Lines Of Code*	Manpower Time (months)	CPU Hours	Number Expected Defects
Less Than 2K	.5 to 3	.2 to 2	0 to 25
2K to 16K	.8 to 5	.5 to 4	0 to 40
16K to 64K	1 to 8	1 to 10	.5 to 50
64K to 512K	2 to 16	5 to 100	2 to 70
Over 512K	4 to 28	10 to 200	4 to 100

**Measured in Assembler Language and operating on an IBM 370/155

Figure 2.5.   Cost of software development. (Data from
IBM Technical Report TR 02.764, January 1977).

The planning of software has not evolved very far from the experience in
the 1960s recorded by Frederick Brooks in his well known *The Mythical
Man-Month* (Brooks 1975). One of the fundamental problems stated therein
concerns the software development process. Experience continually shows
the sheer difficulty of estimating at the outset the size of a software project
and the schedule for its delivery. This problem is illustrated by statistics from
a software development estimating study reported by Datapro Research Corporation (Figure 2.6). Note the tremendous variance in estimating from one

ESTIMATED COSTS IN DOLLARS

PROGRAMMER	15 MINUTE QUICK ESTIMATE	ONE WEEK DETAILED RE-ESTIMATE	% Δ
A	180	74	− 59
B	80	89	11
C	130	155	19
D	150	129	− 14
E	90	122	36
F	60	90	50
G	125	101	− 19
H	61	80	31
AVERAGE	110	105	− 5

Figure 2.6.   Estimating software development cost (Source:
Datapro Research Corp.)

individual to another and for the same individual over a period of time. The ratio of project dollar cost varies by as much as 3:1 for the quick estimates, and 2:1 for the detailed estimates.

While the average for each of the "quick" and "detailed" estimates closely conforms, how much significance can be attached to this fact from one experiment? On the other hand, estimating by informed consensus may be the best one can do.

Part of the problem in estimating software development budgets relates to properly identifying the various stages of the project and breaking the problem down into small enough functional units. Lines-of-code production is one technique that is often used. This technique calls for sizing pieces of program modules that are in the range of 50 to 100 instructions. This approach may suffice for certain simple steps making up a software system, as for example, the number of lines of code required to do a typical edit of a character string.

More complex projects—those involving the interaction of many people—require detailed analysis in two directions:

1. Assessing the scope of the problems to be solved.
2. Providing enough time for integrating all of the pieces making up the whole.

Much has been learned over the last 20 years to aid in this task. For example, the architectural aspect of software construction is eased by:

Modularizing to the utmost all aspects of the program.

Separating data from program steps.

Developing table- or parameter-driven systems.

Utilizing standard software pieces developed and checked out in prior projects.

Relying on major support systems produced by other (e.g., data base management systems).

Certain technologies are emerging to help this process even further. These are the design and specification techniques advanced with such systems as the Program Design Language (PDL) of Caine, Farber & Gordon, Inc., (Caine and Gordon 1975); the Structural Analysis and Design Techniques of Softech, Inc. (Ross and Schoman 1977); and the Design Methodology of Jackson (Jackson 1975).

But no matter what the design and programming aids, or the organizational ingenuity in motivating and achieving goals, time generally cannot be traded for manpower, as Brooks so aptly argued in *The Mythical Man-Month*. As shown in Figure 2.7, there is an optimum point in project staffing

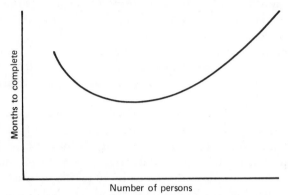

Figure 2.7. Tradeoff of time and manpower.
(Source: F. Brooks, "Mythical Man-Month.")

for software construction. Beyond that point, adding people only serves to create confusion, additional costs and further delays.

Furthermore, the development budget must recognize certain inescapable truisms whose impact increases nonlinearly as software projects grow in scope and time. One such fact is the cost of defect removal relative to the phase of the life cycle in which the defect is detected. Boehm's article (Boehm 1976a) on software engineering reflects experiences at IBM, TRW, and GTE. Shown in Figure 2.8 is the exponential increase in time (hence money) needed to find solutions to fix errors in software as the life cycle passes from the requirements to the operational phase. This empirical data indicates that we should go to great lengths to catch errors (in program or logic) as early as possible.

Boehm also reports that the ratio of design to coding errors is 3:2. This evidence further supports the observation that the more effort that goes into a front-end design, the better the payoff in total life cycle software performance.

J. H. Frame of IBM, in a talk entitled "Major Trends in Software Quality: 1978–1985," given at the December 1977 Conference on Software in Washington, D.C., stated that 50 percent of the total effort in software development is attributable to defect removal. He also said that correcting software errors is 38 times more expensive during the machine test phase than during the initial design effort. Even more dramatic is the cost of defect removal after software is operational—114 times the cost of early code correction.

Frame further reported achieving software productivity improvements at IBM by adopting modern programming techniques. Seventy-five to 80 percent of potential defects were found before testing began. The results of this improvement in initial software quality led to a 15 percent reduction in cost per line of code.

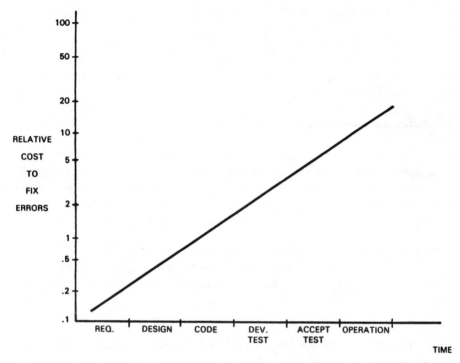

Figure 2.8. Cost of fixing errors during software life cycle. (From Boehm, IEEE Transactions, December 1976).

This 15 percent improvement is impressive when compared to the generally accepted 3 percent per annum increased productivity often cited (Dolotta et al. 1976) and the claims that software costs are continually rising. The question is, of course, whether continually improving quality can net an even greater cost reduction.

In summary, the situation regarding software's critical factors and the areas of potential pay-off for enhancing software production means are:

A. Faster Realization of Operational Codes

The faster one moves from a requirement or concept to an operational state, the fewer manpower and computer resources are expended. Although moving fast could be mistaken for "cutting corners," this is not the intent. Moving fast simply means that one uses the highest level of programming capability in the most specific application environment. In other words, trade computer operating efficiency and generality of scope for more gross operating performance and narrower but specific requirements. This concept is called by Kendall, "install it now, program it later."

B. Minimized Maintenance

Since the maintenance activity occupies a very large percentage of the total expenditure in support of software, it behooves users to identify very carefully the source of software defects (e.g., design!) to minimize defect impact on the maintenance task.

C. Software Selectivity

Clearly, not every computer program has equal value in a user environment, either from a performance or relevance point of view. It goes without saying that productivity increases should not necessarily be sought across the board for every software task, but rather on a highly selective basis as a function of the type of usage an organization might give to the software it owns.

Each of these three major productivity-related aspects deserves separate consideration. For any one organization, some combination of attention and remedy is appropriate in achieving higher-quality and better-operating software.

2.3. THE CRITICAL FACTORS OF PROGRAMMER PRODUCTIVITY

Everyone wants to help the programmer increase productivity, typically measured in rates for generating lines of code. By these terms the history of programmer productivity is bleak. While we have improved organizational and motivational techniques and procedures, we still seem unable to improve performance.

To produce a line of code today costs about the same in current dollars as it did some 25 years ago. At that time, however, applications were less sophisticated and the code generated was less complex. Today a problem requires the generation of many more lines of code than would have been necessary years ago. Hence the challenge and the roadblock.

In a May 5, 1980, article carried by *Information Systems News*, an IBM executive cited experience in programmer productivity improvements. The actual lines of code produced per person-year had increased over a 25-year period by a factor of about three, and the errors per 1000 lines of code had decreased by a factor of 10. Nevertheless, in the same time frame, the demand for total lines of code increased by about a decimal order of magnitude. While the productivity improvements in code production and reduction of errors were substantial, they were dwarfed by the total lines of code needed. As a result, even with a good improvement in productivity, the company still required a substantial increase in staff.

This point perhaps needs further explanation. It is almost impossible to compare programmer performance in developing an application from one time period to another. The payroll program requirements of 1960 are substantially different from those of payroll systems in the 1980s.

Some of the differentiators that now exist over the requirements of a few decades ago reflect the greater complexity of contemporary life as well as our increasing demands on computer system development and performance:

More encompassing functions and reports.

Need for integrated systems among a variety of tasks.

Demand for real-time information.

Rapid response for information needs.

Round-the-clock operations.

Larger data files.

Remote communications.

Availability of data security.

Fail-safe performance.

The literature is replete with statistics related to measuring lines-of-code production. Of specific interest is the data summarized by Raskin and Whitney in Table 2.1 (Raskin and Whitney 1981). The data reflects other research and reporting from Brooks *The Mythical Man-Month*; and an article in the February 1977 issue of *Datamation* by Johnson entitled "A Working Measure of Productivity."

Actually, the cost of a line of code varies as a function of:

Type of software—application versus system.

Size of program—small or large.

Ultimate use—personal versus public.

In Table 2.1, three levels of program complexity (batch, compiler, and operating system) are related to four levels of program usage. The first level of usage is limited to an author's own application. The second category generalizes the software and therefore requires reasonable documentation. The third level involves integrating the program into a system and, consequently, it must observe appropriate interface rules. Finally, the fourth type represents a commercial software product that must not only observe the requirements of the other three levels, but also be operable by independent parties.

The range of cost can be $1 to $100 for a fully debugged, documented line of code; $6 and $15 are often cited as the relevant costs for business applications and systems programming, respectively.

What has been the "real" programming productivity improvement over the first 30 years of the computer era?

An often quoted productivity improvement factor is the negligible 3 percent per annum reported in the SHARE-sponsored Silt Committee book,

Table 2.1.   Lines of Code per Hour of Production

	LEVEL OF COMPLEXITY		
PROGRAM LEVEL	BATCH PROGRAMS	COMPILERS	OPERATING SYSTEMS
One-purpose program	27	9	3
Generalized program	9	3	1
Integrated program	4.5	1.5	0.5
Commercial product	3	1	0.33

Data Processing in 1980–1985 (Dolotta et al. 1976). This, of course, is hardly a perceptible amount, contrasting sharply with the order of magnitude growth in hardware's cost effectiveness and the increasing size of the industry as is shown in Figure 2.9. Indeed, the authors of this book stated that "programmer productivity is (the) potential bottleneck to future growth of data processing."

Constant efforts are being made to improve the situation. Among the latest techniques in organizing programming projects are those employing aspects of structured programming, including top-down processes, walkthroughs, and chief programmers. Boehm cited some results in his "Structured Programming: Problems, Pitfalls and Payoffs" (Boehm 1976b). While no definitive conclusions were reached, it appears that it is possible to achieve up to a 50 percent improvement in the cost of developing and operating software when employing these techniques, mainly because the error rate is reduced.

In other studies, the use of on-line, time-sharing methods for coding and debugging are advertised as beneficial in increasing program production, again by factors which, on a composite basis, are of the order of 50 percent.

DATA PROCESSING INDUSTRY TRENDS (NORMALIZED TO 1955): OVERALL GROWTH, HARDWARE PERFORMANCE/COST, AND PROGRAMMER PRODUCTIVITY 1955-1985

INDICATOR	1955	1965	1975	1985
INDUSTRY GROWTH	1	20	80	320
PERFORMANCE/COST	1	10^2	10^4	10^6
PROGRAMER PRODUCTIVITY	1	2	2.7	3.6

Figure 2.9.   Data processing productivity factors. (Source: Dolotta, T. A., "Data Processing in 1980–1985: A Study of Potential Limitations to Progress.")

But we return to the comments of the authors of the study, *Data Processing in 1980–1985*, who warn:

> *Improvements in procedure-oriented languages such as PL/I, COBOL and FORTRAN do not have the potential for improving productivity by as much as a factor of two, while an improvement of at least one decimal order of magnitude is a necessity, and more would be desirable if we are to solve 1985 problems in 1985.*

Unfortunately, there is little hope for any significant software technology breakthroughs during the 1980s that will make the production of programs easier, faster or more economical. We know of no research and development today that holds such major promise. Rather, the existence of a wide spectrum of software firms producing standard implementation tools and application packages is about the only way to get a quantum jump in productivity. This alternative exploits the utilization of existing software over a wide base of users.

An appropriate strategy to increase productivity, therefore, is one which minimizes new internal development and applies these guidelines:

1. Use as much existing software as possible to reduce new development costs, leaving these latter expenses to be borne by commercial software producers who can spread costs over a wider base.
2. Never develop in-house system programs; use available general-purpose software products such as data base management systems.
3. If you must build your own application programs:
   a. Use modern implementation systems.
   b. Build a prototype, or "breadboard," system as fast as possible to get the application up and running with live data.
   c. Then sit back and think—is it what is really needed?
   d. Revise the prototype as required and put into use as fast as possible.
   e. If necessary, then refine the programs for production efficiency.

When all is said and done, however, the ultimate factor in software productivity is the capability of the individual software practitioner. Even in the presence of better techniques and aids, productivity in the software process is heavily dependent on individual performance. In "The High Cost of Software" (Boehm 1973), Boehm cited two sources who reported individual performance differences of 26:1 and 10:1 in producing software. The most important factors in productivity as reported are not the programming languages and organizational techniques, but the individual's innate talent. Assembling a super team of software producers can thus be considered the sine qua non in tackling these issues. Unfortunately, this is usually not a viable alternative.

2.4. THE CRITICAL FACTORS OF SOFTWARE MAINTENANCE

Software maintenance, as noted in Section 2.1, is the most significant factor in the software life cycle. We have already observed that the maintenance portion of the software life cycle can consume more than three to five times the effort initially expended for the basic implementation itself. Further, up to 60 percent of the ongoing efforts in programming departments are occupied with modifying previously written software.

The intensity of this effort can also be noted by the following observations:

1. Programs grow over time, doubling or even tripling in lines of code over the life cycle, from the initial development size.

2. Individual instructions are replaced rapidly so that the half-life of a written piece of code is only a few years.

3. Program maintenance is expensive because practitioners have limited tools and incentives to do a cost-effective job.

4. Employment turnover among maintenance personnel is exceptionally high.

Maintenance is the iceberg that is bound to scuttle budgeteers who fail to incorporate sufficient resources into their tables of organization as new applications make their appearances. That is to say, for every programmer who develops new software, the organization must anticipate adding two-thirds of a maintenance person to the staff annually just to stay in place, if the software has a life cycle of eight years.

There is, therefore, a substantial economic motivation for containment of the maintenance monstrosity. Suggestions come from four directions:

1. Do a better initial design job to eliminate, or at least minimize, the ultimate defect-removal process during systems operation.

2. Do a better programming and documentation job through structured methods; perform careful checks in order to minimize operational bugs and to facilitate their fix.

3. Use programming development tools and aids which simplify the statement of problems and, to the extent possible, employ previously generated, checked-out code.

4. Use packaged software that is centrally maintained by a qualified vendor for many users.

We do ourselves a disservice in treating software maintenance as necessarily bad and avoidable. We are too prone to associate the word maintenance with "repair" and connect this function with the use of the term in a hardware context.

Hardware maintenance is generally expected and accepted because all machines wear out over time. On the other hand, we tend to feel defensive about weaknesses in software, since they may imply inadequacy on the part of the individual creator—who should be in control of the situation.

But hardware and software maintenance is different! As illustrated by Fred Braddock (Braddock 1980), the objective in coping with hardware maintenance is to achieve consistency of its operability. In software, what we call maintenance is, for the most part, a concern with chasing change.

In other words, in hardware maintenance we wish to insure efficient machine performance by avoiding breakdowns and causes of errors. We are therefore even willing to shut down operations when necessary and to pay for preventive maintenance.

Software maintenance is concerned with "repair," that is, correcting defects in logic design or error in the code, but for the most part, the effort is expended in adding capacity or capability to existing functions. Because we live with change, there is a certain inevitability about software maintenance. Over time software must adapt to changes in user needs and in the operating environment. That is why it is *soft*ware and not *hard*ware to begin with.

If we cannot eliminate software maintenance, how do we cope with it? First of all, we should recognize it for what it is, then organize and handle it. There is a subtle and important difference between the process of correction or repair, which is one part of maintenance, and the other part, which is both the production of enhancements and the reconciliation of older features to new environments. Understanding the maintenance process begins with better accounting records reflecting these differences.

Initial budgeting and subsequent cost feedback of expenditure in maintenance to the user will soon get the message across as to where the real problems lie. If too much is expended in repair, then remedial action can be taken with the analysts and programming staff as it relates to the implementation process. If a large effort is ultimately identified regarding basic redesign of the application, then the user must accept responsibility for having misunderstood or misstated the problem in the first place.

On the other hand, if the bulk of the effort is in response to change, then the user will better appreciate the nature of software as distinct from hardware. Such changes, functional or environmental, should be at the discretion of the source of financial support of the application. The change should be entertained only if there is a cost benefit to be achieved.

But maintenance is not only a reactionary process. Also, there are aggressive steps that can be taken to further the performance and stability of a system by:

1. Streamlining ongoing procedures to avoid operator errors.
2. Adding more safeguards in security as well as data validation.
3. Enhancing machine performance via software tuning.
4. Checking for system and processing integrity of the data as well as the application logic.

In this broader context, maintenance really becomes a specific and continuing software life cycle function which must be anticipated and funded.
This ultimate requirement must be imposed during the initial system design
so that the following will be accommodated:

1. The application will be specified to operate for varying performance
    parameters relating to numbers of users, size of buffers and tables,
    number of transactions, and size of files.
2. The application logic will be modular and data independent, parame-
    terized as much as possible.
3. The application will have standard interfaces to systems software and
    will have defined entry and exit points.

In placing these limits and restrictions, software is generalized so it can
operate with broader scope and in varying circumstances. By giving up very
specific and custom-built requirements in software, the problem of subsequent maintenance is minimized.

Additional Readings

The material in this chapter can be further developed by referring to the
following articles in the Bibliography at the end of the book: Boehm, 1973;
Boehm, 1976a; Boehm, 1976b; Boehm, 1981; Braddock, 1980; Brooks, 1975;
Caine and Gordon, 1975; Chen, 1978; Christensen et al., 1981; Clapp, 1981;
Cornym, 1977; De Roze and Nyman, 1978; Dolotta et al., 1976; EDP Analyzer, 1981e; Jackson, 1975; Jones, 1978, 1981; Kendall, 1977; Lientz and Swanson, 1981; Putnam, 1978; Raskin and Whitney, 1981; Ross and Schoman,
1977; Snyders, 1979; and Zelkowitz, 1978.

THREE

The Development
of the Software
Environment

The architecture and functionality of software has been heavily influenced over the years both by hardware economics and by application needs. Another factor that has affected software is the advance made in its design and construction. All of these elements make up the software environment.

Section 3.1 begins the discussion of software environment by tracing continuing levels of abstraction that have pulled system software apart into major functional modules. These modules have been generalized, creating significant pieces of software within which new applications can be implemented more easily. The latest important such module is the emerging transaction processor discussed in Section 3.2. These introductions to operating systems modules are followed in Section 3.3 by an explanation of the terminology used to describe the environment.

The ongoing improvement in hardware cost-effectiveness has also determined software directions. Section 3.4 analyzes the changing relative economic balance between manpower and machine costs. This leads to a discussion in Section 3.5 of the significant impact of microcomputers on software issues and design. In Section 3.6, the newly emerging influence of office automation and the associated word processing activity are reviewed for their impact on software.

The chapter ends with a discussion in Section 3.7 of the potential changes on software due to the proliferation of semiconductor technology and the emergence of "firmware."

3.1. THE SOFTWARE ENVIRONMENT'S THIRTY-YEAR EVOLUTION

In the early 1950s there was no software environment in the sense of today's operating systems. After switch-on, machines stood bare of information content and instructions. In fact, at start-up, the computer memory registered a random pattern of zeros and ones (the bit values).

But presto, in response to a button push or switch setting, the automatic bootstrap was loaded into the first few positions of memory and the system was go.

Next came the external response. This typically involved input processing by the "booter" of a sequence of characters. This data augmented the very primitive, hardware-based (the first version of hardwired software?) bootstrap itself. The process was repeated several times and, as soon as the memory-based code was suitably extended, the system was prepared to read in the prepared object code of a specific application run. That was environment!

Input to the computer was more often than not via punched paper tape, although punched cards came very quickly thereafter. The specific run program had to be preceded by a specially spliced header, if the medium was tape, or, when employing cards, preloaded with a fixed set of binary-punched cards. This header, which extended the bootstrap, was the first instance of the more complex world of the Job Control Language (JCL) of today.

The run program also had to be manually combined with support software such as the core dump routine, the trace program, the elementary function subroutines, or the input/output utilities. Each user, therefore, generally defined and produced a software operating environment for each run on an ad hoc basis. Machines in the early 1950s were word-oriented (36 to 40 bits) and had at most 1024 words. Hence, users were very conservative in their development of such an environment.

In the beginning the coding itself was machine language, often expressed in hexadecimal notation. But then came the assembler which gave the first assistance to the programming implementation process. These early assemblers, being one-pass, had very strict constraints, requiring code assignment to specific memory locations and the requirement for specifying certain parameters and values in a regimented order. That was how it was in 1954.

Assemblers became more complex, multipass vehicles absorbing more of the bookkeeping tasks and, therefore, freeing the implementor of certain notational chores. They also could include, on call, certain standard subroutines.

By 1957, the assembler was extended and became known as a compiler—mainly because it now had sufficient capability to do more than convert one source statement to one object code line. The system could fully manage its operation via a number of reporting documents, mapping out the code and providing glossaries, as well as automatically generating a good amount of object code from much less source code. These capabilities led to the adoption of the term "automatic programming," although very little was really automatic.

The compiler was extended by the input/out control system (IOCS) which was the first significant step in softening up the difficulty in using the fixed hardware. Through the IOCS the programmer received assistance in communicating between the program and the peripheral world surrounding the central processing unit (CPU). The interface between the input and output calls from the program to the IOCS became the most important function of the embryonic operating system.

Thus, in the late 1950s, the application programmer had available a general compiler (or sometimes a special higher order language), the I/O control function, and the beginning of the operating system.

CPU memory had now grown to more substantial proportions. The typical UNIVAC 1103 had 1024 words of 36 bits each and what amounted to the first virtual memory, being able to extend its kilobyte of internal memory by automatically addressing 16K words on a magnetic drum. The IBM 1400 series was subsequently introduced and provided up to 16 kilobytes of character positions of memory. The resident software environment supporting the application program in the early sixties occupied a few thousand bytes of the typical-sized memory.

The next wave of innovation took three paths. First, the operating system took on more responsibility and became more complex. Secondly, the I/O system was expanded to incorporate an ever-increasing number of access methods to the stored data, as well as more I/O handlers to a variety of peripheral devices and makes.

The third contribution represented a new direction. This was the teleprocessing monitor (TP) which absorbed a number of I/O functions and operating system responsibilities. The TP monitor entered the scene in the mid-1960s in answer to the beginning incorporation of computers in communication environments.

At that point the application software implementor was obligated to provide the processing logic and the data file structure and organization. The other needs could be filled by the three environmental components of the day: the Operating System, the I/O Control, and the TP Monitor. This software complex had now grown to require tens of thousands of bytes while the total CPU memory increased from sizes as small as 4 kilobytes (kb) to 512 kb or even 1 megabyte. The more sophisticated environments actually began using more than 100 kb of memory.

The time was ripe to lay the groundwork for the next stage, which ultimately provided a quantum jump in enhancing the software development process and enriching the implementor's environment. The end of this process was the emergence of the data base management system (DBMS) in the early 1970s. But these systems were preceded by the file management system of the late 1960s.

File management systems never became part of the operating environment. They typically became application program instances themselves. A good example was RPG, representing the nonprocedural language approach to implementing applications, standing in parallel and as an alternative to the evolving variety of procedural languages which were also proliferating in the 1960s.

The DBMS era began in the early 1970s and continued through the decade. The application program was now surrounded on four sides—by the operating system, the I/O handlers, the TP control, and the popular DBMS. It would appear that the application implementor was at a zenith, given the ultimate support at the cost of an extended software environment. Typically, this environment required hundreds of thousands of bytes of committed CPU memory and some additional hardware resources to make all the pieces work together.

That's where technology has led us as we begin the 1980s, where a software environment of one million bytes is no longer unusual. Another amoebalike splitting of functions has taken place with the separation of further capability from the operating system utilities and the DBMS. Emerging is another major module in the software environment, the data dictionary, which is rapidly achieving status as the central focal point for definition and control of all data elements.

The data dictionary is a bookkeeping device for defining data elements in terms of their attributes and accessibility. Maintaining such information in a neutral table makes it possible to develop computer application programs independent of specifying characteristics of data, while simultaneously and separately controlling the storage and organization of the data itself. In essence, the data dictionary serves as a reference point between application programs and data on which they operate.

There is now another major element of the software environment emerging which will be given equal recognition with the five basic modules already enumerated. This component is the Transaction Processor, an important contribution which will mature in the mid-1980s to enhance the overall software environment. This topic is detailed in the following section.

3.2. THE TRANSACTION PROCESSOR

In the previous section we discussed the software environment in which application programs operate. A trace of history showed the evolution of that environment from simple hardware-based bootstraps of the early 1950s to the complex four-part systems of today, i.e., the operating system, the input/output control mechanism, the teleprocessing (TP) monitor, and the data base management system (DBMS). The new kid on the block, the data dictionary, is making its entrance in the 1980s.

Users pay for these facilities in the form of hardware extensions, additional memory and storage resources and the execution of a good number of machine memory and I/O cycles. In return, the same user achieves standardization and convenience, which should gain higher application software implementation productivity as well as improved maintainability of the operating programs.

To this structure now is added one more software addition in support of the on-line, terminal-oriented systems proliferating in today's world of lower-cost video devices and distributed processing. This increment to the software environment is the transaction processor.

As in the past, this new software element is derived by peeling off certain functions that are partially resident within one or more of the existing environmental modules. These existing facilities are brought together and, by adding new capabilities, are further generalized. Thus the transaction processor module will draw heavily from the TP monitor, have a strong link to the data dictionary, depend upon the I/O system, and become somewhat competitive with the standard operating system.

This transaction processor, however, brings with it a new emphasis and some new features. The software is both a framework for structuring the interactive application and the mechanism for executing the on-line dialogue in a video screen-driven setting.

Earlier systems focused on individual lines of input and lines of output. This one-dimensional view of computing life was conditioned by the line of code, the individual card image, and the line of printer output. The view was heightened even further when computing went on line with a preponderance of terminal devices that were functioning line-at-a-time, as, for example, the ubiquitous teletype. This practice persisted even with the introduction of video screen devices which more often than not simulated a piece of paper, virtually rolling across the display surface.

But several observations were made. Video displays are two-dimensional and can heighten the performance of the user if the full screen is used simultaneously. Furthermore, structure and format of the screen display can be abstracted and, hence, generalized for presentation purposes. Finally, the flow of program logic is dictated by the sequencing of the screen display as viewed by the user. This flow is in opposition to the more conventional programming dictated by a procedurally oriented main body of code.

The transaction processor, therefore, must have the following five components:

Screen definition capability
Screen generator and screen library capability
Dialogue composer
Processing logic
Binder and execution module

Recognition that screens may have an inherent common structure was no doubt motivated by the same factors that led to the abstraction of an output page, which earlier had quite naturally led to the report generator. It was seen that the abstracted features of a report are the title, page number, date, control break, column headings, detail line items, and summary controls, as well as physically related features concerned with the number of characters per line or number of lines per page. Once this commonality was recognized, the generalized report writer/composer was not far behind (see Figure 3.1).

The screen abstractions are similarly derived. They can have unique names that are managed through a screen library system, and can be addressed or called from other screens so that a dynamic dialogue of sequenced screens can be generated.

As shown in Figure 3.2, the screen layout is composed of three parts: the protected area and the unprotected areas making up the presentation portion, and the control area for guiding the user. The first part consists of the fixed and nonmodifiable information displayed on specified portions of the screen and protected from change by the user.

The second area is the location on the screen, which invites change through input of data or change of a setting under the control of a marker or cursor. The unprotected areas are often suitably displayed through various enhancing means such as underlines, reverse video bars or a number of special character symbols suggestive of the solicited entry type and data structure.

It is also desirable to display which of the unprotected input areas are mandatory input points and which are discretionary. In addition, there is the optional feature for presetting default values directly into the unprotected fields. In this way the input most likely to occur is already present at screen presentation time. Hence, the actual user input, measured by keystroke, is minimized.

Graphic indication of permissible input form through COBOL "picture" notation or other prompting information completes the architecture for the generalized screen presentation structure.

However, a control function is still necessary. This is achieved by dedicating a third special area. Often the first line or last line of the screen serves a dual function. The first function is to provide prompts for alternative moves or actions based on the particular status of the screen information. One or the other line is also used as the response location for error and remedial messages. Often this single line is augmented by special function keys physically available on the keyboard itself.

Given these screen composition rules it is possible to develop a display definition and generation system inclusive of the following features:

1. Naming the screen.
2. "Painting" the screen on the physical video just as it would ultimately appear at time of use.
3. Specifying data entry or selection points including associated variable label, format, presentation attributes, default values, validation criteria, and associated error messages.
4. Compiling the screen and incorporating it in an accessible library.

SALARY REPORT

AS PERCENTAGE OF
MAXIMUM SALARY

PAGE 8

DATE → PAGE CONTROL BREAK → TITLE → PAGE NUMBER → HEADING

DETAIL ITEMS · COLUMN OF DATA · COLUMN HEADING · SUMMARY LABELS · SUMMARIES · SUMMARIES ON "SALARY"

MDC	GROUP	WORK-CL	SEX	NAME		EMP-NUMB	SALARY	MAXSAL
	A	MGR	M	CALENDAR	JULIAN G.	118	35,124	58,657
	A	MGR	M	KRIEGSPIEL	WARREN J.	32	18,256	67,073
GROUP A TOTAL COUNT						2		
MAXSAL PCT.							53,390	
							42.45%	
	B	MGR	M	LAXLOVE	HOWARD J. JR.	64	18,714	68,757
	B	MGR	M	LEWIS	JOHN A.	88	20,612	75,731
	B	MGR	F	LOVELESS	MARY ANN	124	22,118	81,262
GROUP B TOTAL COUNT						3	61,444	
MAXSAL PCT.							27.21%	
	C	M.T.S.	M	DUCKY	DONALD R.	70	35,988	60,099
	C	M.T.S.	M	LUMPKIN	ROBERT M.	127	20,285	74,528
GROUP C TOTAL COUNT						2	56,273	
MAXSAL PCT.							41.79%	
	D	M.T.S.	M	LONGACRE	GLENN J.	113	32,964	55,049
GROUP D TOTAL COUNT						1	32,964	
MAXSAL PCT.							59.88%	
	X	M.T.S.	M	EGGE	EDWARD	116	34,980	58,416
	X	MGR	M	KAY	GEORGE J.	17	20,743	76,212
	X	M.T.S.	M	KOMTOW	BILLY J.	28	38,724	64,669
	X	DIRECTOR	M	LENIENT	HAROLD S.	77	25,783	94,729
	X	DIRECTOR	M	MACK	STEVEN J. JR.	138	23,820	87,514
GROUP X TOTAL COUNT						5	144,050	
MAXSAL PCT.							37.75%	
DIVISION TOTAL COUNT							348,111	
MAXSAL PCT.							37.72%	
GRAND AVG.							27,727	70,450

Figure 3.1. The general purpose report format.

43

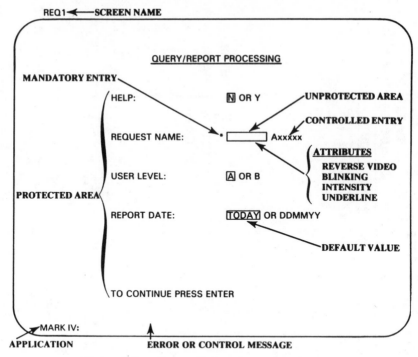

Figure 3.2.   Generalizing the screen format.

Screen design and dialogue composition should not be arbitrary or random. At the very least, screens of one application should look as if they belong together. Hence, a good screen generation and composing system will also enforce certain rules concerning screen structure and sequencing such as:

Selection from a list is better than requiring entry of data.

Names are better to deal with than numbers.

Diagnostics should be self-explanatory.

Entry points should be minimized.

The system should be engineered for errors.

The system should be easily forgiving.

Redundancy of information is desirable.

Alternative actions should be prevalent.

Execution of a screen should be rapid.

Successive screens should maintain consistency and a constant tempo.

Screens should always lead to a goal and have no dead ends.

Every action should be reversible.

Tutorials should be strategically available.

Structured sequences of screens should be amenable to short circuits for those who develop familiarity.

The dialogue composer is the piece of the transaction processor which causes screens to be laced together to form a specific interactive application conversation. In essence, the composer describes the hierarchy and the logic flow of moving from one screen to another.

The screens and associated interactive dialogue are further supported by the presence of the function keys. These function keys initiate general-purpose, application-independent facilities. Examples are initiating tutorials, allowing for hard copy prints of selected screens, and most important, temporary escapes to browse directories and catalogs to assist the user in responding to the forms and selection alternatives posed by the application screens. In addition the function key will also be used to facilitate various exit options during the course of executing the application, ranging from restarting input to the current screen, reinitiating the application, or aborting the present operation.

Coming to the binding and execution module, there is an architectural question concerning implementation. Current systems go in two directions, procedural and nonprocedural.

The procedural approach ultimately leads to a standard, compiled program, typically COBOL, wherein "calls" or "includes" are stated that pick from the screen library the appropriate code or tables to generate the desired screens and cause the entire application to execute. Here the control is under conventional program management (e.g., COBOL) and most of the transaction processor is really the screen definition and generator phase.

In the nonprocedural approach, control of flow is dictated by the logic and structure of the screen sequencing as defined by the dialogue composer. Processing is incidental to the screen, either through an external call or directly as part of the screen handling itself, as defined in the processing logic module. The actual execution of the application is then carried out by the execution module of the transaction processor subsystem which initiates the screen presentation flow, and responds to the terminal operator's input to the screens.

In many older systems, especially for mainframes, transaction processors are not yet part of the basic software environment. Instead, there are special implementation tools such as the Development Management System offered by IBM and commercially available products like TAPS® of Informatics General Corp. On many newly offered systems, however, and especially at the low end scale of computer lines, the transaction processor is already a vital part of the basic software environment. This will also become the case for newly emerging mainframe computers and minicomputers in the 1980s.

3.3. THE COMPLEXITY OF EXECUTION ENVIRONMENTS

It is not uncommon to see a computer system advertised as multi-user and multi-tasking. In addition, such terms as multi-processing or multi-programming are often used to describe the application execution environment.

When all these attributes are joined by the options of background and foreground performance, with some buffered input/output operations and the spooling of print files, it is not surprising that the exact nature of the operating environment seems to need further explanation.

This array of terminology is suddenly coming back into focus as the microcomputer evolution moves to more sophisticated environments and as more complex operating systems emerge. An entirely new population of participants in the grand computer adventure are suddenly faced with terminology dating back several decades. The following questions now arise: Is the terminology adequate and, are words being used consistently and correctly?

We offer a framework within which to view and particularize the meanings of these words. This analytical structure is derived from the threefold approach to data processing: first from the perspective of the user, second from the point of view of the programmer, and third from the implications of the hardware itself.

Systems are characterized as single user or multi-user. "Multi-user" means that many users can simultaneously share the computing resources, independently and at the same time. This denotation does not necessarily dictate the nature of the computer operating environment itself. Both single- and multi-user systems may offer equally complex operating environments, since a number of application programs or jobs can as easily be initiated by a single user as by a group. Nevertheless, the circumstance of group use may necessitate a difference in design. This involves the degree of control required for memory and data file sharing by many parties who can inadvertently interfere with each other. Such conflicts could, of course, occur for a single user as well. In this case, however, the individual is often expected to shoulder the obligation of managing control and integrity mechanisms.

This brings up the important issue of internal program operations of systems ranging in capability from simple, one-program-at-a-time execution to complex, simultaneous processing of a number of individual jobs. The former is often termed serial program execution, while the latter is more accurately described as interleaved processing.

In simultaneous processing two basic kinds of interleaving may occur. One, the inter-program, presumes the initiation and execution of more than one program at any one point in time, where program is defined to be a specific job, self-contained and unrelated to the performance of the other programs. Hence, the operating system facilitates the execution of these jobs in a completely independent manner, simply allocating computing resources to whatever job requires them according to some established priority system. This process is known as multi-programming and was the earliest method aimed at improving the overall efficiency of computer processing. By expeditiously taking advantage of the slower computer peripheral facilities, overlapping processing can be performed independently and simultaneously with the higher speed computing facility of the CPU itself. Multi-programming was first introduced when the input/output involved with file transfers from cards or magnetic tape took place while some other program was already in an intensive processing execution state. This mode of performance was given a special name, buffering. The output printing process which takes place while a second program is executing is another example of specialized multi-programming, with a very specific name, spooling.

One might be tempted to call time-sharing a multi-programming process. This is not correct. Time-sharing is really the allocation of the available computing power of a machine among a number of users, according to some predetermined scheme, and in conformance with a schedule of priority. This could well be accomplished without multi-programming. However, most time-sharing systems would employ some multi-programming capability in order to enhance the productivity of the overall process.

Recently, the term—concurrent—has crept into the vernacular with the announcement of the Concurrent CP/M operating system of Digital Research Inc. This, however, is the type of processing already associated with the term multi-programming, which implies concurrent or simultaneous computing.

The second form of interleaving processing is the intra-program. This approach is called multi-tasking and refers to the simultaneous execution of a number of program modules, all of which have some affinity to each other. Multi-tasking implies that there is a relationship between the tasks that are being "simultaneously" executed. In a sense, multi-tasking is much like multi-programming except that the tasks are all part of a specific job and the steps in the execution sequence are related. That is to say, one task may depend upon the results of another task, or may have to execute in a specified sequence, as it is related to other tasks. Multi-tasking is therefore a much more complex and difficult facility than multi-programming. It requires establishing appropriate synchronization procedures between tasks. The actualization of multi-tasking requires two basic functions that are exemplified in the ADA development environment described in Section 6.3 of Chapter 6.

The multi-tasking capacity of ADA is facilitated by language features allowing for task concurrency and task scheduling based on priorities and interrupts. Sequencing of such related and interacting tasks is dictated by the "rendezvous" function. Tasks can either declare an "entry" point awaiting results from other tasks or declare an "accept" indicating that they are ready to deal with an entry call. Working together, the "accept" and "entry" features cause the rendezvous.

As can be seen, the multi-tasking process requires a multi-programming capability, with an additional requirement that a conditional logic must apply to the precedence relationship of the tasks themselves.

The term, multi-tasking, is sometimes assigned to computer programs with a structure and organization that allow concurrent execution of that program by more than one task at a time. A program with this feature is also often described as being either reusable or reenterable. These terms refer to two different ways in which a program can be initiated and shared by different users without having to restore the program individually or having separate execution copies for each such user. We prefer, however, to distinguish such computer programs from serial program execution, or single-thread programs, by referring to them as multi-thread programs. We restrict the term multi-tasking to the definition already offered above.

This brings us to the influence of the hardware on executing environments. The first important consideration is the availability of more than one CPU. If a computer system includes more than one processing unit, then it is possible to introduce another concept, the notion of multi-processing. The overall environment now can really get complex, as one imposes the programming facilities already described above. It is, for example, possible to simply run two programs quite independently of each other in each of the available processors of the system and consider this to be a multi-processing facility. Or, one could impose the multi-programming or even the multi-tasking environment on more than one processor. Whatever the case may be, one should be very clear as to what is intended. Without any clarification, the term multi-processing, or, as it is sometimes called, parallel processing, should be reserved for the following meaning: A system which executes jobs assigned by a master executive to more than one processor unit.

Another hardware-related operational environment is the time-sharing system discussed above. As already noted, time-sharing can simply be a hardware usage issue, which typically invokes a "time-slicing" algorithm to further the interleaved usage of a single processor by many simultaneous users. A special case of time-sharing is the popular execution mode often found in memory partitioned systems, the so-called foreground/background operating environment. This structure affords a hardware manner of dividing up the computing resource and making it possible to have independent application programs execute according to some controlled priority scheme.

How then should the hardware vendor describe the operating system environment associated with the computer offering? Based on the above, it is suggested that confusion would be eliminated if such descriptions were to be limited to picking the applicable terms from each of the following four categories:

1. Number of simultaneous users
   a. Single User
   b. Multi-User
2. Number of processors
   a. Single Processor
   b. Multi-Processor
3. Operating system performance
   a. Serial Programmed
   b. Multi-Programming
   c. Multi-Tasking

4. Programming execution
   a. Single Thread
   b. Multi-Thread
   c. Time-sharing

3.4. HARDWARE ECONOMICS
AND ITS INFLUENCE ON SOFTWARE

From the outset of computing, the design and structure of software have been determined by the physical limitations and constraints of the hardware, coupled with maximizing the use of these hardware resources. The needs and convenience of the programmer and user were a secondary consideration. Today, however, these priorities are reversing, and we must reevaluate our approaches to software implementation philosophies, the associated architecture of computer-based applications, and the functionality of such programs.

A brief review of the evolving history of programming the computer shows that during the past thirty years there have been periodic shifts back and forth in overall design consideration from monolithic, freestanding system operations to shared resource configurations. Such architectural differences have, of course, affected software development.

In the earliest days, at any one point in time, there was one computer and one user. Today we have once more embraced this approach with the introduction of the personal computer.

The environment of the early 1950s saw the individual "user" in complete control of all the computer capability, ranging from the memory and CPU cycles, to the use of storage, and including the I/O peripherals as well. During any given period the machine was dedicated to one purpose—a specific job—and controlled by one user, who more than likely also served as the computer operator. Those were the days when an $8,000-per-year programmer took command of a $2.4 million machine for a scheduled one hour of checkout or operating time. The man-year-to-machine direct cost ratio was, therefore, 1:300.

This apparently adverse ratio called for better exploitation of the hardware. Typically, the capacity of the system was not utilized fully by any one user during any given period of time due to the disparity of CPU and I/O performance in conjunction with the usual mismatch of a job's need for processing versus data transfer. Hence, came the notion of multiprocessing and time-sharing, permitting the overlapping use of machine resources—as well as sharing of devices—by memory cohabiting and coexecuting jobs.

The serial utilization of the computer by successive users was then displaced in the early 1960s by increasingly sophisticated operating systems acting in the role of a systems manager and resource scheduler. Subsequently, the time-sharing notion was introduced which facilitated simultaneous multi-user access and operation with respect to a centralized system. While good measurements are not now available, these moves—coupled with the then favorable trend in hardware economics—probably shifted the man-to-machine cost ratio by as much as a factor of 10, bringing the relation to 1:30. This ratio, however, was further affected by the then-inflating trends in labor costs, which led to an effective ratio of 1:20.

While time-sharing and complex operating systems were primarily motivated by a desire to lower unit costs of computing through better exploitation of resources in any given time notch, a secondary and most important contribution evolved, the possibility of program and data sharing.

This need arose because of the emergence of data processing applications where multiple users had simultaneous needs for accessing and operating with the same data (e.g., airline reservation systems, missile and space flight, command and control) and for performing similar functions.

But then came the minicomputer and the possibility of returning to the earlier environment of one application and one machine. We saw a separatist movement emerge which discouraged the centralized sharing approach, and encouraged a disengagement to freestanding and dedicated systems. In terms of man/machine economics, we probably then reached a cost imbalance of $20,000 to $300,000, or 1:15. Normalizing, however, the computer power of the mini to the earliest of the mainframes, this ratio more correctly should be 1:3.

The mini environment afforded the opportunity of near-simultaneous access by a number of users so that further hardware exploitation was possible. For an appropriately configured four-terminal system, the normalized man-to-machine cost relationship approached parity.

The underlying trends shaping system configuration and software structure in the early 1970s were motivated by two primary considerations: maximizing the exploitation of the system's most valuable hardware resource, and sharing of data whenever the application required multi-user access.

Together, these factors influenced software construction over the years with the following results:

1. Evolution of multi-level interrupt capabilities and interrupt scheduling.
2. Need for data control mechanisms regarding access, maintenance, and coordination.
3. Requirement for multi-level and multi-source security measures.
4. Demand for complex contingencies in case of failures.
5. Requisite for reentrant programs.
6. Need for centralized data definition.
7. Necessity for standarized interfaces between software modules.
8. Need for audit trail and accounting-related performance statistics.
9. Requirements for highly efficient programming languages and oper-

ating systems that could maximize memory utilization and through-put performance simultaneously.

Software was also influenced in yet another way. This was the result of the changing demands of the man/machine interface itself. In the beginning (after we escaped the tangled world of punched paper tape), the punched card served as the basic unit for both input and output. The world was made up basically of 80-character strings of information transfers. This soon changed to an orientation that focused on asynchronous exchange of single bytes caused by the use of character-at-a-time teletype communication. Finally, the economics of terminals evolved so that video screen displays became widespread in use, bringing with them the need for attendant support. Software needs, therefore, were extended to include:

1. Remote access via a variety of communication handlers and protocols.
2. Excessive new processing loads on the CPU regarding message and data transfers.
3. Buildup of more automated error and recovery methods operable in an on-line mode.
4. Evolution of full-screen-oriented communication in support of the movement to "user friendliness."

All in all, in terms of software, this has meant more complexity in the operating system, more sophistication in interface design and coordination, more need for storage capacity, and more demand on throughput performance to match the on-line interactive needs. In a word, the overhead in processing built up enormously, and relatively fewer resources were available for applications.

Then came the microprocessor, which changed the fundamental economics once more. We now have the most remarkable reversal in balance, matching a $24,000 per year DP user with an $8,000, fully configured microprocessor-based system. Such capability is no less than that which was available to individual users employing the earliest million-dollar computers.

Our present day man/machine ratio of 24,000 to 8,000 is, therefore, in a relation of 1:0.33. Contrast this with the starting point of 1:300 of 30 years ago—a switch in economics by a factor of almost one thousand. By 1985, we foresee this ratio eroding even further—on the order of 1:0.10. This inflection point has an effect on software structure which will be noted in the following section.

3.5. THE MICROCOMPUTER'S INFLUENCE ON SOFTWARE

The fundamental direction of software architecture has been guided by the following cardinal needs:

1. To exploit the most valuable resource in a hardware environment.
2. To account for the requirement to share data in performing certain applications.

In recent years these goals have been joined by the desire to provide a satisfactory user interface via terminal devices.

For a long time, the first requirement was influenced by CPU and memory sharing and the second by storage sharing. The third was ignored, or at best, given second class treatment.

In today's world of low-cost microprocessor-based systems, a sudden shift of favorable economics finally has placed human value at a premium over the machine's cost. Hence, there is an inflection point in computer utilization economics that permeates the software issues. The question, then, is how does software architecture change in a multi-user, distributed, and interactive computing environment?

Deja vu! With the microcomputer, we are once more back to the situation of the one-user, one-application, one-computer environment that marked the early days of data processing. In those days, however, many users had only sequential access to the machine. The low-cost, personal computer of today, on the other hand, is a dedicated appliance that does not involve the sharing of resources and that can pay for itself, even if used only sporadically.

As the evolution of microcomputers proceeds from eight-bit chips to their 16- and 32-bit cousins, the temptation to share "most valuable resources" reemerges. How does one build multi-user systems? Does one use cheap, dumb terminals and powerful, shared CPU and storage devices (shared cluster systems) or intelligent, freestanding terminals that have occasional access to commonly used data as the need arises (distributed intelligence systems)?

We are still in a transitional phase and the answer may not yet be overwhelmingly clear. There are very strong arguments and benefits supporting one scheme over the other. This means the situation must be evaluated from the point of view of system operability, cost economics, and software demands.

The shared cluster approach, be it mainframe- or minicomputer-based, ultimately has operating limitations, either in CPU performance or in the ability to share data among many users. Forcing such a system into a time-sharing mode may achieve data sharing, but at the expense of system performance. Most important, however, the system becomes critically vulnerable, given its monolithic composition with respect to certain crucial elements, especially the CPU itself. Also, contention for peripherals, such as printers, can easily develop. Needless to say, there is also the convenience factor; complete end-user control is lacking in a distributed processing sense. On the other hand, full distribution of computing power to a microcomputer, with attendant peripherals, provides optimal performance, unimpeded access, and ready and convenient availability of printer output.

Many arguments supporting clustered systems point to a seemingly higher cost for freestanding intelligent terminals (distributed logic) than for the multiterminal, shared centralized configurations. Such views, however, are, or soon will become, outdated. With the very low cost of high-volume-manufactured chips and boards, the question of "sharing" the electronics becomes moot. What sense does it make, for example, for users to share a 16-bit CPU chip, currently priced at less than one hundred dollars, that will rapidly decline in price to $10? Computing system costs are moving in the direction of the material elements themselves, such as the plastic cover, the tube and the keyboard—not the electronic components.

Hence, the degree of terminal intelligence should not be the significant factor in deciding on an appropriate overall hardware topology or architecture. In fact, the completely decentralized and distributed micro-based systems of today can readily compete in price with mini-based clustered configurations. If one adds the additional elements of reliability, individual control, and ease of use, then the comparison overwhelmingly favors the dedicated, intelligent desktop computer.

This approach does not, of course, satisfy the requirement to share data in a multi-user application environment. However, this can be handled through the local networking capability of these intelligent terminals, either with a serial loop lash-up or a comparable Ethernetlike communications facility. Thus data sharing is achieved via mutual access to fixed disk storage devices which indeed become the "most valuable resource," both in terms of hardware cost and in terms of system component vulnerability.

Now we come to the heart of the issue and our chief interest, the software.

Most serious application software seems to be moving quickly to a bifurcated mode of operation reflecting the duality of computing possible in a workstation/larger-computer environment. One portion of this software will be executed by a microprocessor-based workstation, with the balance of processing done by a larger computer, be it a standard mainframe or minicomputer. Data entry, interactive dialogue, query, and some selected computing will be performed at the workstation in substantially stand-alone fashion.

Intermittent transmission of requests and data will take place between the workstation and the centralized computer. Certain main processing activities necessarily will be supported on this latter computer, as well as the storing and maintenance of large common data banks. This appears as a loosely coupled distributed network of workstations and larger computers.

Software for such modern hardware systems must, therefore, be viewed as stand-alone operations in the microcomputer, and as an adjunct to software that operates centrally. In the first case, software is structured for the detached, local mode, whereas for the latter, the software must interface with, and be a component of, a foreign system. Both views have a major impact on future software design for such networked systems.

First, there is a common and simple environment for software at the workstation. Software designed for a single desktop computer needs few, if any, security measures and essentially no operating priority scheme. Physical and priority control are at the on/off switch, and data control exists by virtue of a portable diskette or a password for transmission. The operating system will be single-channel, or, at most, it may have some spooling facility. There is no teleprocessing monitor and no need for reentrant code. Resource scheduling is unnecessary, as is the sequencing and controlling of jobs. Even machine accounting is unnecessary—at least as it affects collecting data necessary for chargebacks or the like. The computing resource has become a "throw away" item, an expendable; the computer, a piece of personal furniture.

Communication for I/O has been localized and can be tuned or even microcoded to specific devices. Generality can be displaced. All in all, the underlying software environment for the workstation has been simplified considerably.

But this environment introduces some new requirements as well. User orientation and convenience become paramount. Not only must the interactive screen be responsive to varying user experience and background, but it must also be adaptive. Steady users, over time, want to be able to dynamically redirect dialogues by short-cutting standard procedures when the path is well known or often repeated. Thus, a user-defined, screen-oriented "macro" becomes a necessary function.

Tutoring and the help function are also desirable features, as are user-directed and performed software and hardware diagnostics. Indeed, this calls for some innovations in software maintenance.

Another impact on software design and structure comes from the decoupling of some operating functions from the "main" computer to the workstation. Application software has to be functionally separated into meaningful front- and back-ended pieces that can rationally be executed at the workstation and at the loosely coupled central computer.

Satisfying this latter requirement is no mean trick. It immediately raises the familiar problem of deciding what data shall be held in the local storage of the workstation and how this local data will be coordinated with the central data bank. The problem is complicated by the need to keep in step with the local data employed by other workstations. These design decisions are related to the degree of local edit and validation intended for the data entry functions and how independent the local workstation can be from the centralized data bank in query and reporting operations.

There is, of course, no simple or single answer. The question needs to be resolved for each specific application. Needless to say, the basic design must accommodate these identified functions, and the system must be appropriately triggered either to operate with local data or to seek access to the centralized files.

A final requirement for this new software will be to provide workstation users with implementation assistance for solving ad hoc processing problems which come up from time to time. While standard information retrieval and reporting may be the most common of such functions, there will also be a need for more specific, application-oriented problem solving. Hence, a set of software tools is called for—tools properly shaped and aimed for different classes of users, ranging from the skilled programmer to the more casual end user. This requirement will surely challenge software designers in the 1980s.

3.6. OFFICE AUTOMATION'S INFLUENCE ON SOFTWARE

During the 1970s it was very popular to speak about the integration of computers and communications. In fact, the relationship of these industries was often described as a marriage of two technologies. Consequently, as already seen in Sections 3.1 and 3.2, communications highly influenced software.

Now there is another integration which, in keeping with the times, may be more of a cohabitation than a true betrothal. This is the coming together of word processing (WP) and data processing (DP). The advertising hype, however, is confusing. It is not clear which of the following propositions are being put forth:

1. The same computer can provide either WP or DP services.

2. In a given computer and given software operating environment, it is possible to switch back and forth between WP and DP.

3. With a given computer, it is possible to share simultaneously the CPU resource for either word or data processing from any two or more terminals.

4. A word processing system is capable of being hooked to a second system which may be a DP system.

5. Word processing documents, thought of as files, can be operated upon by the DP software, and vice versa.

6. Data from files derived from DP can be accessed, coordinated, and integrated into WP-generated documents.

7. WP capabilities are enhanced beyond the mere handling of text to include additional functions, more often identified with DP, such as sorting and arithmetic operations.

8. DP capabilities are enhanced beyond the mere handling of numbers and character strings that are associated with formatted files to have the facility to manipulate text and manage documents.

9. WP equipment and functions are a part of a more complete system inclusive of communications, DP, and reprographics so that capture of information in any one medium or system becomes channeled and available in another.

10. WP can be used to manipulate and reformat any file, whether originated under WP or DP.

11.   A common data base management system (DBMS) underlies both WP and DP.

12.   The terminal device and associated keyboard is designed to operate so that it can be used interchangeably between WP and DP.

13.   Both the WP and DP responsibilities throughout an organization are centralized within the same unit.

Perhaps integration is meant to suggest one or all of the above. It certainly is not clear from the promotional campaigns of the vendors whether the intent is to achieve synergy or compatibility. One way to analyze "integration" is to review the changing aspect of DP and WP.

DP first took on an aspect of word processing when the edit function was introduced through the popularization of time-sharing. This quickly led to early text-handling technology through mainframe-oriented systems such as IBM's Administrative Terminal System (ATS). Following this, two related capabilities emerged, the processing of text into a form suitable for photo-composition and the handling of text-oriented data bases for library-type browsing and reporting. These capacities were all big-computer-oriented.

In the meantime, the electric typewriter was extended in capability by introducing electronics and magnetic recording. Such systems were freestanding and independent of the DP center management, as well as separate from the computing tasks themselves. As the CPU decreased in price and increased in capability, and the video display became a lower-cost device, the freestanding, enhanced typewriter became a freestanding electronic word processor.

The stage had been set: DP operated on files, WP produced documents, and communications handled mail. These three functions seem to belong together and yet they were emerging in use and control in different parts of the organization.

However, a number of observations were made:

1.   Information collected under WP or DP could be of mutual use to the other system. For example, a personnel file contains names and addresses useful for generating letters. On the other hand filling out a form, under WP, collects certain information which should find its way to a formatted data file.

2.   Documents generated under WP are at once transmittable over communication wires and subsequently displayable on distant terminals. Text capture by WP is the single most important step toward realizing electronic mail and/or the paperless office.

3.   WP is a convenient way to restructure or reformat an output print file generated by a DP application program. In this way, the WP function could be used to generate more richly endowed text-oriented reports incorporating selected output information from formatted data files.

4.   The WP function is really a form of source data entry that has become a major focus for DP systems. The concept of one-time capture, no duplication of keystrokes, can be exploited via WP and the benefits passed on to DP.

This brings up the basic question of what is meant by integration. At a minimum, integration connotes the effort at control and consistency in use of hardware and communications to achieve information exchange between WP and DP. Such integration would be manifest if the following were possible:

1. The WP device could interface through a standard communications protocol to a DP system and send text files (documents) for storing and/or forwarding.

2. Information entered via WP could be selectively identified and peeled off into separate files which could subsequently serve as input files into well-defined DP applications.

3. Text captured by WP could be processed further into specialized and structured files suitable for formatted handling within the capabilities of the modern DBMS.

4. Data files derived from DP operations could be operated on by WP functions such as: format redesign, cut and paste, column movement, column arithmetic operations, repagination, search and replacement of phrases, introduction of annotations, updating or revising, and automatic checking for spelling.

But standing in the way of this integration is the present absence of standards and structure in WP like those which have developed on the DP scene. For example, there is the issue of the special characters embedded in a text file generated by WP, present to facilitate that document's handling for output. How will DP dispose of such symbols? Then there are simple procedural issues such as the emphasis on the personal files aspect in WP versus more public file attitudes within DP. The disciplines of DP must be inserted into the world of WP before a successful marriage can be completed.

In reviewing and analyzing this question of WP and DP integration, an interesting phenomenon comes to the surface. WP, at the outset and as a goal in itself, was an excellent candidate for a specialized and dedicated computerized function. In fact, if anything, is not WP an example of an operation where software could be eliminated and a hardwired solution be most applicable?

Nevertheless, once this application was isolated and perfected, the next step of the vendors and users was to seek integration with other ongoing activities. We are now on the threshold of this bringing together. Will the wave of specialization soon overtake us again, break asunder these very same functions, and seek their independence once again? This is a distinct possibility, to be considered in the following section on specialization of software to the point where it can be embedded in hardware.

3.7. IS SOFTWARE GETTING HARD?

Some visionaries expect a substantial breakthrough in software technology through the widespread use of chip technology. They hope that software committed to hardwire or firmware will provide better implementation productivity and user economies.

The idea of hardening up the software process is not new. Asher Opler first coined the term *firmware* in the 1960s to suggest the approaching significant change in software production and its form of execution. The concept was to construct software at one level lower than what the standard machine code would allow, in order to achieve the following benefits:

1. Specialized operations, custom designed to maximize performance in a specified environment for certain functions.
2. The ability to simulate the instruction or execution repertoire of one machine environment on a second, object machine.
3. The ability to produce a dedicated machine that optimally performs a specific application or function.
4. Protection to systems and application developers in "locking up" access to the software.

These concepts have led to variations on the theme ranging from completely operating microprogrammed machines such as the 1968 RW530 computer produced by the then Ramo Wooldridge Division of TRW, to the more common approach adopted by IBM through the control program technique utilized in its standard line of computers.

More recently the concept of hardwiring has been exploited in the microcomputer by committing certain functions to a read only memory (ROM) for execution. Even entire applications have been burned onto a chip.

There is, of course, a semantic problem in the apparent interchanging usage of the terms *firmware, hardwired,* and *burned* programs. Unfortunately, these words mix methods of implementation with functionality.

We can have the notion of "locked up" software that is not accessible to the application programmer or to the end user. Such software need not necessarily be hardwired nor does it have to be microprogrammed. We can have hardwired software which, by its very nature, is locked up—but it could well be executing standard machine code. "Hardwire" here is meant to convey ROM-based software and not conventional software executing "hardwired instructions."

Finally, we could have microprogrammed software in any one or more states, locked up, hardwired, or operating in a conventionally accessible memory.

"Firmware" could designate any one of these implementation modes, although the term should be limited to convey "a microprogram stored in a control memory unit."

What has all of this to do with increased software productivity, production, and operation? The proponents for hardwired software seem to believe that the following benefits can be achieved from this technology:

1. Faster production.
2. Cheaper distribution.
3. More efficient performance.
4. Better safeguarding.

In a *Computerworld* article dated June 12, 1978, one observer has stated that the current cost of conventional programming, pegged at $10 per line of code, can be reduced in 1990 to five cents a line by adopting the process of "putting software on silicon chips."

Typically it is the hardware-oriented person or organization that believes in the economic potential of hardened software. Statements such as the following from IDC's EDP Industry Report of November 4, 1979, have been quoted in trade journals in recent years:

The semiconductor makers . . . will . . . solve the software price barrier by embedding software into firmware.

We expect to circumvent a predicted shortage of programmers by offering plug-in logic modules in lieu of custom designed software.

The decade of the '80s will see the software package largely replaced in the marketplace by the firmware package.

Future small computers will trim software costs since custom software will be built into the computer as firmware.

It should come as no surprise that the semiconductor firms advocate such a direction because it serves their direct interests. But do they understand the intricacies of software? That's really what it is all about. To commit a procedure to firmware or hardwire implies complete *a priori* understanding and definition of that process or function. That is to say, the entire solution must be carefully worked out in no less detail, nor with less care, than if the end product remained as conventional software.

But that's only the start. Having developed the design, and even implemented the logic, the next step is the checkout. But how many computer programs developed over the years have successfully passed the checkout process and still ended up in the field with an undetermined number of undetected errors or defects?

Aside from the ongoing enhancements that most software systems demand, the process of evolving a hardwire solution is not different from the conventional programming process itself—but with the subsequent downside risk of requiring retrofit hardware maintenance. What remedy will the supplier of hardwire software provide in the case of a single detected error? How will this supplier deal with the continuing need for improvement and extension?

One quantitative assessment in the IEEE *Computer* issue of June 1981 states that "algorithms implemented in hardware are 10 to 1000 times faster than those implemented in software, they are also 10 to 100 times as costly to implement or change."

There is the hardware manufacturer's dilemma of becoming a fixed target, or sitting duck, to the more flexible software innovator. Thus Radio Shack, given its ROM-based BASIC Level II system for the TRS-80 Model I, is challenged by the random access memory (RAM)-oriented offering of Microsoft Consumer Products, Inc., in the form of a Level III BASIC compiler for that same machine.

Some other arguments are made in support of fixed programs on chips or ROM. One such position is put forth by Texas Instruments, Inc., in defense of its solid-state ROM integrated circuit chips. The company claims that this is a less expensive way of making programs available than requiring a one-time, larger RAM.

A directly opposite argument, however, is put forth by Radio Shack® in support of RAM over ROM for the TRS-80® Model II. Radio Shack states that RAM will allow maximum utilization of the available memory without losing resources that may be idly sitting by in the ROM.

A similar changing view can be gleaned from the brief history of Amdahl Corporation. At the outset, Amdahl designers avoided microprogramming as a means of achieving enhanced performance. Instead Amdahl put all of its efforts and resources into building a CPU with overall higher performance executing conventional software. Lately, however, this company seems to have changed its mind and is now moving in the direction of exploiting firmware.

We can expect to find this flip-flop of design decisions repeated over the coming years, since no one really seems to understand the full significance of the economics of hardwiring the software. We can conclude, however, that at present, the hardwire approach to developing and executing computer programs is really a hardware advance and not a software productivity solution.

Additional Readings

The materials in this chapter can be further developed by referring to the following articles given in the Bibliography at the end of the book: Auslander et al., 1981; Champine, 1980; Chen, 1978; EDP Analyzer, 1979; EDP Analyzer, 1981d; Enos and Tilbur, 1981; Gutz et al., 1981; Hayes et al., 1981; Jones, 1978; Proceedings, 1979; Rauscher and Adams, 1980; Soltis, 1981; and Wasserman, 1980.

FOUR

The Economics of Software Productivity

Most industries throughout the world are focusing their attention on increasing productivity. This seems to be a natural reaction to inflationary tendencies. It is not surprising, therefore, that productivity issues have also come to the fore on the data processing scene.

The hardware people can take pride in their enhanced productivity performance over the years. Continual improvement in cost-effectiveness of delivered hardware is testimony to ingenuity in engineering design and production. Software, on the other hand, seems to fail on all counts. Consequently, when discussing the necessity for improvement of computer productivity, what is usually meant is improvement of software productivity.

Section 4.1 identifies the issues concerned with software productivity. This is followed, in Section 4.2, by an analysis that accounts for possible productivity improvements emphasizing current technology. Section 4.3 assesses the potential impact of productivity improvements on the EDP budget. Finally, in Section 4.4, there is a review of some specific approaches to achieving increased software productivity.

4.1. IDENTIFYING SOFTWARE PRODUCTIVITY ISSUES

Software is both a product and a process. Software productivity enhancement, therefore, must be related both to the activity of developing software, and to the activity of operating software.

With respect to software development, productivity issues relate to software project performance and the development cycles which are typically unpredictable. This leads to manpower and machine utilization overruns as well as tardiness in achieving project completion. Further adding to this problem of project performance is the fundamental question of whether software meets the user's expectations, both by functionally achieving what is desired and by meeting the necessary performance level, or throughput. All of these problems are, of course, exacerbated by the continual switches to better and faster hardware which accentuate every difficulty encountered with software.

Even when software initially functions acceptably, the problems are not behind us. Productivity issues continually enter into the operation and performance of the software. There are constant demands for changes and enhancements, as well as simple maintenance activities for the correction of defects and adaptation to a changing hardware and systems environment.

Too often, improving technology is expected to achieve enhanced productivity. Unfortunately, this will not actually occur in the foreseeable future. Improved computer languages, new system development methods, and better-performing hardware simply will not increase productivity to the degree desired in software implementation and operation.

Proposed solutions to the problem of software productivity as expressed in the current literature are often diametrically opposed to one another. The solution for the 1980s is either the development of hardwired code, or "firmware," as it is sometimes labeled, or the development of super-software in the form of high-level application generators.

The hardware-oriented answer to the productivity dilemma comes as a result of the chip revolution referred to in Section 3.6. Some observers even expect, rather naively, that software will be replaced by wired-program machines, employing read only memories (ROM) or containing microcoded control memories. As noted in Section 3.6, these fourth-generation approaches are actually hardware advances rather than software solutions.

Often the term *firmware* refers to both of these quite different approaches to the incorporation into hardware of operations earlier reserved for software. There is, however, a distinction. More correctly, the term *firmware* refers to computer programs that are stored in a control memory. In many cases, this control memory can be modified by privileged instructions or by selecting special machine states. Under such conditions it is possible to replace microprograms by new and different code. The implication of firmware is discussed in more detail in Chapter 3, Section 3.6.

The capability of highly specialized code operating in a control memory allows the object machine state to maximize its performance against certain prespecified application or system requirements. The technique is useful for increasing computer performance because it is more difficult to change the hardwired logic of a computer than it is to recode microprograms.

In any event, the motivation is to gain more hardware capability and processing capacity than would be possible by simply using operating programs in the standard machine instruction and system repertoire. This is, therefore, one way to achieve increased productivity from already operational software.

An excellent example of how such a facility could improve performance in a given system is to contrast the microcoding of a terminal's screen image extract module with the writing of the same program in native machine code. The latter code may take an order of magnitude longer to process.

Another example is the performance improvement achievable on IBM 370 mainframes operating in the Virtual Memory (VM) environment and relying on the microcoded features of VM Assist and External Control Program Support. Throughput improvements of 20 to 30 percent are being claimed.

This movement toward firmware, while potentially improving performance significantly, does very little to meet the fundamental needs of software design, production and maintenance. One might just as well build an entirely new CPU with improved performance, as Amdahl Corp. did in the late 1970s with its V series computer line. Such a faster computer has had, however, no impact in better software productivity.

Since firmware does not seem materially to affect software productivity, the search continues for other ways of enhancing software productivity. As already mentioned, the application generator is another current attempt to reach the elusive "automatic programming" and "implicitly programmed" systems promised in the early 1960s. It is unlikely that these will fully materialize before the late 1980s, if at all. This phenomenon is discussed in more detail in Chapter 6, Section 6.1.

Productivity issues fall into three clearly distinct activities relating to the creation and operation of software. The first is the actual process of developing or implementing the software. A second aspect of productivity is the operability and maintainability of the software after it has been produced. The third factor is the performance of the software/hardware combination, and includes the issue of productivity from the conventional unit cost improvement point of view. Although all three aspects are related, they deserve independent study if one seeks to enhance overall productivity.

The problem is one of measuring productivity in a fast-changing environment. Computer professionals waste a lot of time in counting and averaging lines of code produced as a means of achieving a productivity indicator. However, the number of lines of code produced by an individual is by itself no more an indication of productivity than is knowing the amount paid for a kilowatt of electricity in operating the computer.

An example mentioned earlier, in Section 3.3, bears repeating. It was noted that an IBM executive cited substantial progress in increasing the productivity and quality for delivering IBM systems control programs. Specifically, data was produced for two 10-year periods which showed a doubling of lines of delivered code produced per staff member and a reduction of errors per 1000 lines of code by a decimal order of magnitude.

This, of course, is impressive and unquestionably shows increases in lines-of-code productivity. However, because of the increasing demand and complexity of the required solution, the total amount of code had increased in these periods by a factor of more than eight, resulting in a quadrupling of the staff. While it is true that unit production had increased, it is not clear that overall productivity had improved.

Productivity is the ratio of output to input where input includes labor, capital, material, and energy. Probably the best we can do in data processing is to track the change in this function over time to determine productivity trends. And the most likely quantifiers of output, for given amount spent, are the measurable quantities of:

Unit cost of a product (e.g., invoice, paycheck, etc.).

Turnaround time for a request.

Ability to meet user deadlines.

Relevance of information received by user.

Number of user complaints.

Computer uptime.

Rerun time.

Average on-line response time.

Length of computer outage.

Appropriately weighted and normalized, a production index can be computed as a function of these measurements and this index can serve to track the DP performance and its improvement.

A word of warning is due, however. Computer applications have a way of becoming more complex over time, either because more data processing details are added (security, recovery, audit, etc.) or because the computing is more demanding (another government report, more deductions, etc.). Thus, the output may not be identical from one period to another and allowance must be made to assure comparability.

The almost desperate need for assistance in meeting the productivity gap in developing and operating computer systems has not been lost upon the various vendors of both hardware and software. Indeed the trade journals abound in advertising claims of productivity enhancers to attract the user community.

A recent review of such periodicals yielded the following claims by various suppliers for their offerings:

Trims software development time by up to 75%.

Boosts programmer productivity up to 75%.

Saves in development 54%, maintenance 70%.

Increases programmer productivity by 40%.

Increases productivity 25 to 40% through improved programming.

Increases application development productivity by two to one and as much as twenty to one.

Increases programmer productivity by 21% and meets completion targets 94% of the time.

Produces results in one-fifth the time for a 400% productivity gain.

Productivity improvements averaged approximately 160%.

As can be seen, productivity claims are related to a variety of functions including production rate, production schedule, and maintainability.

The quantifiers are also mixed because, in some claims, we are told of improvement potentials and in others of potential reduction in a variable. These measures are, of course, related by the expression:

$$P = \frac{100\,R}{1 - R}$$

where P is the percent improvement and R is the realizable reduction. In other words, trimming a measure of work by 25 or 75 percent leads to a productivity increase of 33 or 300 percent, respectively.

One might deduce from any one or more of the preceding assertions that productivity salvation is at hand. Indeed, it may be feasible to increase productivity in one particular activity of the overall application cycle, and it may even be possible to increase such productivity by a substantial amount if the particular application meets certain limited criteria and constraints. Unfortunately the matter is not that simple.

Let us take three representative examples and analyze the potential productivity increase that is realizable with today's technology. First let's select the optimal situation. A business is in need of a general ledger system and has the choices of purchasing such a system or building it in-house.

It is now clearly established that ledger systems have evolved to a point where they are state of the art and available off the shelf. The alternatives for a business seeking a ledger system are therefore economically viable. Purchasing a system from an outside source displaces internal development costs as well as eliminates the risk of undertaking a software project with all its known economic pitfalls. The purchase also makes the system available immediately, thereby achieving opportunity costs. The system is maintained by an outside organization so that maintenance costs are supported by many users.

Given the applicability of the off-the-shelf software to the business, productivity achievement is maximized by this purchase option. Under these circumstances there can be no better solution for more cost-effective data processing.

In a second example, the user wishes to maintain a file of information relating to specific transactions that occur from time to time. The user requires a variety of periodic reports reflecting the content of the file information and wishes to make ad hoc queries from time to time. Hence the data processing functions are quite simple and standard.

The problem is one that occurs quite frequently among end users. It is also a general problem inherent in many commercial activities for which computers have not as yet been utilized. Users are often deterred from employing a computer because they feel access is difficult or because individuals are not aware that computers could easily be used to help process such information.

But self-contained, "solution" systems, often offered by the commercial time-sharing services, are the answer to solving such problems and providing a highly productive and cost-effective remedy. Thus is made the case for any standard data management system, providing it has an appropriate front-end user query and reporting system. Commercial examples are the NOMAD system of NCSS and RAMIS II of Mathematica. Productivity improvements can be astounding for those instances when results are achievable by stating a problem instead of programming a solution. Such systems are further discussed in Chapters 6 and 7.

This brings us to the third and most difficult problem, namely the design and implementation of a new application that cannot directly benefit from existing off-the-shelf software nor be implemented efficiently through a solution system. In this case all of the classical life cycle activities of an application must be engaged, beginning with establishment of requirements, development of the design and specifications, detailed programming, thorough testing and subsequent operation and ongoing maintenance. Here we must bring to bear the best approaches and techniques that technology affords. The possibilities available to software implementors are discussed in the next section.

4.2. LIMITS TO PRODUCTIVITY IMPROVEMENTS

Recent literature has highlighted the many application development problems facing the typical installation. They include the following:

Sites face sizable backlogs, often expressed in terms of the existing staff's capacity—that is, two to three calendar years of effort or 10 to 20 applications.

As much as 60% of the budget is devoted to maintaining or rewriting old systems.

Less than 20% of the systems staff can be deployed for new development efforts.

Programming costs are increasing and outpacing dollars spent for hardware.

A good part of developed software is never effectively used.

A number of voices cry out with varying views and suggestions for alleviating this pressure. The most notable and useless advice is to employ only the very best personnel. As stated in an earlier chapter, the variance in capability between the average and the best of programmers and systems people is enormous. But the shortage of skilled DP personnel, and the inability to concentrate the top performers, makes this productivity-enhancing suggestion a dream.

Another group seeks to avoid the basic problem of programming in the first place. These individuals advocate that new development activities be minimized. They recommend quick, and perhaps "dirty," solutions by using existing general purpose data management systems, or as they are often called, application generators. They belong to the "install now, program later" school popularized by R. C. Kendall (Kendall 1977). This group also recommends prototyping or breadboarding a solution and incrementally modifying, evolving, and improving a solution. They would maximize the use of existing software modules and build an application within the framework of available systems.

A third set of recommendations comes from those advocating productivity enhancement tools and techniques. These suggestions support the efforts of modern technology to better organize the process of developing and operating software systems.

Included in this set of suggestions are better use of existing programming languages and the development of improved languages. Coupled with this focus on language are the various methodologies advanced for structuring the design specifications and programming process itself. With this structured discipline, its advocates argue, the construction process is enhanced and under better control.

Related to the program construction process is the notion of the programmer workbench. This approach to increasing productivity assumes that the ready availability of a combination of software and hardware tools for organizing and controlling the programming process will enhance programmer performance.

A slightly different approach to improving productivity is advocated via performance enhancers. These aim at improving the operation of a completed system by either more efficient execution of existing code through a tuning process or the enhancement of the operating environment with better utilities.

Vendor products for improving productivity address various parts of the overall application development and operation cycle. One might conclude from vendors' assertions, such as those enumerated in Section 4.1, that using any one of their offerings would immediately and dramatically benefit the end user. It is tempting to conclude that, by using many of the suggested improvement techniques, one could achieve a tremendous gain in productivity. We set about testing this hypothesis by identifying the various component steps in system development and system operation and analyzing the productivity potential of each.

Consider first the system development process made up of nine component steps with their associated cost breakdown. Shown in Figure 4.1 are the

	CURRENT COST	% IMPROVEMENT	NET COST
OBJECTIVES/REQUIREMENTS	2	0	2
EXTERNAL SYSTEM DESIGN	8	25%	6
INTERNAL SYSTEM DESIGN	10	20%	8
PROGRAMMING SPECIFICATIONS	12	40%	7
CODING	13	75%	3
UNIT TESTING	24	50%	12
INTEGRATION TESTING	13	30%	9
DOCUMENTATION	6	30%	4
SYSTEM TEST	12	25%	9
TOTAL	100	40%	60

Figure 4.1. Productivity improvement potential in development.

maximum improvements feasible for each component step based on the best available technology today. It will be noted that the coding process can achieve a maximum improvement of 75 percent, whereas the statement of objectives and requirements will probably remain a totally manual process with no real improvement possible.

The impact of maximal improvements for each component step, assuming independence for each such step, is seen to be 40 percent for the overall system development process, or a productivity increase of 67 percent.

These results, taken one step further, can determine what overall improvements are achievable during the total life cycle of an application. Figure 4.2 shows, in addition to the system development process, what can be achieved during the installation and maintenance phases. In this model, the maintenance effort is assumed to have a cost three times that of the development cycle. Furthermore, the maintenance breakdown is assumed to be 20 percent for defect removal, 20 percent for environmental changes, and 60 percent for enhancements made to the basic application.

The total improvement during the overall life cycle of the application is 43 percent, leading to a net cost which, at best, is 57 percent of the current expected life cycle costs. In other words, by employing currently available techniques, productivity can be expected to improve by 75 percent. Since each predecessor step in the software construction process affects subsequent events, it may even be possible to achieve somewhat better results over this entire process.

This expectation of potential productivity improvement for customized systems at the overall 43 percent level should be contrasted with alternatives such as purchasing off-the-shelf finished software products or using a data management system. For certain applications the latter two options may provide improvement factors that are several times better.

4.3. THE IMPACT ON THE EDP BUDGET

The previous section estimated the limits to productivity improvements when applying the best available methodologies and tools in support of custom application development projects. A productivity increase of 75 percent, or a 43 percent cost reduction, is generally considered the outside achievable limit.

What does this mean in terms of dollar value and DP budget implications? The annual expenditure analysis of DP budgets performed by International Data Corporation (IDC) noted that almost 50 percent of the DP installation's costs are consumed by manpower (see Figure 1.4). Of this amount, roughly one-half is devoted to the programmer/analyst staff, including supervision and management costs.

If an overall cost reduction of 43 percent is possible in application development and operation, then by using all available productivity tools it should be possible to save nearly $6 billion on the 1980 estimated personnel budget of $26 billion. Since most installations already employ some of these techniques, and not all of them necessarily apply, a more realistic potential savings might be $4 billion or about 8 percent of the total DP budget.

	CURRENT COST	% IMPROVEMENT	NET COST
SYSTEM DEVELOPMENT	100	40%	60
INSTALLATION CONVERSION TRAINING	15	20%	12
MAINTENANCE (= 3 X DEVELOPMENT)			
DEFECT REMOVAL (20%)	60	75%	15
ENVIRONMENTAL CHANGE (20%)	60	30%	42
ENHANCEMENTS (60%)	180	40%	108
TOTAL	415	43%	237

Figure 4.2. Productivity improvement potential for life cycle.

SOFTWARE PRODUCT IMPACT
ON USER ORGANIZATION
REDISTRIBUTION OF STAFF

		NOW		PROPOSED
MANAGEMENT		15		12
PROGRAMMER/ANALYST				
DEVELOPMENT	16		12	
MAINTENANCE	25		12	
		41		24
OPERATIONS		25		25
DATA ENTRY		9		9
TECHNICAL SUPPORT		10		10
TOTAL		100		80

A STAFF REDUCTION OF 20% GIVING RISE TO A COST REDUCTION OF 25%

Figure 4.3.   Re-allocation of staff. (Data from IDC).

An alternative way of improving the productivity of the in-house development and operations staff is to shift expenditure from in-house staff to the purchase of software developed outside. Its effectiveness can be judged by observing its impact on the EDP budget.

Note the staffing organization shown in Figure 4.3. This indicates that 41 percent of all the line personnel are devoted to development and maintenance. By removing some of the programmer/analyst team and a portion of management, the result is a 20 percent reduction in total staff. This reduction in the higher paid manpower could have an overall favorable expenditure variance of 25 percent.

Apply these observations to the 1980 user expenditure figures shown in Figure 4.4. By reducing staff costs 25 percent and doubling expenditures for purchased software, the overall savings is approximately 10 percent of total cost. This conclusion rests, however, on the assumption that $4 of in-house staff costs can be replaced by $1 spent on purchased software.

Unfortunately, no one knows what the trade-off is between building custom software with an in-house staff and purchasing off-the-shelf software products. But one can do a parametric study to see how sensitive this function is to varying assumptions. Figure 4.5 shows the shape of the trade-off curves for several cases.

Basically, the "savings" potential, as a percentage of total expenditures, varies slightly for these cases. A realistic range of staff reductions, up to 25 percent, shows the saving potential is bound to be 15 percent.

This leads to a final observation concerning the remaining potential open to users for exploiting productivity increases. Again using IDC data, the relative DP installation expenditure rates are:

Total expenditure—33.

Hardware and communications—12.

Operations and software maintenance—12.

Miscellaneous—5.

Internally developed software—3.

Purchased software—1.

The figure for internally developed software is derived by assuming that 20 percent of staff budget is spent on new development efforts.

These ratios tell us that for every $33 spent in the typical DP installation, only $1 goes to purchased software. This sharply contrasts with the $12 going to hardware and communications, $12 to operations and software maintenance, and $3 to new development.

Users, therefore, have quite a bit of flexibility available for helping their budgets and improving their operational efficiency. Productivity increases can be achieved in two independent ways, when applicable:

1. Incorporation of implementation tools and procedures.

2. Use of purchased software.

IMPACT ON USER EXPENDITURE
SOFTWARE PRODUCT
PURCHASE SHIFT

	MODEL I*		MODEL II*	
	$M	%	$M	%
PURCHASED SOFTWARE	1,665	3.0	3,330	6.6
STAFF	26,250	47.4	19,688	39.0
TOTAL EXPENDITURE	55,380	100.0	50,483	100.0

- -

DOUBLING EXPENDITURE ON SOFTWARE PRODUCTS CAN LEAD TO AN ANNUAL SAVING OF OVER 10% ON TOTAL EXPENDITURE, OR FREE PERSONNEL TO TACKLE DEVELOPMENT BACKLOG.

Figure 4.4. Budget impact from re-allocation of staff. (Data from IDC for 1980).

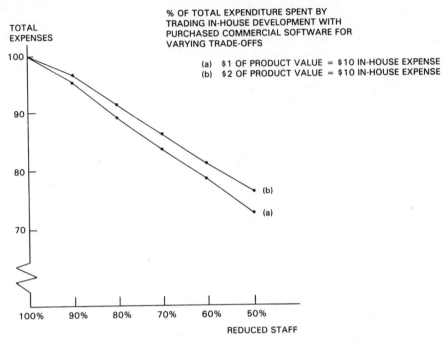

Figure 4.5.   Impact on budget by staffing expenditure.

In summary, the improvement in total user budgets when adopting these alternatives to productivity enhancement can range to 8 percent and 15 percent, respectively, and, in combination, may even be able to reach 20 percent. Such benefits can either serve to reduce overall costs or make it possible for an organization at a fixed expenditure level to perform more processing and cut down its backlog of application needs.

4.4.   OTHER APPROACHES TO SOFTWARE PRODUCTIVITY

Previous sections have dwelled on productivity problems and issues concerning software production. We discussed popular views and approaches that attempt to alleviate these difficulties and cited a variety of aids and methodologies which have been proposed to improve the construction and operation of software.

One observer, Ed Lee of Pro-Log Corporation, questions the general enthusiasm for "development systems." In a number of published articles (Lee 1980) Lee takes issue with generally accepted views and asserts that the electronics industry today has a sufficient number of personnel to design production software. Furthermore, he states that software implementation can be successfully undertaken without a development system or a higher level language.

Lee contends that development systems are the bane of today's programming efforts, and that these systems seem to be right for implementors only because we are told they are right. Furthermore, because development systems became available before correct software design methods had evolved, they have stifled better methods, and have, in fact, given us the problems we now face in producing software.

Lee also attacks the notion of the high-level language as a bad partner of development systems in furthering software design. In this context the current interest in the programming languages Pascal and FORTH is seen by Lee to be a fad.

Lee's focus is on the professional electronics engineer rather than on the hobbyist or applications programmer. He makes this distinction because he believes the aim of the latter two implementors is to achieve a single system that works for the least cost and is achieved in the shortest time.

In contrast, the aim of the engineer is to produce a software design to be manufactured for many users. Therefore, the product of the professional engineer is viewed differently. The engineer must document the software solution for manufacturing and field service in order for these entities to produce the product and then maintain it. This documentation must be of sufficient quality and detail so that less skilled personnel can comprehend it and produce end products.

There lies the crux of the difference in viewpoints. The conventional approach to software shared by most is the step-by-step process of design, development, and maintenance, which requires interpretation and individual expression. As aids, we use development systems and higher-order languages.

Lee, on the other hand, advocates a standardized documentation system which, when utilized by the design engineer, will produce a tested and debugged software design ready for delivery to the manufacturing division.

This process is called STD Modular Methods, where STD could mean any of the following: simple to debug, simple to develop, or swift to deliver. Lee views computing from the confines of the microprocessor field and divides the world between the "computer culture" and the "engineering culture." He believes that adherents of the computer culture have a limited perspective and that their approaches are dictated by dependency upon the computer. Exemplars of the computer culture are practitioners who "forget how the hardware actually works and are taught to speak to a powerful black box."

In contrast, according to Lee, members of the engineering culture are production-oriented and in control of problem-solving by direct and uninhibited understanding of how the computer works.

The STD Modular Methods for program design and documentation derive from adapting the hardware module design approach for use with software by observing the following steps:

1. Break the problem down into component modules.
2. Create a flow chart for each module using standard presentations.

3. Write a specification for each module.
4. Design the program using a precise form with standard notation.

The last step involves describing the module's function through a series that is, in essence, a mnemonic code consisting of three parts: labels, instruction, and modifier. With this series, we have arrived at the threshold of an assembler, with the redeeming value of a proposed standard instruction set having universal application.

To complete the process, the engineer must do a dictionary look up of the instructions for a particular object CPU and hard code the appropriate machine language in hexadecimal. Upon completion of this translation, the resulting code can be inserted into a programmable read only memory programmer and unit testing can begin.

Lee advises that the weakness surrounding the data processing culture is the almost unheard-of practice of writing program module specifications (Step 3 above). He also feels that computer-aided design tools generally get in the way of good designers. Also, assemblers lead to bad practices, causing the user to forget the machine code nomenclature and creating unstructured program results. Furthermore, higher languages intrude on the intimacy of being able to converse directly with the computer. They lengthen the program and the execution time of a task.

Lee has challenged the semiconductor industry by his fundamentalist views on program design and his denigration of development systems for microprocessors. He has obliquely included in his challenge the applications programmer as well.

Perhaps coding in hexadecimal still has a small place in developing minimal storage and high-performing control programs ultimately destined for residence in read only memory. Beyond that point, however, it is hard to see how automated aids and development systems can deter and limit productivity and the effectiveness of engineers or programmers.

In fact, there are two other approaches that reflect the mainstream thinking of the software development community and do emphasize the use of tools and techniques opposed by Lee. One such system is based on the principle of minimizing the development of new code and the second depends upon the use of high-powered development systems.

The example of a system aimed at minimizing the development of new code is the Reusable Code Productivity System reported by a team of software developers at the Missile Systems Division of Raytheon Co. (Lanergan and Dugan 1980). The basis for this approach in developing and maintaining business applications software was the observation that 40 to 60 percent of actual program code was redundant from one application to another.

The evolution of the reusable code system was based on a solid foundation of experience for a sizable DP requirement at Raytheon. The professional programming staff numbered about 120 people and the annual work load consisted of 1200 new programs, with an additional 2000 programs requiring enhancements.

To test the hypothesis that programming redundancy was widely present, a functional classification was made of more than 5000 production COBOL programs. The findings showed that the modules fell into three well-defined DP categories: edit or selection programs, 29 percent; update programs, 26 percent; and report programs, 45 percent. Subsequent examination showed 40 to 60 percent of the code in these modules was redundant and, hence, a candidate for standardization.

The actual reusable code system takes advantage of two independent techniques. The first consists of well-defined, standard functions and operations that are completely prewritten and become available on an off-the-shelf basis. These COBOL modules perform tax computations, date conversions, part number validations, and so on and are callable from the reusable code library.

A second set of aids consists of prewritten logic structures supporting the updating, selection, and report function. These modules are really program outlines, in terms of COBOL structure, which require "fill in" for a particular application.

Applications built from either or both of these types of modules will have a uniformity of style and structure, thereby aiding in their subsequent maintenance.

But what is the bottom line impact of utilizing this approach? Raytheon personnel have stated that at least one major application was implemented in 36 man-months, rather than an expected 126 man-months, and a second application was developed 40 times faster. More recently, through private communications, Raytheon representatives indicated programmer productivity improvements of 75 percent were being achieved.

This brings us to a second approach, recognizing the same fundamentals of functional redundancy from one application to another, and coupled with a focus on transaction-oriented systems. This is a system which has evolved at Data Concepts Inc., where they view a data processing flow as a manufacturing production line. This concept has emerged into the Data Conveyor™ System, comprised of the Fully Automated Specifications/Structuring Technique (FAS!ST™) and the System Implementation/Executor (SIMPL!E™).

To highlight the claimed performance increase over COBOL, statistics are presented by Data Concepts for one complex casualty insurance application yielding the following:

	COBOL	SIMPL!E
Development cycle	4–8 years	1 year
Man-years	100–300	10
Program size	20–30 megabytes	500 kilobytes

The Data Conveyer concept treats a series of transactions as a discrete set of processes, just as might be performed on an assembly line. FAS!ST defines and enters transactions, whereas SIMPL!E executes them. Operations on the transactions can either be automatic or performed by human operators at workstations.

FAS!ST and SIMPL!E are examples of the emerging number of development systems referred to as application generators, implementation systems, or enabling systems. Rather than requiring programming, such systems are basically nonprocedural, calling for the statement of specifications and desired operations. These are then executed within the framework of an existing system. Conventional programming steps are thereby minimized, if not eliminated.

One of the neat features of such systems is the ability to evolve solutions. One can approximate the desired interaction and processing and then further refine it to detail more closely the user's needs and expectations. At each step one has a production system. The remaining challenge is to insure that the underlying framework provides reasonably high performance results.

The authors of SIMPL!E claim an increase in productivity over COBOL by a factor of 10. Furthermore, since SIMPL!E is independent of particular hardware, there is the potential of developing transportable software as long as the Data Conveyor system exists on a target machine. A final advantage to the system is the ability to create running applications which are approximately one-fiftieth the size of conventional application programs, thereby permitting ease of use of minicomputers for complex applications normally executed on mainframes.

There seems to be no single answer to the problem of making software production more efficient. As if the preceding three approaches outlined were not enough, even more varying approaches are described in recent conference proceedings on application development systems. The reader wishing to examine these is referred to the records of the conference sponsored by Share Inc., Guide International Inc. and IBM (Proceedings 1979); and of the conference sponsored by the Association for Computing Machinery, IBM, MIT's Sloan School of Management, and UCLA's Graduate School of Management (Data Base 1980).

Additional Readings

The material in this chapter can be further developed by referring to the following articles in the Bibliography at the end of the book: Chen, 1978; Data Base, 1980; EDP Analyzer, 1979; EDP Analyzer, 1981b, c, f, g; Electronic Design, 1981; Jones, 1978, 1981; Joslin, 1981; Lanergan and Dugan, 1980; Lee, 1980; NBS, 1980; Proceedings, 1979; Putnam, 1978; and Wasserman, 1981.

FIVE

Managing the Software Process

In Chapter 4 we saw that there are various tools and procedures available for enhancing software productivity. These methodologies break down into two major categories—those associated with managing the software process, a topic considered in this part of the book; and those related to the implementation activity itself, a topic reserved for Chapter 6.

In Section 5.1, some problems associated with software production are illustrated by documented experience in the U.S. Government. This story reaches the depth of despair about software—it cannot be worse.

In Section 5.2, a brighter and more promising world unfolds. Software production management is discussed employing quality control methodology called "inspections."

Section 5.3 discusses the issue of managing software production for hardware-compatible environments as well as the problem of software transfer, or portability, between unlike machines.

5.1. PRODUCTION OF SOFTWARE IS A PROBLEM

A report to Congress by the Comptroller General, General Accounting Office (GAO), FGMSD-80-4, November 9, 1979, cites the continuing problem of developing software within the federal government. The report title summarizes the issue: "Contracting for Computer Software Development—Serious Problems Require Management Attention to Avoid Wasting Additional Millions."

This report reflects the views of 163 software contracting firms and 113 federal government project officers, as well as experience with specific contracts for software development. The summarized indictment is severe:

1. Dollar overruns are fairly common in more than 50 percent of cases.
2. Calendar overruns occur in more than 60 percent of cases.
3. Of the nine contracts examined (eight of which were admittedly in trouble), of $6.8 million expended, the results were:
   a. Software deliverd, but never used: $3.2 million.
   b. Software paid for, but never delivered: $1.95 million.
   c. Software extensively reworked before use: $1.3 million.
   d. Software used after changes: $198,000.
   e. Software used as delivered: $119,000.

As the report concludes, "The government got for its money less than 2 percent of the total value of the contracts."

Can software development be so unpredictable and troublesome in this age of enlightened practitioners who have access to higher-order languages, sophisticated operating systems, a variety of implementation tools, and various structured procedures and disciplines?

The report cites some causes for these problems:

Lack of specific contracting skills for solicitation and subsequent administration of software efforts.

Premature rush to develop systems before adequate requirements analysis is completed.

Tendency to commit to the entire project without proper planning or defining checkpoints.

Tendency to ignore final inspection and test conditions and related acceptance procedures.

The report also identifies some popular observations of the software process including:

Projects cost more and run longer than expected.

The "prototype" system usually ends up as a production system.

The ultimate operational system is often achieved after fixing the prototype at a cost equal to or greater than the initial development itself.

The GAO called for action by the federal government to remedy the situation, suggesting that specific guidelines be generated which would assist agencies in custom software development. In this regard, the report provides a provisional checklist of items that can serve as a basis for a more comprehensive attack on the problem.

But can better organization in itself, by the federal customer or any other software purchaser, really affect the fundamentals that operate in software construction? Regrettably, the customer's organization and procurement process has little influence on these factors.

What can be done? The single most important and influential step that can be taken when contracting for software is to require a "break-in" phase. In this phase, the contractor must review and feed back his full understanding of the requirements and the development objectives as a prerequisite to the start of the actual implementation. This process is part of the procedure technically called "inspection," which shall be dealt with in detail in the next section.

This procedural step—while possibly retracing earlier in-house activities which may have established the user requirements in the first place—will:

Reconfirm and authenticate operational requirements.

Provide expected performance parameters.

Establish test and acceptance procedures.

Validate the vendor's understanding and commitment.

After this step is satisfactorily completed, schedules and prices can be established and the customer can then organize to monitor and manage the software development.

In fact, the serious buyer may well wish to purchase this initial phase of the project from two qualified sources to provide a check and balance. It has been clearly established that most of the serious defects in software occurring during the operation of a system can be traced back to initial design flaws and oversights. Hence, extra dollars spent early in the game are the best investment that can be made to minimize post-contract problems. Yet it is this step that is too often expected by government procurement officers to be provided gratis.

But that isn't all that matters. The report overlooked two other important points. The first is the unrealistic belief that establishing "correct" specifications at the outset, and maintaining adherence to those requirements, will eliminate problems in developing software. Unfortunately, there are not many systems that can be definitively prescribed at the outset. Customarily, as development progresses, changes proliferate. Even more important, the client or end user often does not really know what is being sought in detail until pieces of the development become visible.

This understanding of the software construction process suggests the need for early completion of a system's basic functions which will help the user to track both progress and direction. This step becomes, therefore, an important and measurable contractual milestone.

Finally, the software buyer should be cautioned about the post-contract, operational phase, when critical maintenance activity begins. The importance of this period is often overlooked. The referenced GAO report emphasizes only the construction and delivery phase of government contracting for software, while ignoring the operational impact of the delivered software. If the maintenance experience had also been studied and evaluated, the federal government's problems with custom-developed software might have seemed even more serious than those reported.

5.2. PRODUCTION CONTROL THROUGH INSPECTION

The previous chapter outlined how bad software construction can be. In this connection, one often hears the criticism that software is always "too little and too late." Hope for improvement evolves from a more accurate understanding of the software development task. When the process of software construction is compared to an analogous process, building construction, for example, the solution to some of these problems becomes clear.

In the building industry, after all, it is expected that most buildings will be finished as prescribed, on schedule and within their budgets. Is it not true that these buildings stand up under their expected use for long periods of time? What is responsible for this kind of success?

The building industry has evolved over thousands of years and has developed an infrastructure that blends the talents and know-how of a number of disciplines—all directed and controlled by the "general contractor." This management function orchestrates the building process, tying together the efforts of specification, design, development, and turnover to the "end user." The team coordinated by the general contractor consists of the architect who designs under the aegis of well-developed, proven principles; the draftsman who translates abstract designs into engineering drawings; engineers who review for structural strength; the various specialty subcontractors who bring expertise in carpentry, plumbing, electricity, and so on, each exercising the particular methods and tools appropriate to this craft. What makes the process especially effective is the industry's commitment to standards and precast parts so that full advantage can be taken of productized modules.

The catalyst that brings it all together and assures a high degree of success is third-party review—the inspections that check for adherence to standards and rules. The process of incremental licensing, as a requisite to proceed, gives the building construction business the necessary discipline and incentives to do a professional job.

Software should also be built by experts, and it should be disciplined by rigorous quality assurance, paced by a similar process called inspection. Inspections are a powerful tool for both programmers and managers. Just as in the inspection of a building under construction, the software in development is compared at various stages to the original plans and specifications in order to identify problems as well as to evaluate adherence to standards. The technical leaders and managers depend on the inspections for checkpoints in tracking a project. These inspections become review milestones that must be passed successfully before further development can proceed.

Inspection is a methodology developed and popularized through the internal programming construction efforts at IBM. Important contributions to the computer literature that describe this IBM experience can be found in M. E. Fagan's article, "Design and Code Inspections to Reduce Errors in Program Development," (Fagan 1976), and in the IBM report, "Inspections in Application Development, Introduction and Implementation Guidelines" (IBM 1978).

Depending on the nature of the programming services, inspections may be conducted at several stages: project goals, preliminary design, detailed design, test plan, or clean compile. Beginning the inspection in the earlier stages is most advantageous because eliminating problems at those points can lead to enormous savings during later phases.

To begin the inspection, a team is formed. Although individual members will vary from team to team, the roles performed remain the same. Each team is led by a moderator who is in charge of the process. A reader, who is not the author of the computer program, paraphrases the materials at the meetings. One or more inspectors are present who will have reviewed the materials. This team meets with the author of the design or code, who has prepared the materials to be inspected according to a list of criteria.

At the first meeting, the materials are distributed, and the general background and philosophy of the documentation is discussed by the author. After the overview, the team members individually review the materials, possibly over several days. They use a formal and often specialized project checklist of possible error types to help locate problems.

After this individual preparation period, one or more inspection sessions are held. While the reader paraphrases the materials, team members point out any problems, inconsistencies, violations of standards, or ambiguities. The moderator carefully limits discussions to the job of identifying problems, and records every problem noted. Checklists are also used to systematically scan the materials for any problem areas. Design or redesign is not discussed at these meetings; the problems are simply identified.

The moderator tabulates statistical results from these sessions in order to locate common problems and to help plan future inspections. The moderator gives the author a complete list of all problems. The inspection process always assumes problems will be found. Consequently, as part of the project plan, time is scheduled for rework to fix problems. Depending on the nature of the errors found and the judgement of the moderator, the materials may or may not be reinspected by the inspection team. The moderator has the responsibility to ensure all rework is performed.

The inspection process should not be confused with another popular review method called the walkthrough. The walkthrough places the author at the helm of the discussion. Thus, impartiality is given up and the temptation is present to go down familiar paths. The author may also view the work from a biased point of view and might easily gloss over the difficult and unknown areas.

Inspections help to shift the emphasis toward more thoughtful design rather than hasty code. Successfully employed, inspections have led to programs that require 35 to 65 percent less debugging and test time. Problems reported after release of the software are reduced by as much as 40 percent. These positive benefits are a result of the basic time shift in discovering the errors inherent in any software development project. Experience has shown that as much as 90 percent of all errors that ultimately reside in a program are detected through the inspection process before unit testing begins.

To be effective as a formal procedure, the inspection must be implemented in a properly prepared, receptive environment. The prerequisites for preparing this environment are commitment, standards, methodology, and tools.

Management commitment is fundamental to installing the inspection process. There must be the desire to produce better software in a more organized fashion, accompanied by a willingness to try new, formal techniques. Besides this fundamental philosophical commitment, success in using inspections requires that both managers and programmers be aware of the various demands which will be placed on the project. These include:

1. A commitment to writing and approving designs before coding. We note that writing down ideas may take a lot of time.

2. A commitment of the time of several team members, sufficient to review software and participate in meetings.

3. A substantial commitment of the moderator's time to conduct the inspection and supervise rework.

4. A commitment that specific software, certain programmers, or selected development stages (e.g., code only) are not "singled out," but are all included in inspections.

5. A commitment to writing down all inspection results, problem reports, statistics, and so on.

6. A commitment to scheduling and performing the rework of software or a design, even if it represents a delay in the project.

The next requirement for successful inspections is the identification of standards. Software designs and code cannot be formally inspected or reviewed without reference to basic standards. The standards represent the discriminating measure of acceptable and unacceptable design and programming practices. Standards can also serve the extremely vital purpose of insuring that the development process is not reduced to simply generating compilable code.

In practice, inspection efficiency improves greatly with better and more detailed standards. Extensive discussions are not necessary. Many differences of opinion can be resolved or at least identified as being subjective. Issues of form and style, very critical to subsequent ease of maintenance, are simplified and become much easier to resolve. The whole process works faster, and more acceptable software will be produced before the inspection starts.

A development methodology is also key to inspection success. When inspections.are used on a project that is developing new software or modifying portions of old software, the development process must be followed step by step. Design inspections will be ineffective if the materials are not sufficiently detailed or if coding has already been done. Code inspections will become frustrating if design-related problems are still unsolved. Software must be inspected in an orderly fashion at its various stages of development. This becomes an indispensable requirement for effective inspections.

From another viewpoint, inspections can be the driving force to properly sequence the steps of development. If inspections are held at several stages (Goals, Preliminary Design, Code) then written materials must be produced at each such stage and the software design and implementation must therefore pass through these stages. This development methodology is thus intimately connected to the inspection sequence which drives the process through "exit criteria" from one project stage to the next.

Finally, inspections must be conducted with adequate tools. Inspections are not reviews held on the spur of the moment or spot-checks of a staff member's work. To be effective and efficient at locating and correcting problems, three types of tools are utilized to shape and define the procedures in a "customized" manner on any project. These tools are: the criteria for inspection materials, the various checklists, and the recording of data and statistical analysis of results. Before implementing inspections, managers and staff members should refine these tools for their particular projects.

The "criteria for inspection materials" specify what the author is to prepare for an inspection and what will be expected in order to pass the inspection. These are the so-called entry and exit criteria. The materials to be inspected should be specified in as much detail as necessary to avoid any confusion on the part of the team.

The criteria for materials are different for each of the Goals, Preliminary Design, and Code inspection phases. Criteria for each phase include: a statement of the purpose of inspection, prerequisites for initiation of the inspection step, a description of the format or outline to be used to convey the information, and a list of materials to be inspected at the meetings.

Each of the inspection phases has certain general requirements that apply to any application. These are identified in the baseline criteria for the materials needed for each phase. In addition, the criteria for materials for each stage should also describe any specialized requirements tailored to the needs of the particular environment. Each project implementing inspections should develop such specialized criteria, referring to items such as the specific operating system, the particular software application, and the implementation language. The items listed in the baseline model can be expanded to meet a project's specific needs.

The second tool is the checklist. This outlines the various categories of problems that may be encountered. Each category contains a series of questions used to locate problems. Although checklists are not intended to be an exhaustive list of problems, they are a representative sample of common types of problems.

Checklists vary for each of the inspection phases. Only code checklists are language-specific. Like the criteria for inspection materials, the checklists include general questions pertinent to any application, as well as additional questions that are specific to a project's environment. Any one checklist may include as many as 100 items to be reviewed in categories such as the programming module's functionality, data usage, control logic, external linkages, computations, maintainability, and readability. While the design review checklists are general in nature, the programming language checklists are specific to languages and systems, such as FORTRAN, COBOL, PL/I, MARK IV Systems, IMS, and so on.

Checklists are used in several ways. Each team member should be familiar with the questions on the checklist to assist in finding problems. During the preparation period, the checklists can be used as a way of reviewing the materials. Based on previous experience, the moderator may advise the team to pay particular attention to specific problem categories during preparation.

During the inspection sessions, the moderator decides how to use a checklist. The checklist may be used with each module, only on selected materials, or it might not be used at all. When a checklist is used at the meeting, each major checklist category is briefly mentioned, and the team is given a chance to scan the questions and locate any problems not previously mentioned. Scanning with the checklist may occur after the line-by-line paraphrasing, or in lieu of the paraphrasing.

Checklists are also used by the moderator in categorizing the major problems found and tabulating problem statistics. Checklists should be revised regularly so that common problems are included in the list and nonrecurring problems are removed from it.

Checklists can shape the inspection process. Very detailed checklists can cause inspections to be very thorough, whereas streamlined checklists can speed up inspections in favor of locating only major problems.

The last tool is the moderator's systematic recording of the events and findings taking place during the inspection meeting. Using well-designed forms, a problem report is developed that records the errors reflecting omissions, violations of standards, wrong logic, and even extra features. These data become the basis for the rework and subsequent reinspection, if necessary.

The data also become input to the ever-expanding statistical data base of discovered problems and problem types. These data, over time, will provide helpful information to management in improving the organization's skills and in eliminating bad working habits. For this purpose, error rates per thousand lines of code or per thousand lines of design statements are tabulated by individual, project, and module types.

The principal benefits of inspections are as follows:

1. Significant reduction in testing time by as much as 65 percent.
2. Significant reduction in coding errors and functional omissions during the software operational phase; as many as five times the number of problems occur during operations for systems built without inspection.
3. Improved quality of the finished product from the functional point of view.
4. Improvement in the professional performance of individuals participating in the inspections, quantitatively seen by a reduction in error

rates over time and increase in lines of code produced per unit of time by as much as a factor of two.

5. Identification of common problem areas for the entire staff, which can then be given proper management attention and correction.

6. Early warning signals of potential problems with individuals and identification of "error-prone modules" when the inspection discovers error rates that significantly depart from the norm.

Inspections provide a subtle and most important contribution to software development and operation. The inspection process shifts the discovery and correction of errors and defects from software's operational period to the early design stages. Since the cost for software corrections during operations is many times the cost incurred in detecting problems during design, inspections provide an unusual leveraging of cost/benefit over the entire life cycle of the software.

Inspections are not free. Design inspections can require from two to six hours per person for 1000 equivalent lines of code whereas code inspections can require between five and fifteen hours per person for each 1000 lines of code. Also the number of detected major errors can vary from a low of 40 per 1000 lines of code to double that number.

The payoff is in higher performance in quality and delivery of the product. Experience has shown that projects starting with stated requirements and undergoing the discipline of inspections were completed close to schedule and, most important, delivered at less than $5 per line of code produced at a rate of nearly 10 lines per hour. Such performance is at least 100 percent better than the performance usually associated with conventional methods of program construction.

In summary, although additional effort must be applied to a project to implement inspections, the impact on productivity is positive—primarily because of the substantial reduction in the maintenance activity resulting from the higher quality of the product.

5.3. SOFTWARE COMPATIBILITY OR PORTABILITY

Since the early days of computing there has been a struggle for universality in the design of hardware on the one hand and the applicability of software on the other. Uniformity associated with hardware has been called *compatibility*, whereas the quality of machine-independence in software has been dubbed *portability*. Achieving compatibility or portability, or both, would go a long way toward more effective management of the software process.

Early attempts at universality were not concerned with conformity in hardware logic or in machine organization. Indeed, word size, register variability, and overall architecture differed from vendor to vendor, as well as from machine to machine for even the individual manufacturer. Conformity was sought through the establishment of language standards. Thus evolved two major and independent efforts, both relying on higher-order languages as a means of crossing over hardware lines.

The first approach depended on the problem-oriented statement facility of languages such as FORTRAN and COBOL. These languages were widely welcomed for their promise of providing uniformity and portability of application from machine to machine. Instead of the evolution of an "Esperanto" for computing, however, there developed a plethora of similar languages, with large numbers of dialects.

Another effort in this direction was made by a group of avant-garde users who were leading member companies of the IBM computer users association, SHARE. These companies committed themselves to a major cooperative venture in sponsoring the Universal Computer-Oriented Language (UNCOL). This effort was supported not only by key user organizations but also by the better computing minds of the late 1950s.

The UNCOL concept was simple. One would first develop applications in any higher-order language. Such programs would then be compiled to generate intermediate language programs in UNCOL. These programs would be accepted by the UNCOL object machine translator, generating object code for a specific target machine.

On a theoretical basis, the concept was sound and presumably feasible. While the scheme permitted statement of the application in a common language, quite naturally the individual transformations which would exist for the various machines could lead to local anomalies (primarily resulting from data representations) such that the processing for two different machines could never be guaranteed to be identical. Whether for this reason, or for some other, the UNCOL project did not materialize. Perhaps it fell apart from its own enormous weight and from lack of user interest. With the passing of UNCOL, it seemed as if the computing world retreated from its early zeal for universality and began to accept the various independent paths taken by both manufacturers and language builders.

Still another technique for transportability was sought in the early sixties through development of a programming system written in its own language. Once a sufficient kernel of that language or an intermediate language was hand-coded or compilable for a particular machine, the system would be self-generating on an object machine. Although such efforts were actually undertaken and demonstrated (e.g., NELIAC), the computing world neither rushed to adopt these experiments nor supported their commercialization.

If anything was to be done to facilitate transportability from one machine environment to another, it would take on a specialized, hardware orientation or at least the vested interest of a hardware manufacturer. Thus was born the general concept of emulation and conversion.

Emulation was a joint hardware/software approach to maintain operability on newer generation hardware of the software developed for older systems. A good example is the emulation of the IBM 1400 series software on the subsequently available IBM 360 and later IBM 370 line.

Conversion was invoked by a manufacturer wishing to transfer (or un-hook) software from one brand of hardware to another. A good example of such a venture, and a highly successful one at that, was Honeywell, Inc.'s Liberator, announced in 1963, which modified IBM 1400 programs to oper-ate on a competitive computer line, the H-200.

Besides such manufacturing efforts, specialists continued to offer software products and professional services for moving software from one environ-ment to another. There are, for example, COBOL-to-COBOL schemes, PL/I-COBOL translators, Autocoder-to-COBOL systems, RPG-to-COBOL or PL/I, and 1400 Series software converters and simulators.

The next great moment in seeking the Valhalla of universality came about in the late seventies. This time the movement was motivated by some very strong economic factors.

Because of the sheer dominance of IBM computers, an enormous invento-ry of application and system software emerged for these machines. This software is valued at more than twice the installed hardware base—a mere $200 billion.

A second important event also took place. Computer hardware engineer-ing had become a highly efficient and mechanized process. Through semi-conductor technology and modern electronic design methods, new comput-ers could be designed and subsequently manufactured with relatively modest efforts.

The stage was therefore set for the advent of the plug-compatible main-frame (PCM). This product would take advantage of the wealth of existing IBM machine-oriented software available in the public domain, as well as that software available on a commercial basis, directly from IBM and from independent sources.

Indeed, since software had become the bottleneck in the evolution of the computer industry, it became a clear economic matter to exploit such soft-ware by seeking to utilize it over longer periods of time. Also, a second strategy emerged—seeking more cost-effectiveness from existing software by improving its performance on better, yet compatible, hardware rather than by reprogramming. And this is indeed what has happened in the large com-puter marketplace, leveraging existing IBM 370-based software by extending its life cycle and performance through hardware evolution.

In the small end of the computer market, a different phenomenon has developed on microcomputers. Rather than solving the transportability problem of software by producing machines that are compatible, manufac-turers are producing software that will operate on a variety of hardware devices.

Surprisingly, substantial software standards have emerged in this low end market where an operating system such as CP/M™ from Digital Research Inc. and the BASIC language systems offered by Microsoft Inc. are de facto universals. In both, the software operates on a diverse number of computing systems, certainly aided initially by the common presence in most systems of a small variety of CPU chips.

Emerging from this environment are applications which are indeed portable because they are programmed in a common BASIC and function in a common operating system. One well-known business application supplier advertises extensive software to operate on 23 varied hardware offerings.

Even when the chip was not common to the software, ingenious portability solutions were sought. For example, Microsoft created the Z80-based Softcard which, when connected to an Apple II computer, allows for ready execution of software developed for the Zilog Z80 and the Intel 8080 world on machines employing the 6502 CPU.

Perfect portability, however, still lies out of reach. A so-called standard BASIC and standard operating system still present differences, including any one or more of the following aberrations:

Applicable release of the BASIC.

Applicable release of the Operating System (OS).

Specific vendor's deviations from the standard BASIC or OS.

The booting or start-up process.

Storage organization and transfer standards.

The physical aspect of storage transfer itself may well present formidable blocks to easy transfer from one system to another. Not only is disk size an issue, but also whether the disks are single- or double-density and single- or double-sided. Another parameter concerns whether the disk is hard- or soft-sectored, and how the storage labels and directory are organized. These variations can easily lead to 128 combinations—although most can be quickly eliminated. Nevertheless, this does show that portability of software is not an automatic process.

At least one vendor has taken transportability to its ultimate destination. CAP-CPP of the United Kingdom has developed a total operating environment with associated language facilities and utilities. Applications can operate in more than 20 different computer environments ranging from the IBM Series/1 to the Digital Equipment Corporation's PDP-11 and even to many of the common microprocessor-based, desktop computers and workstations.

Application builders in this environment are truly independent of the hardware as long as the system, called MicroCOBOL, is available for the object hardware system. From the user's point of view, the functionality of MicroCOBOL is independent of the host hardware to the point where neither the applications developer, nor the end user executing the interactive applications, needs to know which machine is driving the screens, nor does he care.

Portability in this system is defined to the nth degree, inclusive of the assertion that program dumps would, if shown in hexadecimal, appear identical—that is, independent of the machine on which the program operated.

An error in one machine would necessarily be duplicated in a second machine, if the error is software. That is to say, "bugs" can be replicated. As a matter of fact, the system is strong enough to be used for identification of hardware defects if it can be shown that the software operating on one system does not reproduce the same results on the second. The leading light of this achievement is Alex d'Agapayeff, who declares that the MicroCOBOL capability has given birth to "immortal software."

The importance of achieving machine-invariant software is not perceived today in exactly the same light as it was by the early computing pioneers. Today we are driven to software universality for a number of other reasons. First of all, there is the overwhelming economic one of cost-effectiveness as reflected in development productivity and maintenance. The more users that can share in the use of a piece of software, the more attractive and cost-effective that software can be. In other words, the only chance for software to begin to match the continuing cost-effective improvements of hardware is to achieve more widespread and common utilization.

A second point is the rapid movement toward distributed data processing. Distributed data and/or programs implies the need for maximizing portability, especially when control in acquiring hardware itself may become more and more distributed. Not only are the equipment types diverse and fast-changing, but the purchasing is distributed so that centralized control, which earlier sought to achieve uniformity in hardware, is no longer possible.

A third key issue is the strong movement to the microprocessor through workstations and desktop computers. These instruments have begun to invade the end-user area, both as entry-level systems, and as sophisticated entry points to networks in centralized systems. The widespread availability of such devices and their variability gives strong support to universality in software.

Whether it's hardware compatibility moving downward from the large mainframes to smaller machines or software portability reaching upward from the micro, both transportability technologies are now necessary to realize the more cost-effective use of computers in the eighties.

Additional Readings

The material in this chapter can be further developed by referring to the following articles in the Bibliography at the end of the book: Boehm, 1976a; Cave and Salisbury, 1978; Christensen et al., 1981; Data Base, 1980; De Roze and Nyman, 1978; EDP Analyzer, 1979; EDP Analyzer, 1981g; Electronic Design, 1981; Fagan, 1976; Felkowitz, 1978; Fisher, 1974; IBM, 1977; IEEE, 1978; Jensen, 1981; Kendall, 1977; Myers, 1978; Proceedings, 1979; Putnam, 1978; Wassermann, 1978; and Wassermann, 1980a.

SIX

Software Implementation Systems

In Chapter 3 the concern for increasing productivity in producing and operating software was explored. Although there is no immediate resolution of this issue, there is hope of achieving improvement by applying better implementation systems. In this chapter popular approaches that purport to meet this problem are reviewed. Section 6.1 discusses the nature of the application generator and illustrates the methodology through three examples. This implementation tool takes on many forms, depending on who offers the aid. In Section 6.2 a more in-depth look is taken at one very popular application generator, the MARK IV System.

Section 6.3 comments on the impact of a new programming system, Ada, which represents the most ambitious undertaking to provide a complete implementation environment based on a procedural language.

This is followed by Sections 6.4 and 6.5, where taxonomy of implementation systems is summarized and described to bring into focus various alternative processes and methodology in developing software.

This chapter ends with Section 6.6, which looks at the popularization of "user friendly" as it pertains to software. It is shown that in software, as in other things, there is no perfect solution to make life easy for everyone.

6.1. THE APPLICATION GENERATOR

"Application generator" is one of the most important alternative means of increasing the production and subsequent maintenance of application software. Is this term a modern day version of the older concepts of automatic programming, implicitly programmed systems, or program generator? Or is it another way of describing a nonprocedural language? Or is it, perhaps, an attempt to achieve the ultimate higher-order language in the form of a report writer, user query system, or parameter driven program?

The precise meaning of the term is in doubt because we apply it indiscriminately to both the manner of implementing an application and the degree of ease in implementation. One of the earlier uses of the term appeared in the book *Data Processing in 1980–1985* (Dolotta et al. 1976), where the application generator is described in terms of desired objectives in enhancing the productivity of application development by:

1. Minimizing the percent of total software in a new application that is new software.

2. Extending the life cycle of a line of code.

3. Permitting new software to be reusable in other development.

4. Reducing skill level requirements of implementations.

5. Significantly increasing productivity of implementations and quality of resulting products.

6. Permitting more direct and unambiguous statement or design of problems to be solved.

7. Eliminating variability in system design by different individuals.

The following definition of the application generator is presented in the Dolotta book:

A tool for implementing an application via user/terminal interaction, in a dialogue setting, where selection choices and responses to posed questions lead to the automatic tying together of hierarchically organized sets of building blocks into executable programs for solving a specific problem.

In more familiar words, an application generator is a computer program that accepts application implementor directives in the form of specifications that are then automatically transformed into an operating computer program. Both of these definitions leave scope for interpretation, which accounts for the wide variation in features existing among application generators.

For example, IBM has introduced two concepts in connection with providing more implementation capability for the computer user: Application Enabling and Data Systems. Both of these terms have been linked to application generation.

Application Enabling offers three choices for enhancing new application development. One is the purchase or lease of off-the-shelf packaged software. The second includes certain licensed software designed for non-data processing personnel to assist in problem solving—for example, query systems, report writers, and special purpose financial planning tools. The key operating theme for this software is an English-like language which purports to simplify the exercise of a functional program by users who have no DP knowledge.

The third member of this enabling capacity is the Application Generator. IBM describes this software productivity enhancer as a "simple fill-in-the-blank technique to specify preprogrammed functions, instead of writing in a procedural language."

Two IBM products are specifically identified to illustrate this concept of application generator: the Application Development Facility (ADF) and the Development Management System (DMS). The former is used with building applications for operation with IBM's data base management system, IMS, and the latter is used in construction of programs for operation in mainframe Customer Information Control System (CICS) or the 8100 Information System environments.

The Data Systems concept encompasses the same objectives as Application Enabling but is limited to construction of programs that are heavily dependent on data base and data communications (DB/DC). The overall environment starts with a data dictionary focal point, adds the DL/1 or IMS/DB data base, is inclusive of CICS or IMS/DC for data communications, and provides a "data delivery" capacity for constructing an application solution. Again, as in the enabling viewpoint, the ADF and DMS program products are classified as application generators that are part of the data delivery portion of Data Systems.

In its use of the term application generator, within both Application Enabling and Data Systems concepts, IBM has proposed software that is a useful and powerful implementation tool but hardly a significant step in the direction of making application development easier for any but trained DP practitioners. Neither ADF nor DMS are designed to take advantage of precoded application submodules, nor are they tools easily learned by novices.

Another way of seeking the meaning of the term *application generator* is to review other software offerings that claim the label. For instance, consider the American Management Systems (AMS) product, Generation 5. This software is contrasted by its producer with procedural languages, and its scope is limited to the development of financial applications. The authors claim that this application generator achieves initial development and lifetime maintenance cost improvement of 60 percent or better over conventional programming methods.

The components of Generation 5 are said to be five: a specialized language oriented to financial systems, a design methodology, a data management capability, a screen generation facility, and precoded functional components common to the application. Included, for the latter, are an automatic audit trail, maintenance of data integrity, data entry efficiency, controlled access to data and, data retrieval facilities.

This software system achieves its productivity-enhancing objectives by employing specialized features that accommodate implementation of the financial application. For example, edit and validation processes are automatically invokable and are designed to support accounting needs. Reports can be requested in form and content that are financially oriented, as in the case of requesting an "aging" report or a cross-footed presentation.

AMS attaches a different meaning to the application generator by contrasting it with four prior implementation technologies beginning with machine language, assemblers, compilers and, finally, parameterized languages or precompilers. Presumably the last three of these methods could be called program generators to distinguish them from application generators, the latter being directly tied to a specific user requirement or function. In this sense, the term application generator does not accord with IBM usage, where the products ADF and DMS are application independent and more procedural in nature.

A contrast to AMS are the Implementation System offerings of Informatics General Corp. These products are best represented by the MARK IV System.

MARK IV, and the related systems ANSWER/2™ and ANSWER/DB™, are powerful nonprocedural systems that generalize the processing functions associated with file definition, file creation, data maintenance, report generation, and query. In their totality these offerings represent the power and capability of data management systems.

It is possible to implement a specific business application by selecting from a choice of parametric settings as well as by stating logical conditions in transaction processing, retrieval, and reporting. In this sense, perhaps 95 percent of the operative computer instructions will have been precoded in MARK IV and will be executed during operations, guided by the selected parameters and logic. The structure and capability of the system is, therefore, preset and limited to the generalized features and functions that have been implemented by the software supplier.

The consequence of this use of MARK IV is to leverage the application production capacity of the implementor in three dramatic ways:

1. Reduces the actual development time by up to 6 to 1 through ease of use; the necessary MARK IV directives require less than comparable lines of COBOL instructions by an order of magnitude.

2. Replaces program documentation by the automatically produced MARK IV output tables.

3. Reduces software maintenance requirements, since the MARK IV System is maintained by the software vendor.

All three of these examples claim to be Application Generators and seem to satisfy the following definition offered by Datapro Research Corporation:

The application generator is a set of preprogrammed functional modules within which are variable parameters, which can be uniquely defined for a particular application, and which can perform automatic application functions. It is also a facility within which data files can be defined, constructed, and accessed by program logic; where input transactions can be defined and accepted for subsequent editing and processing; and where outputs can be defined and produced in accordance with operational, functional, and peripheral equipment needs.

Yet we have seen at least three different views of what an Application Generator is and does. As in many areas of data processing, words by themselves do not necessarily tell the story nor are they used consistently. The term Application Generator is another one of those buzz words that floats around and hasn't settled. Accordingly, we see the need for better terminology to distinguish between systems such as DMS, Generation 5, and the MARK IV System.

6.2. THE MARK IV STORY

One of the first commercial efforts at producing software was the MARK IV System of Informatics General Corp. This product was mentioned in the previous section as an example of an application generator. To demonstrate the implementation leverage provided by an application generator, we will now describe the system in more detail.

MARK IV was initially offered in 1967 as a proprietary software product by Informatics. It was the culmination of years of thought and development by John A. Postley, and had emerged from a number of predecessor systems—the Generalized Information Retrieval and Listing System (GIRLS) and the three earlier MARK systems.

MARK IV is today one of the most widely used proprietary software implementation systems. It ranks in usage as a nonprocedural programming language behind Assembler, COBOL, PL/I, BASIC, and FORTRAN. More than 20,000 individuals have received formal training in MARK IV usage and more than 40,000 have employed it for implementing applications in a worldwide installation base of over 1700 facilities.

Computer languages, like the computer itself, have been in a state of constant evolution for the last three-and-a-half decades. In general, the evolution has been from machine or procedure-oriented languages toward nonprocedural or task-oriented languages. This process is depicted in the language evolution chart of Figure 6.1, where the development of procedural and nonprocedural languages are shown over time. Also noted is the relative importance of operating environment dependencies associated with each of the identified language types.

Users of procedural languages focus on the dynamics of providing a proper sequence of instructions so that the computer will perform a set of desired functions. Nonprocedural languages provide automatic triggering of most standard computer procedures after users state the problem requiring solu-

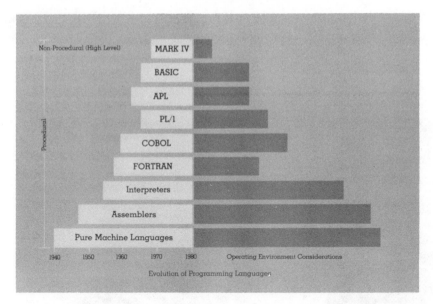

Figure 6.1. Evolution of programming languages.

tion. Such languages are also spoken of as "high-level" or "people-oriented." MARK IV is such a language.

MARK IV is not only a very powerful high-level computer language, but is also simple to use and economical. Programs written in MARK IV are brief and efficient. A program written in MARK IV, for example, requires approximately one-tenth the number of statements required by a COBOL program.

Just as COBOL is a higher-level language than Assembler, MARK IV is at a higher level than COBOL. In fact, MARK IV is to COBOL as COBOL is to Assembler. Features and programming techniques that must be manually generated with lower-level languages are provided automatically by MARK IV.

MARK IV incorporates hundreds of the most often-used programming techniques and makes them available to the user in the form of automatic features and intrinsic capabilities. The user who takes advantage of the more than 2000 completely automatic functions of MARK IV can concentrate on task definition, relieved of virtually all procedural concerns. Actual programming and key-entry times are reduced by 90 percent over the same program written in COBOL. In most instances, execution times equal or surpass those of COBOL.

With MARK IV, functions such as reading input files, file coordination, transaction updating, table lookups, text editing, data base access, report formatting, and many more are performed without a single line of code being written. This means that users of MARK IV can regard systems and applications not as lines of coding but as blocks of programs designed to meet their needs.

The net result of the use of MARK IV is a dramatic return on investment via improved application systems implemented and maintained in a fraction

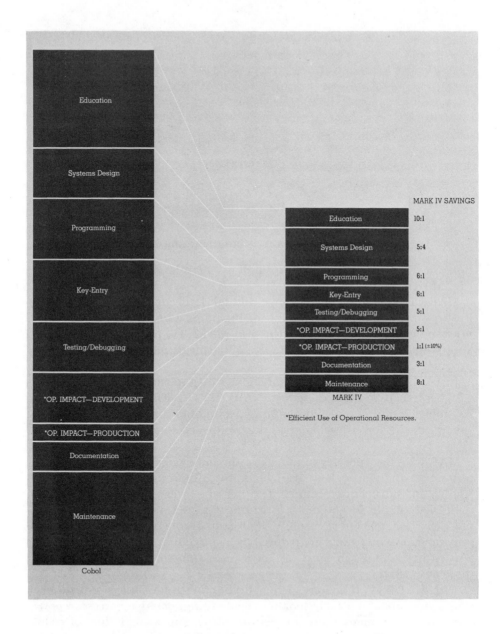

Figure 6.2. Comparison of COBOL-MARK IV.

CAPABILITY/FEATURES	1968	1981
Cumulative Quantity		
Revenues	$2 Million	$115 Million
Installations	50	1,700
Releases	1	26
Development Dollars	$1 Million	$17 Million
Training Classes	— —	3,000
People Trained	— —	24,000
Base Price		
Minimum System	None	$15,000
Top-of-Line System	$30,000	$90,000
Count or Number		
Models	1	8
Operating System Environments	2	6
Options/Special Features	1	25
Lines of Code	25,000	600,000
Program Modules	72	935
Overlays	8	92
Pages Documentation	200	2,000
Diagnostic Messages	284	2,100
Training Courses	5	10
Installation Parameters	1	60
Typical Host Computer	IBM 360/40	IBM 3033
Minimum Host Computer	IBM 360/25	IBM 4331
Maintenance Fee	None	7 to 10%/year

Figure 6.3.   Thirteen years of the MARK IV system.

of the time and at a fraction of the cost of conventional methods. This productivity enhancement is illustrated in Figure 6.2 by comparing the application implementation steps of a COBOL approach with the use of MARK IV.

But the real MARK IV story is best represented by the progress of the product over its lifetime. When the package was originally made available, its life expectancy was four to five years, coinciding with the expected life cycle of the then-prevalent IBM 360 family of computers. Since then, however, MARK IV has evolved as a family of capabilities in its own right, enjoying a longer life span through the continued use of the 360 computer family, the follow-on IBM 370 series and, now, because of hardware life-cycle extenders, the IBM series 30XX, and the IBM-compatible CPUs. Figure 6.3 provides a view of how this software product evolved, showing the progress of the system for over a decade of service.

After 23 releases and expenditures for development exceeding $17 million, the MARK IV System has been improved and expanded in a variety of measurable ways. Not only does it operate in more environments, but its capability and capacity have expanded by more than a decimal order of magnitude as measured by lines of code, program modules, overlays, documentation, error messages, and available options.

What has not changed are the 11 basic implementation specification forms. The language externals, while enhanced, have not been compromised. Software written for the early releases will also function under the current MARK IV.

It is interesting to note that the top-of-the-line system price, with much enhanced capability and functions, has increased by 200 percent in a decade during which the Consumer Price Index, measuring the inflation rate, rose by a like amount. The price increase, therefore, is washed out by the inflationary impact. Hence, the increased capability of the system, estimated to be a factor of fifteen, becomes the cost-effectiveness improvement of this software over the 13-year period.

Users who have employed MARK IV over the years have truly benefited considering that their total expenditures, including the annual maintenance fee, will have been substantially less than $100,000. Given the product's productivity enhancement over COBOL programming by as much as a six to one factor, as illustrated in Figure 6.2, the investment can typically be recouped in as short a time frame as a year.

What is MARK IV and why does it have such unusual power and attractiveness? Fundamental to MARK IV is the ability to manipulate files of data without the user ever needing to be aware of where the files are located, how they are organized or how they are accessed. The MARK IV processing cycle is shown in Figure 6.4.

Simply stated, MARK IV has three basic features:

Input control—the ability to access and manipulate files from a variety of storage media.

Processing control—the ability to manipulate and alter (update) the state of stored information.

Output control—the ability to retrieve, format, and transmit data in reports or other output media.

With MARK IV the basic unit is the file (or data base), and the logical structuring and processing of the information in the data base is the programming goal. MARK IV can process files that already exist within an installation or can be used to create new files. In either case, the description of the file is completely independent from the file itself.

MARK IV processes a wide variety of files with various formats and record structures. The format of the files and the structure of the records are defined to MARK IV using a simple file definition form. This form specifies the physical file format, the logical record structure, and the attributes of the individual fields within the records. The file definition form is shown in Figure 6.5.

The structure and format of a file and the records within that file are defined to MARK IV and stored in its library. This is the one and only time these files need be defined. The independence of this description of the file

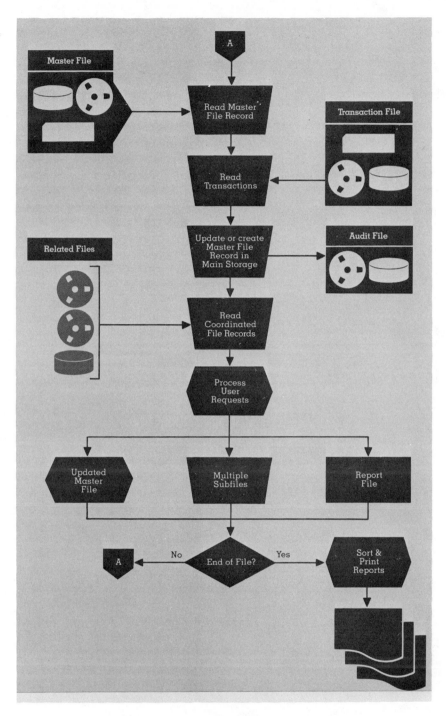

Figure 6.4. Standard MARK IV processing.

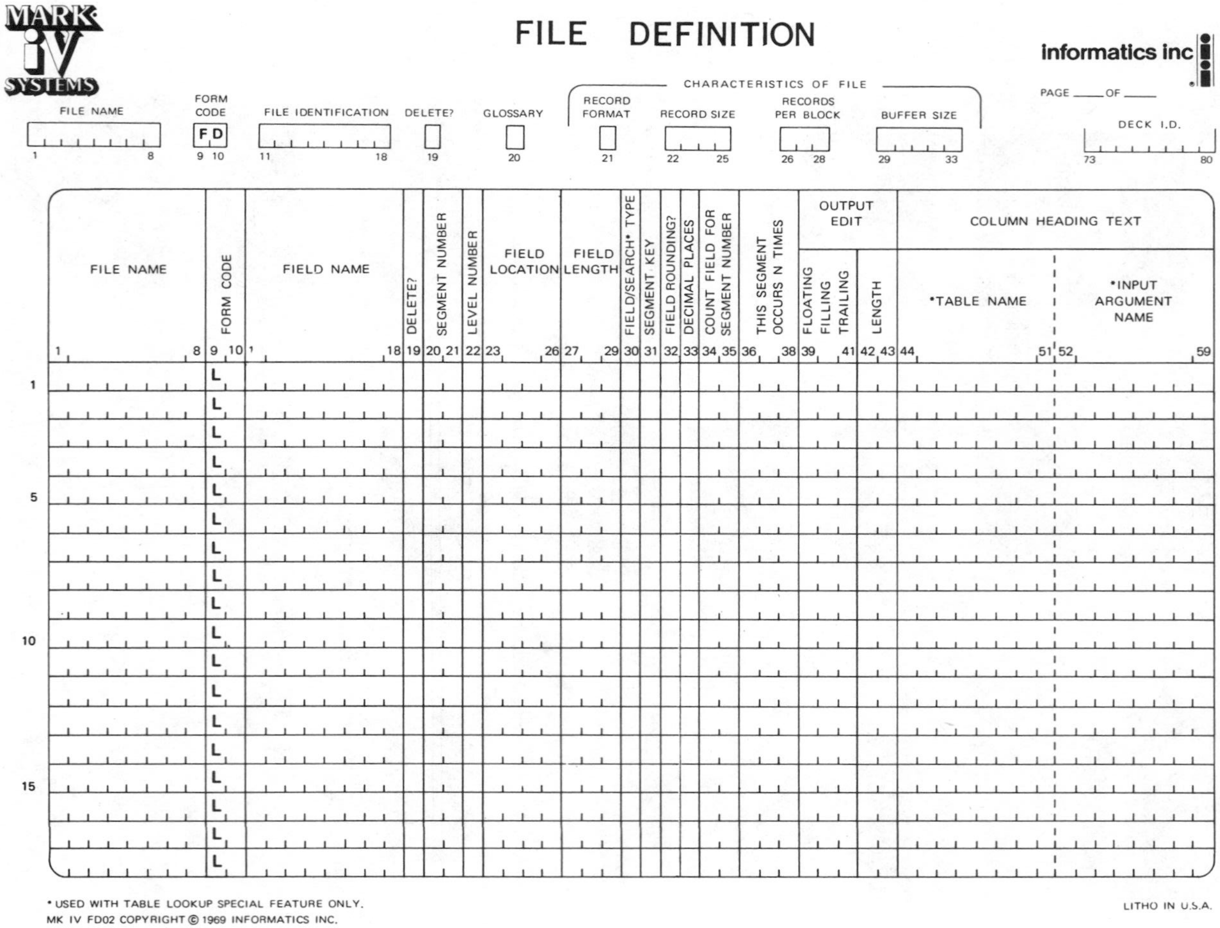

Figure 6.5. File definition form.

structure from the file itself allows the file to be described in a logical manner regardless of the physical structure of the actual data.

The MARK IV Information Request form makes programming an easy task for any newcomer to data processing. To illustrate, picture a busy accountant who has just received a request from his manager for the total year-to-date activity on one vendor's account for 1979. The manager wants the information by 5 p.m. today. The accountant reaches for his MARK IV request forms and begins his "programming" effort to extract accounts payable information for the vendor whose identification code is 2386.

The following steps correspond to the Roman numerals on the MARK IV Information Request Form of Figure 6.6:

I. Taking an Information Request form, our accountant writes in a Request Name, any name that fits the allotted space.

II. He writes TODAY in the Report Date box (to get TODAY's date on the report).

No other information is required in the heading area of the form. MARK IV provides automatic default conditions for everything left blank. In this example, MARK IV will produce a single-spaced report on standard-sized paper.

III. To be able to request information from a file of data the file would have to be previously defined to MARK IV. MARK IV stores this definition, and a printed glossary of the names is available at any time for any users of the file. The file definition provides our accountant with a glossary showing the names of the pieces of data which make up the file.

Therefore, when our accountant wants to refer to the data on the file, he just looks at the glossary for the Accounts Payable file and uses the names that were assigned to the pieces of data in the file. For instance, the piece of data that is the vendor number is called VENDOR, and since the vendor in which he is interested is ABC Manufacturing (vendor number 2386), he "selects" that vendor by writing VENDOR EQ(ual) D(for Decimal) 2386 in the Record Selection area of the form. When looking at the Accounts Payable file, MARK IV will pick out only the data about vendor 2386.

IV. Since only the activity of 1979 is of interest, the accountant writes A(for AND) INVYEAR EQ D 79 to select only the activity concerning ABC Manufacturing Company that has taken place in 1979.

If no such special selection criteria were required, (e.g., all activity for all vendors is desired), then the Record Selection portion of the form would be left blank. The default condition for MARK IV would then report on the total contents of the Payables file.

V. Now that our accountant has specified the selection criteria, he can particularize the data he wants to see on the report itself. He wants the vendor's invoice number, date, amount, check number, check date, and amount paid. He writes the names for those pieces of data (taken from the glossary), one on each line in the Report Specification section of the form, in the sequence he wants them to appear across the report.

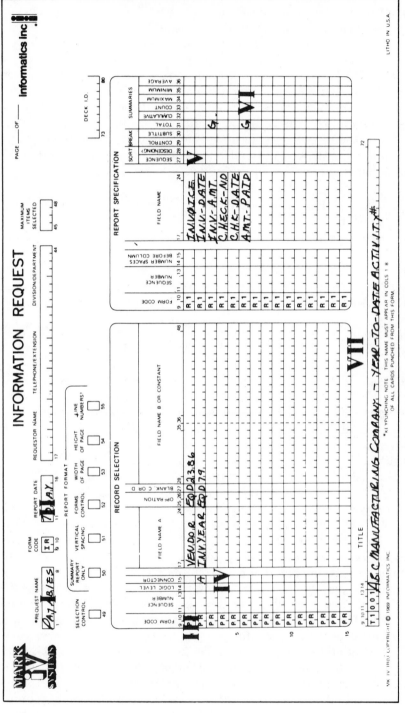

Figure 6.6. Information request form.

VI. To get a total of the activity being reported, our accountant simply enters a G(for Grand) in the column marked Total on the same lines as INV-AMT and AMT-PAID. MARK IV will provide a grand total of all the INV-AMTs and AMT-PAIDs in the report.

VII. Finally, to give a meaningful title to his report, our accountant writes his own title in the section of the form labeled Title.

That's all there is to it. Of course, at this point, the accountant will give his filled out Information Request form to someone in the data processing organization who keypunches the form, enters the data into the computer, and delivers the resulting report. The requested report will look like the output shown in Figure 6.7, for which all of the formatting will have been done automatically. In essence, we tell the computer system via MARK IV *what* we want and not *how* to solve a problem. This is the fundamental difference between employing a nonprocedural language and a procedural language.

If an on-line terminal is available, the accountant could alternatively submit the request to the computer directly and receive the requested information back at the terminal. For example, the following request entered at a terminal is also possible, employing MARK IV as the retrieval and reporting mechanism:

LIST INVOICE INV-DATE INV-AMT CHECK-NO CHK-DATE AMT-PAID

TOTAL INV-AMT AMT-PAID

TITLE 'ABC MANUFACTURING COMPANY-YEAR-TO-DATE ACTIVITY'

WHERE VENDOR EQ 2386 AND INV-YEAR EQ 79

```
04/28/79      ABC MANUFACTURING COMPANY - YEAR-TO-DATE ACTIVITY        PAGE  1
```

INVOICE NUMBER	INVOICE DATE	INVOICE AMOUNT	CHECK NUMBER	CHECK DATE	AMOUNT PAID
51-03917	01/12/79	3.47	002571	02/15/79	3.47
51-07242	01/14/79	60.43	002571	02/15/79	60.43
51-11275	01/21/79	152.40	002571	02/15/79	152.40
51-12336	01/27/79	104.53	002571	02/15/79	104.53
51-14514	02/03/79	14.44	002819	03/15/79	14.44
51-17180	02/14/79	102.42	002819	03/15/79	102.42
51-20992	02/29/79	63.00	002819	03/15/79	63.00
51-21541	03/02/79	189.12	002819	03/15/79	189.12
51-23730	03/07/79	19.72	003093	04/17/79	19.72
51-24226	03/10/79	1,092.46	003093	04/17/79	1,092.46
51-28859	03/27/79	605.00	003093	04/17/79	605.00
51-29331	03/31/79	5,486.00	003093	04/17/79	5,486.00
51-31155	04/07/79	19.09	003095	04/18/79	19.09
51-33126	04/11/79	187.55	003095	04/18/79	187.55
51-34568	04/15/79	28.90	003096	04/19/79	28.90

```
GRAND TOTAL                          8,128.53                          8,128.53
```

Figure 6.7. Output for information request.

This example is, of course, fairly simple, but the situation illustrated is common in most businesses. What is uncommon is the ease with which this hypothetical problem was solved. With the MARK IV Information Request form, solving similar problems easily and quickly can become a common occurrence.

For more complex processing and reporting requirements, additional MARK IV capabilities enable the professional analyst or programmer to ply his trade in a more sophisticated manner, employing a number of other, more powerful request specification forms. It is this aspect of specifying an application solution and automatically generating the operational program that justifies calling the MARK IV System an application generator. Indeed, as will be seen in Section 6.5, MARK IV is also classified as a complete, integrated solution system.

6.3. ADA, THE PROGRAMMING SYSTEM FOR THE EIGHTIES

Application generators are the focal point for enhancing productivity with nonprocedural techniques. Much of data processing, however, still continues to be procedurally oriented, especially in areas of building systems software and real-time applications. Effort is still directed, therefore, toward the development of more productive and more easily used algorithmically based implementation systems. One such project is Ada, the newest entry in the continuing search for better computer languages and implementation systems. The system is named in honor of the "first computer programmer," Ada Augusta, Countess of Lovelace, who lived in the early nineteenth century.

The role of the U.S. Department of Defense, DOD, in sponsoring Ada places a silver spoon in the mouth of this creation. DOD notwithstanding, there are also other powerful forces behind Ada, including the military establishments of England and Germany. This phenomenon currently ranks among the leading topics of computer interest and discussion. Therefore, Ada, like most women of today, must be taken seriously!

Is another computer language necessary? By the tone taken in many quarters, the answer is neither simple nor uniform. Let us cite a few comments:

A headline in *Computerworld* of April 13, 1981, "Turing Award Winner Warns of Ada's Dangers."

A quote in the February 1981 issue of *Datamation* attributed to an authority on programming language design, "Do not allow this language in its present state to be used in operations where reliability is critical."

An *Electronic News* column asking whether "DOD created a software albatross that has a limited cadre of programmers to support it and adopt it for military use?"

A feature story in *Mini Computer News* (8/12/80), "At the moment, the new language ADA is literally a paper tiger, that is, a work of rhetoric and precise planning, but not an implemented reality."

An editorial in the November 1979 issue of *Mini Micro Systems* worrying about a product sponsored by "a military establishment that's often perceived as an exasperating customer, and whose contributions to the advancement of technology, rightly or wrongly, are often viewed as destructive."

Some quotations carried in a *Business Week* article (3/23/81) that Ada's complexity "might sink of its own weight" and its "standardization won't help because it takes a tremendous amount of retraining of programmers."

The most biting comment, however, comes from one of the industry's most critical observers, Herbert Grosch. Writing in the August 21, 1980, issue of the British journal, *Computing*, Grosch compares Ada to the old aphorism describing the camel as a horse designed by a committee. Ada, he says, was "suggested by a corrupt committee, specified by a lowest-bid committee, designed by an overseas committee, trained by the Pentagon, and promised to the knackers while still a foal."

Of course, as Mr. Grosch and everyone else knows, a camel possesses qualities that a horse could never equal—namely, reliability and the ability to survive in an environment of extreme conditions.

There is, of course, another side to the coin. And we give due recognition to the more positive positions:

A more recent *Electronic News* headline proclaiming that the "Ada language finds wide acceptance" and reporting that a "rush is on to implement the new military programming language" by at least 25 publicly disclosed entities in the commercial, industrial, and military communities.

A favorable report in *Electronics* (2/10/81) describing the many advanced features of Ada and quoting the positive views of those who predict Ada will become the "ultimate language" and that "Ada will replace FORTRAN."

A similar feature article in *Mini Micro Systems* (4/81) heralding Ada as a language system for shortening "the conceptual distances from problem to program" and supporting the premise that it is "a significant software engineering tool."

An entire issue of the IEEE's prestigious monthly magazine *Computer* (6/81) devoting six articles to very positive reviews of Ada's current status as well as stating that it is "destined to become the dominant programming language of the 1980s."

An *Electronics* article (2/24/81) relating the endorsement by Intel. The Ada construct is favored as the basis for the architecture of Intel's multi-user 32-bit microprocessor, the APX432, and an early Ada compiler has been produced.

This is not the first time that the DOD has attempted to improve its own lot with respect to programming language uniformity. In earlier days the motivation was primarily portability. The military did not wish to be too dependent on any one manufacturer, nor on any particular computer family, in what was then already a rapidly changing technological environment.

Indeed, it was the DOD that convened the industry-wide Conference on Data Systems Languages which led to the specification of COBOL. Were it not for the DOD in the late fifties and early sixties, COBOL might not be the widely used language that it is today. But other efforts were not as successful as, for example, the standardization sought by the DOD with JOVIAL in the mid-sixties. Even today, service-oriented standard languages such as the Navy's CMS-2 and the Army's TOS or TACPOL software systems, are not expanding in use.

So what makes Ada different? Rather than portability as the primary objective the current emphasis is on improving the software construction process based on the goals of:

1. Increasing programmer productivity.
2. Increasing the software's reliability.
3. Improving the implementation process for real-time systems.

The last of these three objectives is of paramount importance to the military. It is desired as a means of reducing the very large commitment (over 50% of all computer activity) of expenditures that continually go into the development and operation of complex, real-time applications. These are the so-called "embedded computer systems" including communications, Command and Control, weapon systems, and tracking systems.

Portability is, of course, still desired. In fact, to assure this benefit, as well as achieve uniformity for other reasons, DOD has actually registered Ada as a trade mark in order to enforce rigid adherence to the adopted standards. Correctness and completeness will, therefore, be essential if a system is to receive validation and be able to use the label Ada. Subsets or even supersets of the language, therefore, will not be endorsed and, in fact, cannot use the name Ada. This restriction has also aroused some controversy. There are those who feel that such limitations will hinder the evolution and utilization of this language.

As seen from the foregoing, Ada is surrounded by controversy and strong opinions—both positive and negative. As one author said in the *Infoworld* issue of April 27, 1981, Ada may be "another unwieldy, inefficient language like PL/I, or . . . a breakthrough in software technology."

What then is Ada all about? One observer regards Ada as a three-ring circus. Perhaps this metaphor illuminates how busy and encompassing the project really is, consisting of a language/compiler, a common programming environment, and a validation capability.

The language of Ada represents a coalescing of all of the good attributes of Pascal, ALGOL, and PL/I, including more recent advances, as well as an overcoming of weaknesses of the past. From this point of view, perhaps Ada represents the best amalgamation of current academic findings, the ongoing European viewpoint, and the avant garde American influence. The Ada language features modularity and multi-tasking, and highlights functionality to support systems programming.

Because Ada addresses the most challenging of large-scale software development, due attention must be given to the structure of that software. Modularity is, therefore, called for at an unprecedented level to support the interaction of the software constructors and to facilitate the maintenance process.

Ada modularity hinges on the notion of the "package," a broad concept as well as the most notable feature of the language. The package is comprised of two components, each an independent file. The first file is the specification or declaration portion, and the second is the execution or operational code. Since each component can be compiled separately, there derives a high-level separation of data, parameters, and procedure declarations and very late binding.

To better control the construction and execution process, the specification file is comprised of a visible and a hidden portion. The hidden portion is private and facilitates another Ada feature, that of "hiding."

Hiding is not necessarily intended only to provide protection or to afford a security function. Rather, it is present to enforce distinction between logical and physical interfaces and to facilitate decoupling of programs. Thus, hiding is a key concept in achieving the capability of separately compiling elements of code.

Another key Ada feature supporting modularity is the compilation data base, or Ada program library. The Ada compiler will maintain a data base reflecting pertinent information for the compilations that have already taken place. Thus, dependencies between compiled units will be managed by the compiler itself. Furthermore, management reports can be generated out of this data base in the event names, procedures, parameters, and interdependencies need to be checked.

The multi-tasking capacity of Ada is facilitated by the language features that allow for task concurrency and task scheduling based on priorities and interrupts. Sequencing of such related and interacting tasks is dictated by the "rendezvous" function. Tasks can either declare an "entry" point awaiting results from other tasks or declare an "accept" indicating that they are ready to deal with an entry call. Working together the "accept" and the "entry" features cause the rendezvous.

The third key facility of the Ada language relates to its capacity to support systems programming. Here we require performance efficiency, execution reliability, and the potential to interface with external languages and physical hardware environments. Ada addresses all of these needs.

Turning now to the Ada programming environment, we note that the objectives of life cycle support, configuration control, portability, and project control should all be supported at the source language level. The Ada Programming Support Environment (APSE) is a response to these requirements. APSE, together with the kernel APSE (called KAPSE), provides the basic mechanism for achieving the implementation structure and portability. KAPSE comprises the low-level and minimal set of functions that are typically machine specific.

This layered approach is designed to achieve the desired capability for "rehosting" Ada from one development machine to another, and the capability for "retargeting," which implies operating the application on a variety of object machines. Interestingly enough, and on a historical note, these objectives of Ada would finally bring about the portability dreams of the late fifties when SHARE sponsored the ill-fated quest for the Universal Computer-Oriented Language (UNCOL).

The validation principle for Ada comprises a quality control function as well as an authorization process. Thus, the principle assures adherence and enforces conformance to Ada standards. This activity is formalized through the Ada Computer Validation Capability (ACVC) which will promulgate the methodology and procedure via a likely DOD-established enforcement unit, the Ada Compiler Validation Organization.

But there is an enormous and fundamental paradox about Ada. The Ada Language System is proclaimed to be the answer to developing sophisticated real-time systems. Hence, the more complex the system, the more applicable Ada should be. Yet the serious warnings of Ada's critics, quoted earlier, indicate that the sheer size of the language structure and features make it vulnerable to breakdown. Thus, it appears that the very complexity of the system may be its greatest weakness, in that it diminishes the reliability for which the system was primarily created.

One reputable source, Professor C. A. R. Hoare of Oxford University, was quoted in the June 15, 1981, issue of *Information Systems News* as stating "Ada represents a far greater risk to our environment and to safety than unsafe cars, toxic pesticides or accidents of nuclear power stations" if the language system is used in programming a nuclear weapon system.

This controversy on Ada is further heightened by two tongue-in-cheek observations that have been made. The first comes from the correspondence pages of the May, 1981, *Communications of the ACM* in which an observer links the name Ada to a Biblical character in Genesis of whom the writer believes that the poet Byron surely was aware. The hope expressed in this letter is that since Ada, who was the daughter of Byron, had poetic connections, the language bearing that name "will encourage poetic programming, so that we may all enjoy reading each other's programs."

This position may be contrasted to a second reference coming from abroad. Appearing in the German language monthly, *Computer Magazin* (5/81), there was a report on an Ada workshop entitled, "Die Geburt des Grünen Elefanten," or "The Birth of the Green Elephant." The green refers to the winning design of the Ada environment, selected in a four-way competition, and the elephant connotes a huge "war machine," or overkill.

The article includes a large picture of the elephant showing the torso and all of the internal bodily parts. Each physical part of the elephant is assigned an Ada attribute. This illustration shows how the language is fed through the elephant's nose, gnashed with the teeth, computed in the brain and processed by the digestive system. Unfortunately, however, the results end in the intestines and the object code is shown as back-end droppings. This is not very encouraging with respect to the future of Ada.

But for the last word, perhaps the views of the most esteemed programmer of today might be in order. In an interview for the Spring 1980 issue of the ICP *Interface Administration and Accounting* issue, Captain Grace Hopper responded to the question on Ada's prospects as follows:

> *It's too all-purpose. Ada is a programming language designed for program-ming language designers. They forgot about the people who have to use it. . . . as for Pascal and Ada, there will be an excitement about them for a while, and then it will die down. Then they'll go back to using COBOL and FORTRAN.*

This is the Ada story. We inject our own, serious doubt about the pros-pects for wide acceptance of this language system, especially in the commer-cial marketplace. There is a notorious resistance to programming language change as it relates to the broad body of computer professionals. Neither the individual practitioners nor their management have the desire and incentive to adopt change. COBOL, FORTRAN, and RPG are hard to displace!

6.4. THE TAXONOMY OF IMPLEMENTATION SYSTEMS

Enhancing the production of computer applications and improving main-tenance support for these programs is the most sought after objective in today's data processing world. Invariably, those who advance recommenda-tions for such improvements will suggest adoption of one or more of the following aids or support systems:

1. A higher-order, user-oriented language.
2. Use of nonprocedural techniques.
3. Incorporation of development tools and a development environment.

Often, however, there is confusion in using these terms. Are the promoters of these three approaches advocating the same or similar ideas, or are there clear-cut differences? In fact, it is the combination of all three that makes up a software implementation system.

Higher-order language is an issue of semantics; it has to do with the connotations or ambiguities of the meaning of symbols. To a specific end user, the symbology used in an application-oriented language has a clearer meaning than does the symbology used in an assembler language.

Nonprocedural techniques is an issue of syntax; it has to do with the structure or sequence in which symbols and statements must be strung together. In a nonprocedural specification the presentation and intent are more readily perceived, understood, and used than in the structure associated with an algorithmic language.

Development tools are issues of programming environment. This has to do with the milieu within which applications are produced. The development environment includes both automated support tools and the application building strategy. An integrated solution system is more conducive to application production than is a potpourri of ad hoc programming aids.

What combination of the three listed suggestions provides an optimal software implementation environment? What options are available in today's marketplace that offer the user, whether programmer or non-EDP professional, easy access to the computer and a friendly environment in which to solve problems? We wish here to clarify and highlight the distinction among the offered ideas as well as their interaction. For this purpose it will be useful to refine our understanding of these three concepts by initially describing each in terms of its own range of possibilities.

First, we have the matter of language from the viewpoint of semantics. Expressing a problem to the computer means employing assemblers, using compilers, and incorporating specialized languages, often called higher-order, or problem-oriented languages. At one extreme is machine-dependent nomenclature, like the highly structured machine language-related assemblers and macro-oriented symbolic languages. At the other extreme are functional or application-oriented dialects, such as systems for modeling or simulating a process, and application-directed languages like APT, a medium for developing programs which perform numerical machine control.

Often associated with these implementation languages are terms such as *host language verbs, macro operators,* and *call statements* at the level closest to the machine. *Higher-order language, high-level language, problem-oriented language, application language* or *end-user language* refer to means of communicating with computers at a more functional or application-oriented level. Language systems are also identified as preprocessors, pseudo code, and intermediate or meta languages. These systems typically serve as surrogate languages to facilitate ease of communication or a degree of abstraction from physical specifics. They are symbolic in nature.

Next is the question of language syntax. The alternatives are usually polarized around procedural versus nonprocedural languages. In directing the computer to solve a problem, this distinction may be described as the difference between the "how to do" process and the "what to do" specifications.

Syntax ranges from the algorithmic approach of conventional computer programming languages to the expression of the problem in natural language, or "free English" statements. Between these extremes are the often-cited Report Generators and Query Languages. Examples of these structures are: COBOL, representing the algorithmic; RPG, a report generator employing specification forms; and SQL/DS (SEQUEL), a query language, requiring an ordered set of statements. The natural language systems are on the forefront of today's technology, with commercially available INTELLECT of Artificial Intelligence Corp. exemplifying this terminology.

The variation of syntax moves along a slowly evolving path. The end points are readily discernible as highly structured and coded languages at one extreme, and natural language expressions at the other. In between, we identify two alternative implementation schemes categorized as follows:

1. Specification form—typically hard-copy-oriented and highly stylized formats that require filling-in-the-blanks or have a graphic orientation. Also included are video-guided entry formats.

2. Ordered statements—stated directions or commands which may require a specified sequence or order but are somewhat free form and near application or Englishlike in structure. Included here are directed prompts, which are computer-led statements presented via terminal devices, soliciting user-initiated responses to available choices.

These syntax variations have led to the coining and labeling of systems by terms such as the following:

Algorithmic	Procedural language
	Computer-oriented language
	Programming language
Specification Form	Nonprocedural approach
	Parameterized system
	Parameter driven
	Table driven
	Data driven
	Decision table oriented
	Fill-in-the-blanks programming
	Graphic forms
Ordered Statements	Fixed format statements
	Command level system
	Directed prompts
	Canned menu style systems
	Menu driven
	Selecting options from predefined lists
	Syntax directed editors
	Structured English

	Englishlike system
	Pseudo English
Natural Language	True English
	Normal English
	Plain English
	Ordinary English
	English-oriented
	Conversational English
	Free format statements
	English statements
	Freeform input
	Free language system

We note that the specification form is called nonprocedural. This designation may seem inappropriate for an approach that is only one step removed from the algorithmic extreme. In truth, however, the degree of "nonproceduralness" is a changing attribute, slowly moving from the absolute procedural aspect of the classical one-pass, algorithmically-oriented computer assembly program to the natural language facilities. Indeed, at each of the stopping points in between, there is some procedural aspect present despite the liberal use of nonprocedural tags.

The third element of implementation systems encompasses the process of building a computer program for either a system or an application category. Program construction takes place in a solution environment which involves software specification, design, development, and subsequent maintenance. The procedure and methodology for this activity is inherent in the chosen development strategy, which ranges from the ad hoc selection of programming tools and aids to employing integrated life cycle construction and support systems.

In the traditional and more formal development environment we include: the use of structured design and structured programming procedures to facilitate software construction; walkthroughs and inspection cycles to achieve higher quality assurance; and exploitation of reusable code and self-documenting systems. But there is a second way to construct solutions to a computer problem. Instead of the conventional programming effort, there are development techniques available today which allow implementors to make parameter selections from offered choices and alternatives by responding to computer generated prompts. From such semiautomated means application code is generated to deal with the problem to be solved. Hence, the term, application generator.

This leads to the interesting question of what is meant by "developing" a solution versus "using" a system. Is the VisiCalc user, constructing a spreadsheet with associated rules and relationships, implementing a specific application or simply exercising the result of someone else's implementation of a program? Is the fully packaged general ledger turnkey system a finished product and ready for use by accounting personnel? Or is there an intermediate end user who specifies the environment, the transactions, and the Chart of Accounts, and who can be considered the real "implementor" of general ledger for the firm? Finally, is the initiator of a query or request for a report an application builder or an application user?

We choose to include all of these cases as examples of the scope of the implementation systems environment, making up the overall spectrum of application development alternatives, as illustrated in Figure 6.8. Furthermore, we seek implementation systems approaches suitable for both the EDP professional as well as the end user, who will have varying degrees of computer literacy. Figure 6.9 shows the four distinct categories of end users.

The solution environment therefore stretches from the EDP-oriented, structured, "anything" approach, to the use of application generators, and ultimately to the incorporation of integrated solution systems.

Examples of these three development technologies include:

1. Structured design and programming disciplines as espoused by the software development methodology of Jackson, Yourdon-Constantine, Warnier/Orr, and so on.

2. The Report Program Generator (RPG), reflecting application generators.

3. Integrated solution environments such as the **MARK IV** System of Informatics, and **RAMIS II** of Mathematica.

Solution environments are often data base management systems augmented by powerful front-end problem specifiers (the request language) and back-end presentation mechanisms (the report generators)—giving an integrated flavor. The ultimate integrated solution environment is, however, a user-oriented turnkey system, combining hardware and software to fit a very specific application need. Although Utopian today, a true solution system ought to respond favorably to a user's proverbial, "Do my job."

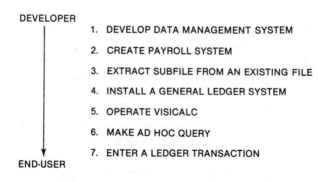

DEVELOPER

1. DEVELOP DATA MANAGEMENT SYSTEM

2. CREATE PAYROLL SYSTEM

3. EXTRACT SUBFILE FROM AN EXISTING FILE

4. INSTALL A GENERAL LEDGER SYSTEM

5. OPERATE VISICALC

6. MAKE AD HOC QUERY

7. ENTER A LEDGER TRANSACTION

END-USER

Figure 6.8. The developer/user spectrum.

	CATEGORY A	CATEGORY B	CATEGORY C	CATEGORY D
UNIT:	DEPARTMENT	PROFESSIONAL	EXPEDITER	CLERK
REQUIREMENT:	FINANCIAL SYSTEM	CASH MANAGEMENT	ORDER FULFILLMENT	PAYROLL ENTRY
FUNCTION:	CONTROL	ANALYSIS	TRANSACTION	DATA ENTRY
HARDWARE:	MINI- OR MAINFRAME COMPUTER	WORKSTATION	INTELLIGENT TERMINAL	DUMB TERMINAL

Figure 6.9. The "end-user" spectrum.

Terminology often used to describe the implementation system elements and schemes supporting the program development environment includes:

Language processor

Subroutine linker

Code generator

Macro generator

Editor

Problem statement language

Requirement statement language

Designer language

Description language

Application development facility

Application generator

Program generator

System generator

Program product

Software product

Canned application

Packaged application

Turnkey system

Solution system

Programming environment

Program constructors

Reusable code libraries

Predefined programs

Program development system

and the IBM terms of *Information Center* and *Development Center*.

More recently, and looking to the future, the concept of the Automated Development Support System (ADSS) has emerged (Wasserman 1980). This is especially emphasized in the Ada program development and its emphasis on support environments, as discussed in Section 6.3. Here the concept is called APSE (Ada Programming Support Environment). ADSS, or APSE, includes many of the tools and procedures suggested by the foregoing list of labels and seeks to reach an optimal system for program development.

The three components of an implementation system are, therefore, the semantics of a computer language, the language's syntax, and the programming development environment. Together these three elements comprise the overall framework for building and operating computer based applications. These components, and some representative points along each axis, are illustrated in Figure 6.10. The means by which one manages the enhancement of productivity in the solution of a computer-based problem is determined by where one operates in this implementation space. These choices are further discussed in the following section.

6.5. EXAMPLES OF IMPLEMENTATION SYSTEMS

In Section 6.4 a taxonomy of implementation systems was developed using the graphic representation of Figure 6.10. As we have already noted, the objective of enhancing productivity is not limited to computer professionals, for example, programmers and systems analysts. The end user also plays a role, and part of solving the software production problem is to provide the more casual EDP user with adequate means for directly expressing his computer-oriented problem and to assist this user in executing a solution. Hence, the appropriate and optimal implementation strategy in the context of the three-dimensional space of Figure 6.10 is determined by the type and qualification of the implementor as well as the nature of the application itself.

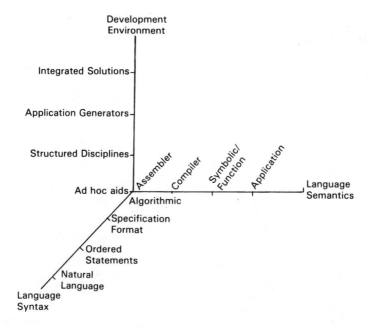

Figure 6.10. Key implementation system elements.

To illustrate, we may have any one of the following problem scenarios for which an appropriate implementation environment is sought:

1. The systems programmer wishing to build a new data base management system.
2. The business systems analyst charged with developing a payroll application.
3. The information analyst wishing to extract data satisfying certain conditions from an existing file.

Each of these situations leads to a different implementation strategy in the sense of the structure dictated by the configuration of Figure 6.10. These differences also raise the relevance of the popular notion of "user friendliness," which sometimes refers to semantics, often to syntax and, implicitly, to the manner of solution. User friendly, therefore, can mean many things, depending upon the experience and the needs of the implementor.

Does this three-dimensional construct adequately reflect the available alternative implementation schemes, and does it help to clarify the meaning and purpose of the various labels that are applied when discussing the subject? In order to consider this question, the characteristics of alternative strategies are studied by analyzing the space spanned by an imaginary cube imposed on the coordinates shown in Figure 6.10. We look for representative examples that fit in this space, as depicted in Figure 6.11. To perform this analysis we assume that the cube has a dimension of three units and employ the following notation to designate its eight vertices:

Axis	Measure	Relative Value
Syntax:	Procedural	0
	Nonprocedural	3
Semantics:	Machine language	0
	Application language	3
Environment:	EDP tool oriented	0
	Solution oriented	3

The raster of 64 points that make up this cube represents the spectrum of implementation systems and gives us the opportunity of imposing a classification scheme. It becomes convenient to look at this cube in successive slices, which are taken at points 0, 1, 2, and 3 along the syntax axis. These planes are better represented in Figures 6.12, 6.13, 6.14, and 6.15, respectively.

Figure 6.12 is filled out in its entirety. The remaining figures are not complete, mainly because some of the intersections are by their nature mean-

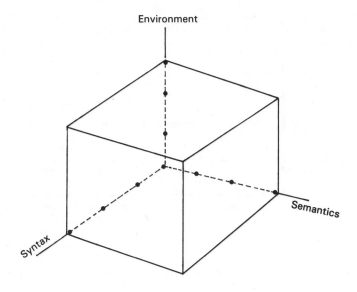

Figure 6.11. The implementation system space.

ingless, or there is no ready representation known to the author. As each figure is described, the cited implementation system component is positionally related to the cube shown in Figure 6.11.

· Consider first, therefore, Figure 6.12. The origin, at (0,0,0), reflects the implementation scheme that employs the conventional algorithmic-oriented, assembler program supported by the operating system, teleprocessing monitor, and basic file access methods. An example is the BAL system of IBM, operating in a DOS or OS environment. This is the environment wherein real-time, custom coded applications are typically implemented, because throughput performance and special input/output requirements are inherently present. A closely related, and more desirable position along the environment axis is the symbolic point (0,0,1) which introduces structured disciplines exemplified by the IBM PL/360 language. This enhances productivity over the (0,0,0) alternative. Further up the environment axis is the symbolic point (0,0,2) which adds the reusable code facility to the implementation scheme.

For professional programmers the implementation environments represented by (0,0,0), (0,0,1), and (0,0,2) yield progressively more productivity. At the point (0,0,3) we reach the integrated solution environment which is a complete system for program development. This must include an integrated capability of the operating system, utilities, development languages, a text editor, file handlers, and file systems. A good example closest to the basic machine facilities is the VM/CMS/SPF system available for large IBM computers.

Integrated Solution	VM/CMS/SPF 003	ADA 013	INTERLISP 023	ACP 033
Application Generator	RE-USABLE CODE 002	MAESTRO 012	ADF 022	SCRIPT 032
Structured Discipline	PL/360 001	PASCAL 011	APL 021	APT 031
Ad Hoc Aids	BAL 000	COBOL 010	IMS 020	DISSPLA 030
	Assembler	Compiler	Symbolic/ Function	Application

Figure 6.12.   Implementation schemes for algorithmic syntax.

Another closely related assemblage of application building systems is represented by points (0,1,0), (0,2,0), and (0,3,0) along the semantics axis. These approaches differ from the first set in that a significant departure is now provided in syntax, the manner in which to state and execute an application. While generality in program construction is retained as one moves out along this axis, the languages become more function- or application-oriented. Ap-

Integrated Solution	103	113	MARK IV 123	PFS 133
Application Generator	102	SCORE 112	RPG 122	GENERATION 5 132
Structured Discipline	101	CORNELL PROGRAM SYNTHESIZER 111	QUERY-BY-EXAMPLE 121	OFFICE PROCEDURES-BY-EXAMPLE 131
Ad Hoc Aids	STD 100	110	DECISION TABLES 120	130
	Assembler	Compiler	Symbolic/ Function	Application

Figure 6.13.   Implementation schemes for specification format syntax.

Integrated Solution 203	213	RAMIS II 223	VISICALC 233
Application Generator 202	SYSTEM 80 212	AIMS PLUS 222	MIMS 232
Structured Discipline 201	211	EASYTRIEVE 221	SAS 231
Ad Hoc Aids 200	210	220	230
	Assembler	**Compiler**	**Symbolic/ Function**	**Application**

Figure 6.14. Implementation schemes for ordered statements and directed prompts.

propriate examples are: the COBOL or BASIC compiler and interpreter, for point (0,1,0); the IBM Information Management System (IMS) macros in support of data base management functions, at point (0,2,0); and DISSPLA, representing point (0,3,0). DISSPLA is a product of Integrated Software Systems Corp. and consists of FORTRAN subroutines which can be called by a user's program in order to produce virtually any type of data display. It is a graphic application support system.

Integrated Solution 303	313	323	333
Application Generator 302	312	INTELLECT 322	PLANES 332
Structured Discipline 301	311	321	331
Ad Hoc Aids 300	310	320	TELLAGRAF 330
	Assembler	**Compiler**	**Symbolic/ Function**	**Application**

Figure 6.15. Implementation schemes for natural language syntax.

Continuing with the analysis of Figure 6.12, we next note the introduction of structured disciplines in formatting and expressing the computer requirement. A foremost example of a structured language is Pascal, shown at point (0,1,1). A number of commercial products, such as Metacobol of Applied Data Research, have also addressed this requirement by enhancing the use of the standard COBOL language.

Representing the symbolic/function category, at point (0,2,1), is the highly specialized language APL. This category could also have been represented by the LISP system, aimed at the artificial intelligence model builder. For the more application-oriented structured discipline at point (0,3,1), we identify APT, the Automatic Program Tool language for stating and controlling numerical control machines.

An interesting combination of application generating capabilities is represented by the MAESTRO system of Softlab Systems, Inc., at point (0,1,2). This implementation scheme supports the generation of COBOL language solutions, imposing both a structured discipline and access to reusable code.

Continuing along the application generation category is the Application Development Facility (ADF) of IBM identified at point (0,2,2). ADF represents a procedural approach to generate applications operating with the aforementioned IMS.

The application-oriented code generator shown at point (0,3,2) is SCRIPT. This is an IBM software product that operates in a time-sharing or conventional operating system environment and provides text formatting facilities. Through a standard editorlike process, a text file is created, having embedded parameters expressed with a specialized command language that directs the ultimate format of the text. Using SCRIPT, it is possible to generate a final formatted result equivalent to that created by a word processing system or a product suitable for photocomposition. Thus SCRIPT is an application generator used to create a variety of formatted documents.

Completing Figure 6.12 are the entries Ada, Interlisp, and ACP, positioned at (0,1,3), (0,2,3), and (0,3,3). Ada (that is, APSE, as described in Section 6.4) is not yet a reality, but it appears in this slot because it is a complete development environment representing a most comprehensive, solution-oriented set of tools and support systems. UNIX™, with all of its workbench tools, might be an alternate occupant of point (0,1,3).

Interlisp is a programming environment based on using the LISP language. This system is geared to sophisticated users exploring applications in artificial intelligence. Hence, the programming problems dealt with are quite different from those more conventionally solved with procedural languages. In fact, LISP addresses those problems that usually cannot be specified at the outset, but require evolution as they are solved. Interlisp is an integrated solution system because it provides all of the support facilities necessary to generate and execute the application.

ACP (Airline Control Program) is the solution environment for the administration of airline reservations and related functions. This IBM software, which is general purpose and industry-oriented, provides the software modules and tools for implementing a system for a specific airline. Although ACP originated in PARS, the Programmed Airline Reservation System, it is now used in a wide variety of fast-response, high-volume functional areas, requiring the handling of tens of thousands of terminals. Applications extend even beyond airlines data processing. ACP has been enriched by a procedural-oriented application language, Sabertalk, a development of Eastern and American Airlines. ACP gives the user an integrated development environment which is application-oriented.

Another example of a total application solution fitting into category (0,3,3) is Informatics Life-Comm. This is a very large application system encompassing the administrative needs of life insurance companies. Life-Comm includes over 30 functional components which perform all necessary data processing in support of the individual life insurance policy, from the proposal stage through the policy's termination. With Life-Comm, the home office of medium- to large-sized life insurance companies are completely automated for a variety of policy offerings and all of the associated accounting.

We now step along the syntax axis of the cube of Figure 6.11 and begin to examine the systems based on nonprocedural approaches. The first stop are the examples representing the specification format approach shown in Figure 6.13. At point (1,0,0) is Pro-log's STD Modular Method for generating programs without employing a development system or a higher-level language. This is the system already discussed in Section 4.4. Related to this approach might be a similar technique using decision tables, represented by IBM's APL Decision Table Processor at point (1,2,0). In both of these cases we visualize the user as an electronics engineer, and the application as almost exclusively in circuit design and/or development of high-performance-oriented microprogrammed functions. Of course, the very existence of forms and tables for these approaches suggests a disciplined environment and the possibility of automatic program generations, so that the range of these implementation schemes might well extend to the points (1,0,1) and (1,0,2).

A different set of users is suggested by the region about the line (1,1,0) to (1,1,3). These are the nonprocedural, front-end processors to conventional compiler systems. The first of the examples is the Cornell Program Synthesizer, shown as point (1,1,1), which is a syntax-directed editor. This system is a facility for constructing a program by forcing a display template on the application developer, who responds by "filling in" the appropriate variable names, processes, and parameter values. This procedure creates a program through a step-by-step, top-down generation of a syntax tree. The resulting program is highly structured, syntactically correct, and automatically documented. Another example of a front-end forms-oriented processor is Score, available from Software Design Associates, Inc. Score is a preprocessor generating COBOL programs and identified as point (1,1,2).

A quantum step in increasing capacity for implementing systems is represented by the remaining entries of Figure 6.13. The IBM Query-by-Example (QBE) system is placed in the specification format category, even though it is a screen-oriented facility rather than the more conventional paper form system dominating this table. QBE is a structured system that generates responses to queries that are symbolically requested. Hence, it is positioned at point (1,2,1). A similar approach, more application oriented, is Office Procedures-by-Example. This is also an IBM development and is assigned position (1,3,1).

The Report Program Generator (RPG) is an application generator that has a nonprocedural structure through its specification request forms and operates within the framework of the conventional IBM OS/DOS and many other environments. The user may specify files and request reports, but must ultimately know some DP-related concepts and functions.

To the right of RPG in Figure 6.13 is the application generator for application systems at point (1,3,2). Here the specification parameters and generations become more functional or user-specific. In this connection we cite as an example the Generation 5 package of American Management Systems. This is an application generator aimed toward building financial and accounting applications.

The MARK IV System described in detail in Section 6.2 is placed in location (1,2,3). It is a complete system for defining, generating, and maintaining files as well as providing the means for complete and flexible information retrieval and reporting. The system is based on responding to general purpose specification forms with a high degree of default capability, requiring a minimum of form details. The powerful file creation, maintenance, and transaction facilities distinguish MARK IV from products such as RPG and give it an integrated solution character.

The remaining entry in Figure 6.13 is the software product, Personal File System (PFS) of Software Publishing Corp., described in Section 7.3. This complete system is a good example of emerging data management systems available for microcomputers. PFS is entirely video forms-oriented. For a given set of application-specific describers, a screen template is generated which then guides the user in the complete solution of his information retrieval and reporting problem.

Just short of the application generators are the various combinations of design and development facilities that aid in implementing screens, data bases, and certain common data validation and processing functions. Examples of such products are IBM's Development Management Systems (DMS) for CICS environments, Informatics' TRANS IV and Terminal Application Processing System (TAPS), and Cincom's Mantis. These facilities are characterized by their specification format and decision table syntax, their data processing language orientation and their very structured presentation, combined with the exploitation of reusable code. Their proper position would be in the right half of Figure 6.13.

Proceeding toward an ever-increasing relaxation of procedural orientation, we next focus on the systems that have as a common base the language structure of ordered statements and directed prompts. These are shown in

Figure 6.14. Examples of such systems are various query languages and report writers as well as the application solving facilities of data management systems. These systems are often incorrectly described as having an English orientation. The semantics vary from directives that are highly oriented toward data processing to application specifics. The syntax could require a stylized, formatted, and ordered set of statements as well as a seminatural language presentation. There is a natural tendency for these syntaxes to cluster in the upper right portion of Figure 6.14.

At the application generator level there is an automatic COBOL code generator represented by System 80, offered by Phoenix System Inc. This product is positioned at point (2,1,2). System 80 is a highly interactive, line-by-line, prompting system which solicits responses from the application developer from which the finished, structured COBOL program is generated. There are three main modules that accomplish this task. First the system prompts the developer for a complete file definition in order to generate one or more dictionaries. Then the user has an option to develop either data entry or processing programs. The data entry generating module creates the program which, upon execution, guides the input of data in order to generate and maintain files. The module developing the processing logic will generate the program that performs information retrieval and reporting. A comparable system aimed at the microcomputer market is The Last One. It has characteristics similar to System 80, except that it generates BASIC code.

As we now move further to the right in Figure 6.14, there is a common tendency by system vendors to describe their offerings as "Englishlike" or "free English." Such descriptions are deceptive and can easily mislead the potential user. True, as will be seen, systems falling into these categories use English (or some other) language—but the style and form are not natural language. An example is:

File Personnel
Segment Department
Select Location if Location = "New York"
Select Name
List Name Location Telephone
Title "Special Report"

This short "program" illustrates the point. It is English in appearance but has a well-structured form and flow, and is performance-oriented by virtue of the action verbs (File, Segment, Select, List, Title) which are predefined commands. The payoff from these "ordered statement" systems is, of course, substantial. They replace the more conventional COBOL programs by convenient shorthand that may be briefer in number of lines of directives by one or two decimal orders of magnitude.

A good example of such a system is Easytrieve, a product of Pansophic Systems Inc., placed at location (2,2,1). There are many other competitive products such as DYL-260 of Dylakor, Answer/DB of Informatics General Corp., and even the most recent, IBM's SEQUEL, which belong to this niche of solutions.

The AIMS Plus system of AIMS Plus Inc., is assigned to point (2,2,2). This system is very much like System 80, its neighbor to the left in Figure 6.14. The difference is that AIMS Plus does not generate or depend on COBOL or any other code. Instead, the user's responses to the interactive prompts are fed into tables, and the resulting "application program" is then executed interpretatively.

Determining the assignment of a system between locations (2,2,1) and (2,2,2) necessitates drawing a fine line between a query system suitable for ad hoc information analyzing and a capability for developing a production-oriented, ongoing application. The complexity of identification and categorization increases as many new systems emerge, especially at the microcomputer end.

We now take another step in the direction of dropping machine dependency by examining location (2,2,3), where we have a nonprocedural language approach and a fully integrated solution environment. This situation is exemplified by popular data management systems enhanced by user-prompted or stylized English front-end languages. NOMAD, of NCSS, and the RAMIS II system already cited are good examples of this technology. RAMIS II is an especially good candidate, since it is much more closely tied to its data base than is NOMAD, which depends to a large degree on its associated operating system for data base definition and the edit function.

At point (2,3,1) the data analysis system SAS, from SAS Institute, is identified. The system generates a variety of statistically oriented reports as a result of writing a number of ordered statements.

The Mitrol Industrial Management System (MIMS) of General Electric Information Service Company represents the point (2,3,2). This nonprocedural approach to building applications is oriented to the special needs and functions of manufacturing. The system includes a data base, a general report writer, and a transaction processing capability. Application orientation comes about because of highly specialized manufacturing-oriented command statements, such as PLAN. Invoking this verb, which operates on variables such as time period, a manufacturer's resource planning explosion for a specific part can be automatically generated. For each chosen interval of time, this shows such items as material required, on-hand, and available, together with planned release dates, and so on.

The last cited example in Figure 6.14 is VisiCalc, at point (2,3,3). This is a complete system, fully prompted to assist accountants and financial planners in defining, building, and manipulating the conventional spreadsheet.

Finally in Figure 6.15, the plane through point 3 on the syntax axis of Figure 6.11 is presented. This area represents the available implementation systems that employ natural language.

What makes a language natural English versus Englishlike? The "almost English" claims have already been cited as attributes of the ordered statement systems discussed in connection with Figure 6.14. Perhaps the line of demarcation can only be clarified with some examples.

A leading contender for a natural language capability is the commercially available software product INTELLECT of Artificial Intelligence Corporation. INTELLECT analyzes an English language query, resolves ambiguities through a prompted dialogue, displays the interpretation of the query, and, if acceptable, responds to the final retrieval step and generates the output.

INTELLECT is deemed an application generator and assigned to position (3,2,2). It is not an integrated solution system because it only facilitates retrieval. The data base will have been generated by some other program and the special LOADER utility will incorporate such data under INTELLECT.

A key to understanding natural language processing as distinct from a more formatted approach is the extension of the indexing feature common to data bases. In order to broaden the understanding of an English sentence relative to a specific data base, it is necessary to enhance the conventional indexing scheme by a supporting system. This system provides additional meaning to possible words used relative to the data base. For example, if the data involves personnel, then the following definition of synonyms might be appropriate:

Employee/People/Anyone/Everyone/Personnel/Person/Everybody/Anybody

Thus, INTELLECT can be expected to accept and process the following queries with equal ease:

PRINT THE NAME OF ALL EMPLOYEES WITH THE NAME JONES
IS ANYONE'S NAME JONES?
HOW MANY PEOPLE ARE THERE WITH THE NAME JONES?

An application-oriented natural language system is Programmed Language-based Enquiry System, PLANES, shown at point (3,3,2). This system, developed at the University of Illinois, is aimed at supporting the data base needs of U.S. Navy aircraft maintenance and flight information. PLANES includes an English language front-end capable of understanding user requests with the ability to carry on clarifying dialogues. The system is also geared to answering vague or poorly defined questions.

PLANES is able to handle query requests such as the following:

1. Which aircraft had engine damage in May 1973?
2. Did any planes which had engine maintenance in May have ten or fewer flight hours in June?
3. What types of aircraft are there?

The first question is a standard type of request which could be asked in any system, though not in the natural form presented here.

The second request is a complex statement which involves a good number of interrelationships and which cannot be handled by the typical menu-driven or prompting query systems.

The third question is general and solicits information about the content of a data base. This facility is not typically available in any other system.

The third example of Figure 6.15 is TELLAGRAF™, a companion product to DISSPLA, which was cited in connection with Figure 6.12. TELLA-GRAF is a conversational computer graphics system allowing the use of natural English to express directives generating a graphic output. It is assigned location (3,3,0). To illustrate, all of the following statements assign "MILLIONS" to the y-axis label:

> Y-AXIS LABEL IS "MILLIONS"
> LABEL THE Y-AXIS "MILLIONS"
> "MILLIONS" IS THE Y-AXIS LABEL
> THE Y-LABEL IS "MILLIONS"
> PUT "MILLIONS" ON Y

Natural language systems of the type described here are "natural" with respect to query only. Defining and generating the data base, developing the indexing system and the semantic extenders are specialized requirements which still depend on more conventional programming techniques.

This survey leaves acknowledged gaps in the array of alternatives for natural language systems. This reflects, of course, the state of today's technology. What looms ahead, and may prove to be even more exciting, are the prospects of natural voice input, permitting a user to communicate with computers in one's own natural language and style. Limited vocabulary systems with this capability are now in an early prototype state, as described in Section 8.3. Systems useful for business purposes, however, may not become productized until the early 1990s.

6.6. USER FRIENDLY AND FRIENDLY USAGE

More often than not, the description of a piece of software includes the claim that it is "user friendly." Presumably this means that the software will duly take into consideration the user's level of computer literacy and make it easy and pleasant to deal with the computer. Thus, we expect software to provide an appropriate interface which will facilitate man/machine communications. In the event of errors, software should be forgiving by allowing escapes to prior points, and retracing of steps already taken; it should also be sufficiently robust so that users cannot bring down the system or cause it to compute nonsense. But can we overdo this business of user friendliness to a point where we reach a state of diminishing returns?

We would probably all agree that a highly prompted, interactive screen-oriented system is the cornerstone for real user friendliness. To this we must add the capability of full screen edit, controlled data entry points embedded in a nonerasable template, and explicitly stated data entry formats with associated validation logic. These features prohibit entry of undesirable data types or data values. This structure is designed both to limit the actions of the user and to prevent the possibility of entering bad data.

What does it really accomplish? It probably has severely limited the flexibility and growth of the system. The features and facilities added will most likely get in the way of the user as his experience with the system increases over time.

Examine an example from real life. In the process of defining requirements for a record keeping and reporting system, a financial expert indicated that each transaction should have a unique identification number expressed in four digits. The programmer/analyst, to demonstrate the power and capability of the data entry validation facility of the data management system, forthwith designated the ID field as numeric and, specifically, as a positive integer. After spending a few weeks building the history file, the analyst discovered that some transactions were allocated to two different profit centers and had to be divided into two separate records. In order to identify the transaction for accounting purposes, the numeric ID had to be enhanced by an alphabetic character. As the ID had now become an alpha-numeric character string field, the definition of the file had to be revised and the file rebuilt.

This experience illustrates the Catch 22 of designing user friendly systems. The interactive prompts guide the user's data entry and processing steps to the narrowest possible limits and constraints, so that due edit and validation checks can be performed. This specificity, however, is the antithesis of subsequent flexibility. It is difficult, if not impossible, to make ad hoc, dynamic changes after the system is defined and operational.

Another observation illustrates how "friendliness" can become overbearing. A well-thought-out set of screens with associated menus and forms may be excellent for introducing a system to new users or refreshing the memory of prior users. But too much prompting can become a tortuous path for the experienced user. A truly friendly system must afford both intimacy as well as distance.

Thus the user should have shortcuts available and be able to bypass screens that, after sufficient use, become tedious and thoroughly understood. This can be accomplished by three techniques:

1. Allowing screen bypasses through multiple direct entry points in the logical procedure.

2. Supporting command level functions that take the place of specified screens.

3. Providing alternate screen logic and procedures that fit the preference level of the user.

In other words, an application should accept user demands communicated in a variety of ways. A corollary to this would be the nicety of being able to dynamically modify both form and substance of screens once the application becomes operational in order to fit more closely the special needs of a specific user.

It may be correct to say that careful examination of requirements and careful development of functional specifications can avert the consequences of unforeseen situations popping up after the system is implemented. In other words, surprises can be forestalled by spending more time in requirements analysis, functional specifications, and programming details. However, this is easier said than done. While it is certainly true that more time spent in such design will minimize problems later, the typical user has very little patience or, for that matter, time to spend in studying a problem. He wants to get on with the solution.

Even if the user were willing to defer the implementation of his system while spending more time carefully pondering needs and postulating his requirements, he would probably still fail to find the "best" design. He would suffer from a kind of myopia caused by the limitation of the human capacity to understand completely and foresee all contingencies affecting an application problem.

For all of these reasons, it is advisable for users to move rapidly toward some form of implementation, cursory though it may be. In other words, given a typical problem amenable to solution with modern data management systems, the best advice is to select whatever system comes most easily, put up a model of the most likely application and play with it. This process is usually called system prototyping.

It is the actual hands-on experience of manipulating data from entry, retrieval, and reporting that provides the best and most convincing understanding of what is really desired and where the limitations might be. With this type of heuristic experience, users are equipped to arrive at acceptable solutions. It is best that the fewest constraints be imposed at the outset in order to allow for experimentation as well as to meet the eventual surprises that will surely arise.

Without a doubt, this dynamic and interactive prototyping will encourage better computer utilization as well as speed up the implementation process. Once a problem is really understood adjustments and corrections can be made if the system allows, or the file definition and file building activity can be restarted.

Users delude themselves if they believe they can get by with a carefully thought-out design and implement the application in only one pass.

Additional Readings

The material in this chapter can be further developed by referring to the following articles in the Bibliography at the end of the book: Allen, 1981; Astrahan and Chamberlin, 1975; Boehm, 1976; Computer, 1981a; Computer, 1981b; Data Base, 1980; EDP Analyzer, 1979; EDP Analyzer, 1981b; EDP Analyzer, 1981c; EDP Analyzer, 1981f; Electronic Design, 1981; Eventoff et al., 1981; Gutz et al., 1981; Hayes et al., 1981; IEEE, 1981; Jensen, 1981; Joslin, 1981; Ling, 1980; Lucas, 1981; Miller, 1981; Proceedings, 1979; Reisner, 1981; Sammet, 1981; Schneiderman, 1979; Teitlebaum and Reps, 1981; Waltz, 1978; Wassermann, 1980a; Wassermann, 1980b; Wassermann, 1981; Wassermann and Shewmake, 1981; and Wilkes, 1975.

SEVEN

The Data Management System Phenomenon

As described in Chapter 6, the impact of data management systems on implementation schemes was profound. Hence, this important software development deserves special focus and emphasis.

In Chapter 7, Section 7.1 clarifies terminology by differentiating among data management system (DMS), file management system (FMS), and data base management system (DBMS). There is also a discussion of the meaning of query systems and their syntax.

Next, Section 7.2 raises the important subject of user prerequisites for employing a DMS. It is much too popular today to disregard formal introduction to computers and instead push the learning into the applications systems themselves by advertising them as "user friendly." This might well be a case of oversell.

The actual use and applicability of a DMS are described in Section 7.3 through a case study of a membership file. A commercial product operating on a microcomputer is evaluated with respect to its suitability to the problem and its users. In the following Section 7.4, a user view of the DMS is presented with the objective of mapping actual experience back on the design of the software.

7.1. CLARIFYING DATA MANAGEMENT SYSTEMS

One cannot engage in a discussion of computer technology without encountering and being confused by the terms: file management system, data management system, data base management system, and information management system. These terms cover three data processing notions concerning structure, procedure, and access of data in a computer system. Underlying these expressions is the rather subtle and very confusing use of the terms *data file* and *data base*.

The issue of structure directly leads to distinguishing between a data file and a data base. Suffice it to say that a data base, as contrasted with a data file, is a more complex structure of data which has interdependence and can be viewed as a combination of a number of data files. There is a secondary implication that a data base, unlike a data file, avoids data redundancy and is able to separate application programs from data base dependency. Today most file-dependent systems can coordinate the processing of multiple files. Furthermore, the movement toward relational systems encourages one to think of data bases as a number of simple files or tables. Hence, making a distinction between data files and data base may no longer be essential or even useful.

Procedure is the means by which programmer or user communication can be facilitated to perform operations on the data files or data bases. This would include query and report generators as well as editing and validation schemes for data accession.

Finally, there is the issue of access. This refers to the mechanism for locating and extracting, according to certain conditions, pieces of data that may be contained in the data file or data base.

Now that the three independent aspects of computer systems have been defined, the relationship between them and the terms *file management system* and *data management system* is easy to establish. Both a file management system and a data management system connote a combination of facilities that includes all three of the indicated components, namely, access, procedure, and structure. The two systems are traditionally differentiated from each other by the implied data structure, that is, whether it is a data file or a data base. As the distinction between data files and data bases becomes blurred, there is a consequent evaporation of the distinction between file management systems and data management systems.

Data base management system (DBMS) is the popular term used to describe the access process to get at the data. To add to the confusion, this nomenclature is often used interchangeably with *data management system* and *data base system*.

This leaves *information management system*. When written with capital letters, the label applies specifically to a product of IBM, usually called IMS, which is a particular data base management system. The naming of a very popular and highly visible data base management system, or, preferably, access system, with the label, Information Management System, is therefore confusing. In these types of systems, one does not manage information. One manages data. A data management system generates information, or, putting it differently, information is produced as a result of operating a data management system. Of course, the specific IBM term, Information Management System, is now no longer a generic description of a process or procedure.

Rather, IMS is the name of a product, whose meaning cannot be deduced from the three individual words making up the name. In fact, IBM designates IMS as a "data base manager," which is a much better description.

This anatomy of terminology shows the lack of adequate vocabulary with which to describe the handling of data. We especially note that "data base management system" is an unfortunate construction which hardly connotes its fundamental objective of data access.

The following suggestions are offered to clarify these seemingly confusing and possibly conflicting notions. Let the overall name given to the process of structure, procedure, and access be "data management system," whether we deal with so-called files or data bases. Let us advocate retirement of the term *data base management system*. The access aspect of a data management system could be referred to as the "data base access system." The procedural aspect of a data management system can be described as "data manipulation languages," which, incidentally, is a phrase already acceptable to the industry.

This discussion mentioned procedure as an important operative element encompassed by the term *data management system*. Procedure includes the means of communication by which users operate on data from the point of view of storage and retrieval. Here again there is an encounter with terminology that is often bewildering. Take, for example, the term *procedural* versus the term *nonprocedural*, as it relates to computer language types. Since there seems to be widespread enthusiasm for nonprocedural languages, it appears that all languages today must take on that label, even though there is a good deal of procedure involved in most of them. As noted in Sections 6.4 and 6.5, computer languages simply do not divide neatly into such a dichotomy.

A popular claim for nonprocedural languages is that they are English-like. This is especially true for query systems. But are there really any differences between competing alternatives? Does it really matter if the conditional statement comes before or after the report specification? Or does it matter if the conditional statement begins with the word IF or FOR or WHERE or WHEN? Doesn't it seem obvious that all of the following statements have essentially the same structure and ease of use:

LIST	A	IF	B
LIST	A	FOR	B
LIST	A	WHERE	B
LIST	A	WHEN	B
IF	B	LIST	A
FOR	B	LIST	A
WHERE	B	LIST	A
WHEN	B	LIST	A

The arguments about the selection of a verb to designate the output mode seem unnecessary. Does it matter whether the word is SELECT, LIST, DIS-

PLAY, PRINT, or just plain OUTPUT? Essentially, there are three types of output that can be requested. They are output to be printed (hardcopy), output to be shown on a CRT (softcopy), or output which is to be retained in the form of a file available for subsequent access. Surely three standard terms can be agreed upon that reflect these three alternatives.

Englishlike is also promoted through the use of so-called noise words. Systems are advertised as having the ability to construct natural language queries by being able to include certain designated words which are ignored by the query parsing system. Thus we are told that rather than make the request:

> Print Personnel, name, telephone, sex, if sex = "male"

we can ask,

> Print from the Personnel file the name, the age, the sex if the sex is equal to "male"

Yes, the second formulation certainly looks like a more natural English language statement than does the first. On the other hand, except for demonstrating a nicety of the system to a first-time user, who would use the second, more verbose, form?

This is not to say that natural language approaches are bad, or useless. Indeed, if it is possible to communicate with a system in a natural language mode, then one has the best of all worlds. Verbosity or curtness can then be at the discretion of the user and one has the most important benefit, namely, freedom from the necessity for certain ordered formats and special verbs.

7.2. PREREQUISITES FOR USING DATA MANAGEMENT SYSTEMS

State-of-the-art data management systems vendors are quick to promote their product as "user friendly." The implication seems to be that this feature removes a usage barrier from the user and facilitates easy communication with the computer.

Data processing professionals may be able to design so-called user friendly systems—but are end users sufficiently knowledgeable to use such systems intelligently? Are there not certain prerequisites that a person must have to be even a casual computer user?

As in everything else, there is no free lunch. The new and casual user of computers has more critical needs with respect to data processing than the support provided by the so-called "friendly" screens. Indeed, anyone proposing to use a computer must come armed with some understanding of fundamental principles of data and data handling. The following concepts and functions comprise part of the necessary background that will prepare an individual for a first encounter with data management systems and the computer.

The most fundamental prerequisite is the notion of a file of information or, if you like, the concept of the data base. Next is the need for an understanding of the components of a data base, including the logical aspect of the record, the concept of a field, and the notion of value or attribute of a field.

Once these data file concepts are in place, then it is necessary to teach the operations of search, retrieval, and reporting. Unfortunately, this implies knowing something about Boolean logic and maybe even the use of parentheses for nested relationships. It is only after the user appreciates all of these elements that he dare turn to the screen and log in for his interactive session. Even when armed with this abstract background, the user has a need for some further systems-oriented skills.

Consider, for example, as simple an expression as the calendar date, uncomplicated by anything beyond the conventional representation in common American usage. First there is the issue of input format and prompting. Shall the date on entry be allowed in free form, that is, May 3, 1980, or 5-3-80, or 5/3/80, or even 050380? The decision on input format is determined by four considerations:

1. The degree to which the input process is to be facilitated and validated.
2. The manner in which one wishes to store the date.
3. The basis on which one might ultimately wish to perform search operations against the value of the date.
4. The way the date is to appear in the output reports.

Overriding all of the these factors is, of course, the degree of "user friendliness" that should be present with respect to the data entry process itself.

In some systems independent control is provided for each of the four specified requirements so that a decision on handling one of them need not affect the others. In other systems, the user must make some commitments and trade-offs which will affect the flexibility and usage of the system. Unfortunately, the typical user may not understand clearly how one of his decisions affects another.

The easiest choice is to select an input form which matches the desired output format. In this case one is naturally drawn to the structure 5/3/80. The amount of data storage is, of course, affected if it is decided to incorporate the two "/"s along with the numerical quantities. Also, the decision to enhance the date with separators probably dictates that the values will be treated as character strings and not numerical quantities. Hence the input validation process may be severely limited.

Now comes the more subtle issue which relates format to processing. It is highly likely that the date will be the object of a search operation when selecting records for report generation. It may be desirable to select records on the basis of whether the date precedes or comes after a given date, or if the date falls within a range. It may also be desirable to select records on the basis of specific day, month, or year of event. For maximum flexibility it would, therefore, be desirable to address individually each component, day, month, and year. Does that mean that date becomes three fields and not just one? Does the chosen data management system have the more advanced feature of subfields, or overdefined fields, which permits doubling up of these requirements?

In the event that the highly user-oriented system does not permit this flexibility, then the likely alternative is the most unexpected solution. The user would enter, store, search, and output the date employing the form year, month, day. Referring to the earlier example, May 3, 1980 would actually be represented by 800503. With this structure, search criteria can be stated to achieve most of the selections normally associated with dates, but now the input format and output presentation will have lost aesthetic value. The "user friendly" criteria will have been compromised.

Would the typical end user's understanding of computer operations sustain the analytical process just described? Even with the most user friendly system available, success in defining fields for a file and subsequently executing queries requires more than a superficial acquaintance with computers.

Next, consider exception handling. In maintaining telephone numbers for employees of a company, assume that 90 percent of these employees are served by one area code while the balance reside in several surrounding coded areas. Would the data management system insist on reserving ten character (or numeric?) positions even though seven would suffice for 90 percent of the entries?

There is no simple solution because it depends upon one or more of the following factors:

1. Availability of storage capacity.
2. Trade-off in storage utilization versus set-up and execution ease to account for the differences.
3. Availability of variable-length field capability.

One simple, but possibly unacceptable, solution is to record only the phone numbers of the 90 percent group and maintain the balance in a separate, possibly even a manual, file.

Dates and phone numbers are not the only complex issues confronting the end user in design and use of a data base. Another issue is the handling of name and address. Again, what are the input, storage, search, and output considerations? Is it valuable to have search access to last name, zip code, or street name? Are mailing labels a requirement? Can search on last name and format for a proper mailing label be reconciled? Setting up the individual field entities and prescribing the order and format of the data becomes a systems design issue of no small proportion. Decisions about the most basic elements, such as field size for names or the format of a person's name, involve much greater expertise than is first apparent.

There are, of course, big computer systems that have evolved functionality that meets many of the above needs. For example, the NOMAD application development system of National CSS, Inc., offers one such comprehensive answer. In this system there are 11 options on format control for date presentation and nine options for presenting a name. Each of these options can be invoked in any order—giving the user a factorial number of variations.

Generally speaking, however, the conclusion is that there are certain conventional systems concepts familiar to trained EDP professionals which are completely beyond the experience of casual computer users. No degree of user friendliness can by itself overcome the need for understanding fundamental concepts and trade-offs in design of computer applications. This knowledge must be acquired through formal educational processes.

7.3.   USER'S POINT OF VIEW OF DATA MANAGEMENT SYSTEMS

Users of data processing are besieged with a variety of software programs to meet the needs for better tools in implementing applications. The most common offerings are data management systems suitable for ad hoc or prototyping use in generating a solution to a computer problem. These systems are now also becoming available in increasing numbers on popular desktop computers for personal and professional use.

Vendors of data management systems make an honest effort to focus on the ultimate user's needs. However, the starting point and perspective for the design of these products are too often those of the computer and the data processing professional. Hence, most attention is directed toward the technical aspects of file design, data structure and data networks, search and retrieval logic, report generation options, and the whole area of data base maintenance and support.

How well do these professionally oriented functionalities really satisfy the user? Only the user can respond and so, adopting that role, we propound the following criticisms and suggestions for improvement of commercially available DMS, especially those offered for popular microcomputers.

The most prominent irritant in commonly available data management systems is the lack of ability to redefine and reconstruct a file definition and the associated data file when the user discovers, after file definition is complete, that some data element is missing. Because of this oversight, an existing file must often be rebuilt unless the user, with inelegant foresight, has included dummy fields in the originally defined file.

A corollary to this limitation is the lack of ability to modify a field size or type when it is found that the number of numeric positions is insufficient or a field must be converted from a numeric to an alpha-numeric category.

Data management system designers seem to have a one-way focus when it comes to data base construction. Too often the assumption is made that data bases start from nothing and build up incrementally. Modest record maintenance capacity is, of course, provided through the ubiquitous record delete function. But what is sorely needed is a global maintenance operator that can, via a command level function, perform operations on an entire file. In this way, families of records can be modified according to some logical selection. Take the simple example of a file maintaining annual sick leave data which must be reset to zero once every twelve months. Can the system do this in a simple way or must one annually rebuild the file from scratch or modify each record sequentially?

Those systems that do possess global commands generally limit the operations to one field at a time. Further sophistication is desired to maintain data that are the basis for generating moving averages or cyclical computations. What is needed is the ability to shift field values within a record from one field to another. For instance, this feature would provide, in the case of 12-month history data, the means of moving data covering 11 months from fields two through twelve, one field position each to the left, and opening up the twelfth field for current month input.

Operations on fields within a record is often not enough. It also would be nice to have some functions which operate on two successive records, ordered according to the output sequence. This would be useful for generating year-to-date sums and would make it possible to have a column that shows successive change in a variable.

Next, consider a typical string search. Most systems limit such a search to exact matches or, possibly, a match against a number of leading characters, which is, in essence, a match on a prefix. Of course, some systems allow for a floating set of characters so that the specified search key will establish a hit no matter where the indicated sequence of characters are located in the field under review. However, if a system goes that far, why doesn't it go just one step farther and allow some wild card capability? This feature, incidentally, would create a general purpose, templatelike capacity for extracting data.

Why can't the output of a data management system automatically provide the query statement along with the printed report? Because modern retrieval systems provide dynamic screen-based interaction, the query, once entered, is lost in the bits of the machine. There are too many times when the user forgets the question for which there is now a bountiful answer.

While on the subject of output, let's go on record for a few other desirable features that would make life easier for the user. Many times a query is made to produce a report destined for general distribution, whether inside or outside an organization. Hence, format is important. Certainly, a minimum requirement is to have some control over page size and layout. It would also be nice if there were a means to overcome the physical limits of paper or screen width. Even more essential is the ability to control output field format, especially with respect to quantities carrying many decimal positions.

Now it is often argued that simple, user friendly systems should not incorporate too many complicating features since this would probably encourage a retrogression to complex operations or even procedural programming. We are not, for example, replicating a report generator in a query system. Perhaps some of these features could be provided through a post-query editor, a facility which does not exist today in any system of which we are aware. A post-query editor would be able to perform reformatting and text-oriented operations suitable for modifying a report file. It would allow the user to change the looks and content of a report file to suit individual needs. Column labels could be modified and enhanced, footnotes added, columns switched, data modified, and so on.

Incidentally, a DMS that requires output of detail lines in order to obtain totals is another irritant that makes users impatient with the designers of the system.

Another desirable feature that is often lacking in a DMS is the generation of interim information on how many records qualify for the query's answer set. This is useful in determining the adequacy of the query that will pinpoint the response, as well as the practicality of generating a report. But there is also another key benefit. By identifying an answer set one has implicitly identified a subfile. It should now be relatively simple to direct the system to subset such a file, either in a virtual or real mode.

Such a file subsetting facility would be further enriched if the DMS also had a file merge function so that more flexibility in modifying data would be possible. This feature would allow for dynamic creation of new files by merging several subsets of existing files.

Finally, there is the importance of the default condition. A typical DMS user usually operates with the same file and similar data updates and queries. The system can take advantage of this by always presenting to the user a default condition for the prompts and specification forms. These defaults would reflect the most recent use of the system for that user. In this way, input keystrokes as well as key errors are minimized. In the succeeding section, we shall see how one such DMS meets many of the situations described above.

7.4. DATA MANAGEMENT FOR THE END USER

In Sections 7.2 and 7.3, data management systems were discussed from the point of view of the users. Certain limits and deficiencies were identified that apply to the wide spectrum of commercially offered products. This section responds to these views by reviewing a popular DMS offered to the microcomputer marketplace. The review is performed through a case study reflecting a life situation. It will be seen that this specific DMS meets many, but not all, of the requirements already set forth.

The chosen software, PFS and PFS:Report, are the related products of Software Publishing Corporation of Mountain View, California. The acronym PFS, though not elucidated by the manufacturer, presumably stands for Personal File System. That is exactly what is offered by this very user-friendly and comprehensive software product which allows for the standard data management features of defining files, updating such files, searching the files, and reporting therefrom.

For $95, one obtains a rather complete system which offers all of the foregoing facilities, given the availability of an Apple II Plus system with 48K memory, disk drive, and video monitor. For a second $95, one gets the reporter portion of the system which allows for a broader range of output generation. In both instances, a printer will add measurably to the operability and usefulness of the software.

The documentation for PFS and PFS:Report comes in a very easy-to-read and pleasant format which introduces one by a natural progression to all features of the system. Illustrations are abundant; the diagrams and examples make it a self-teaching experience.

In one word, PFS is elegant. The expertise of the people who produced PFS is founded on prior experience with big machines. This is reflected in the packaging of the software, the features of the system, and the supporting documentation. Indeed, the excellent software ideas have obviously been influenced by the much higher-priced and more powerful Hewlett-Packard systems, IMAGE and VIEW. Compared feature by feature, PFS stands up exceedingly well against systems with substantially higher prices expressed in five figures.

Consider, for example, file definition and record creation. Defining the file is tantamount to defining input screen formats which are subsequently used as data entry forms in building the file itself. The screen painting capability of PFS is quite natural and simple. The software's authors call this process an automatic schema generator.

The system does not have any data entry validation capacity because all field values are treated as variable-length character strings. This characteristic allows several unique features often not found in systems that are a thousand times as expensive. First, data entered for a specific field need not have consistent format. Dates, for example, could be entered as 6/8/81, as well as 6-8-81, or even 6 August 81. Telephone numbers may appear as 213-555-1234, or simply 555-1234, or even 5551234. This flexibility in telephone number representation could be useful in storage saving. Using the example in the previous chapter, if 90 percent of the telephone numbers are in a known area code and remote area codes occur in the remaining 10 percent, the prefix for the former can be ignored. In other words, the system is designed to handle exception cases on an ad hoc basis.

During search or reporting time the field values can be dynamically interpreted as either an alpha string or a numerical quantity. In the latter case, all embedded nonnumeric characters are simply deleted and the numbers concatenated to form a numerical quantity. (The data, represented as either 8/10/81, or 8-10-81, will become 81081 when treated as a numeric quantity; the values $100, 3.99, 10 and 4 dollars will automatically be converted to 100.00, 3.99, 10.00, and 4.00.) This facility provides a dual advantage. Field values can be in proper format for output presentation purposes on the one hand, and available for numerical operations on the other.

Another important aspect of file design is that of storage requirements. The variable length field and record facility allow dynamic expansion of data as long as there is sufficient entry room on the screen opposite each of the protected item labels. Therefore, zip codes expanding from five to nine characters will pose no problem as long as there is space on the screen opposite the item "ZIP: " for at least nine positions. In this system one can avoid the often unpleasant task of deciding *a priori* how many character positions to leave for names, addresses, and so on. As field values increase or decrease in character length, storage of the data is automatically adjusted.

Files are automatically indexed by a hashing technique with respect to the very first data item in the record definition. This limitation to a single index is acceptable for a system geared to the personal computer. Each of the other fields, however, can be employed as a sequentially accessed search key.

The retrieval logic operating in field searches can be against fully or partially matched character strings or matched on a numeric basis. This makes the system incredibly flexible, allowing for retrieval logic that can find any record as long as a specified field contains a stated character string or numeric quantity. Further, the search can be qualified to be either a string at the beginning of the field value in the form of prefix, at the end in the form of a suffix, or floating somewhere in the middle. The numeric search is activated if the field is tagged for numerical processing.

Unfortunately, the retrieval logic is limited and therein lies one of the chief weaknesses of PFS. First of all, only "AND" logic is allowed, and secondly, numeric searches are limited to greater, less, or equal comparisons. The system would be very much more powerful if "OR" logic were also permissible and at least the "NOT" function were available for both character strings and numerical operation. These features are now under consideration by the software vendor.

In the report generation area, one can employ either screen or printer for selected output from the retrieved records. PFS will even provide simple reports in free format, including field selection and page control. This capability, for example, can be used to generate mailing labels.

PFS:Report enhances the output capacity of the system by producing tables with up to nine columns and allowing for two levels of sort. The user-nice features of table centering, column header aliases, ad hoc titles, pagination, and paper control are handled as with big system report generators. One can even derive as many as three new variables as a function of already defined entities. Summaries include total, average, and count, as well as one level of subtotals, subaverages, and subcounting. Given the ability to control the paper in terms of lines, width, selected breaks, and paper type, one has enormous options at his fingertips.

So far, the description of PFS has been in the usual computer vernacular. PFS, however, introduces itself to the user through documentation that never employs the typical jargon of the trade. Rather, the term *form* is utilized to suggest a concept, which is presumably better understood by end users than is the term *record*. Screens, screen painting, and file definition are replaced by the more familiar terms of *form design*, which results in a *blank form*. Fields are called *items of a form* and records are simply an instance of a filled-in form. From this point on, all explanations are easy to grasp.

But to do real justice in evaluating a programming system such as PFS, one needs to explore its limitations and benefits by testing its usefulness in solving a real problem. For this purpose, an opportunity arose with which to challenge PFS.

The problem is to generate a membership file for a nonprofit senior citizens center. The membership roster for this organization numbers 6000 and is growing by more than 10 percent per annum. The usual individual personal information has to be recorded, consisting of 15 data elements, four of which comprise name and address of the individual, and 10 that reflect descriptive information about the persons. One more refinement, however, makes the problem nontrivial. Monthly and year-to-date reports are required by funding agencies to count the total number of participants in each of 50 different activities, grouped into four categories, as well as to count the total number of unduplicated names participating in each activity and category. Similar totals are also required for subsets of the membership, aggregated by satisfying certain search criteria that are based on social and demographic factors.

In addition, the management of the center wants to keep track of each individual's participation in the program. Such data would provide overall general usage trends as well as the individual's degree of activity. One management objective in maintaining a time-related log of activities by individuals is to become aware, over time, of decreasing participation and thus be able to take appropriate action to get inactive members reinvolved.

To accomplish this tracking of member activity, it was necessary to allocate recording space, recognizing, however, that it would be highly variable for each member. The variable-length field facility and partial field search capacity of PFS became important capabilities that made the system really useful. The fifteenth data item became the recording point for reflecting the monthly participation of each individual in the various activities using a coding scheme MXAB, where M = numerical value of the month, X = a single character reflecting category, AB = a two-character activity identifier.

The problem seemed ideal for PFS. All of the functionality of PFS was utilized and some of these functions were stretched to the limit. But most important, the ease of use of the system provided a painless introduction to computer utilization for users who were completely uninformed with respect to data processing. The design of the screen format for data entry and form presentation is shown in Figure 7.1.

The first and most important impediment turned out to be limitations on storage capacities of the disk systems associated with personal computers.

```
┌──────────────────────────────────────────────────────┐
│   LAST NAME, I :                                       │
│   ST ADDRESS  :                                        │
│   CITY        :           ZIP      :                   │
│                                                        │
│   PHONE       :           MBR ID :                     │
│   ETHNICITY   :           DATE   :                     │
│   FINSTAT     :           STATUS :                     │
│   REL PREF    :           SEX    :                     │
│   MAR STATUS  :                                        │
│                                                        │
│   ACTIVITIES  :                                        │
└──────────────────────────────────────────────────────┘
```

Figure 7.1.   Data entry and presentation format.

The 128-byte blocking of data by PFS leads to a maximum of 1000 records that can be accommodated on any physical disk. Unfortunately, the PFS storage overhead supporting variable-length field capability became a negative factor for the fixed-length information and a positive contributor to the variable-length name/address and activity fields. It became apparent that the membership file would probably use two blocks of disk storage per record, so that perhaps only 500 names could actually fit on a physical diskette. In other words, the membership files would have to be spread over 10 or more discrete diskettes in order to design the system. This would ultimately severely limit the generation of certain management reports that depend on a presentation sequence bouncing back and forth between portions of the file on different disks. While this does not necessarily reflect a shortcoming of PFS, it does indicate how rapidly small personal computer systems can be exhausted by real-life application needs of the beginning user.

Applying PFS to the solution of this problem yielded all of the desired reports except one. Also, some of the application update and maintenance requirements revealed a few significant system shortcomings which are described below.

First is the issue of the reports. The most difficult objective was to invert the file for each of the recorded values of MXAB and derive the necessary counts. These counts had to include overall totals as well as unduplicated totals. A member might have an undetermined number of participations during any one month, including multiple occurrences of the same activity.

A special and unique feature of PFS provided the solution. PFS, being text-oriented, has a special reporting operator that inverts a specified field containing keywords and automatically produces a report, sorted by these keywords. For each keyword it is possible to associate other field items of the record. This feature was designed to generate the classical library keyword index listing.

This automatic feature of PFS, coupled with allowing suppression in printing of repeating values, yielded the necessary agency reports giving total and unduplicated counts by activity and categories of activity, by month, and year-to-date. This was accomplished by treating the fifteenth field as a keyword field where the keywords really represented the MXAB activity tuples. (See sample report in Figure 7.2, which illustrates the output for the first two months and presents the unduplicated participant counts in the second column with the total count in the third column.)

ACTIVITY REPORT

ACTIVITY	MEMBER #	NAME
1AIN	2342	JONES, R.
		JONES, R.
	4150	SMITH, M.
	COUNT: 2	COUNT: 3
1ATR	2342	JONES, R.
	5110	BROWN, T.
	COUNT: 2	COUNT: 2
1BED	2342	JONES, R.
	4150	SMITH, M.
	4575	ALVAREZ, J.
		ALVAREZ, J.
		ALVAREZ, J.
	COUNT: 3	COUNT: 5
2AIN	4150	SMITH, M.
	5110	BROWN, T.
		BROWN, T.
	COUNT: 2	COUNT: 3
2BED	2342	JONES, R.
	4575	ALVAREZ, J.
	COUNT: 2	COUNT: 2
2BOV	2342	JONES, R.
	5110	BROWN, T.
		BROWN, T.
	COUNT: 2	COUNT: 3
	COUNT: 13	COUNT: 18

Figure 7.2. Sample report with control breaks and subcounts.

One report was not feasible. There is no way to select members for which there has been no activity for, say, the last three months, unless one does a brute force record-by-record inspection. This limitation is related to the unavailability of the "not" selection logic, which is as useful in data processing as is the "equal" operator.

As already mentioned, the activity data is accumulated on both a monthly and a year-to-date basis. At the beginning of each year, it is necessary to reset the activity field values to blanks. It would therefore be desirable to have field control of the files to do global operations such as a replace operation. Unfortunately, this is not possible with PFS. The only system global operator is the delete capacity, which can be invoked for a given set of search parameters and, when a match occurs, that particular form is erased.

Another limitation of PFS is its inability to directly and selectively search and extract records from an existing file in order to create a subfile. This may be accomplished, however, by copying a file and then performing the "remove" function which deletes records according to the chosen search criteria. Again, the "not" selection option is a critical need.

Both of the last two requirements, as well as the earlier mentioned desire for global operators, could be accommodated if there were an additional option in the "copy file" facility. If it were possible to copy a file by selection logic designating which fields are to be incorporated in the target output file, then one could, with this single feature, achieve the desired operations. Of course, once more, the "not" operation would be essential.

The opportunity to review PFS provided an interesting experience in examining how protection of software is practiced in the microcomputer arena. Software Publishing Corporation does not concern itself with identifying a particular piece of software by any serial number. Ownership, or license to use, is simply established through the purchasing transactions. The software is sold with a three-month warranty for the operability of the physical diskette itself and not the computer program. The diskette is protected from duplication by a proprietary process. The owner may obtain a second copy of the software by mailing in the "backup copy certificate" and $15. A copy of the system will then be sent as long as the purchaser has filled out and submitted an owner registration card to Software Publishing Corporation.

Despite the limitations, the user friendliness and capability of the PFS software make it an unusual entry into the race for better and better data management systems. The lay personnel of the senior citizen center readily understood the process of form design and screen-controlled data entry. System prompts and flexible operation make the software suitable for new computer users who obtain functionality that is more often associated with big computers and sophisticated large scale software. Let's not forget, however, that even the most ordinary problems may tax both the software and the hardware limitations of a particular system.

Additional Readings

The material in this chapter can be further developed by referring to the following articles in the Bibliography at the end of the book: Astrahan and Chamberlin, 1975; Data Base, 1980; EDP Analyzer 1981a; EDP Analyzer, 1981d; Hayes et al., 1981; Ling, 1980; McGee, 1981; NBS, 1980; Reisner, 1977; Reisner, 1981; Shneiderman, 1979; Sisson, 1980; Snyders, 1981; Wassermann, 1981; and Zloof, 1981.

EIGHT

Impact of Microcomputers on Software

In Section 3.3, we noted that the economics of computing observed an inflection point as a consequence of the sudden availability of low-priced desktop computers. This marketplace event has led to two phenomena:

1. The creating of a substantial consumer base with large purchasing power.
2. The stimulation of new hardware and software technology which will affect all of data processing.

In Section 8.1, we discuss the pervasiveness of the microcomputer, describing how it affects the marketplace and identifying sources of information as well as pinpointing some of the innovations.

Section 8.2 is concerned with the deep impact computers are making on the youngest generation and what the long-term implications of this computer literacy might be.

Chapter 8 is concluded in Section 8.3 where we show by example how software is being seriously affected by the microcomputer. The example is the BASIC computer language which has been adapted to the microcomputer. Within this environment BASIC has blossomed to take on many new characteristics and capabilities.

8.1. THE PERVASIVENESS OF MICROCOMPUTING

With nearly one million microcomputer units now in the hands of end users, is it any wonder that a rich, new industry has emerged almost overnight in support of that market? And with almost one-half of these small systems emanating from only two suppliers (Radio Shack and Apple), it should be no surprise to see a heavy emphasis and support for those brands alone.

This new industry involves software suppliers, peripheral manufacturers, and, to facilitate distribution, a new breed of retail computer stores and mail-order houses. Add to this a rich and flourishing software publications business, and you have the new world of microcomputers.

This world, in fact, is an underground network, since so much has transpired in it with little or no recognition by the computer community at large. Let's look at some of these activities and offerings.

The throngs attracted to regional personal computer shows attest to the grassroots interest and commitment to the microcomputer. As an example, there is the well-known West Coast Computer Faire held in the San Francisco area, which chalked up its sixth show early in 1981, and attracted more than 20,000 people. California also hosts an annual Computer Swap Meet.

That a new business is in the making is shown by the spreading Business and Home Computer Show, which boasted attendance of 31,000 at its first event in Boston during 1979. Computer conventions hold special and concurrent seminars and exhibits solely dedicated to the smallest end of the data processing business as, for example, the Personal Computer Festival at the annual National Computer Conference. The manufacturer has gone the way of the road show, as did Radio Shack with its TRS-80 Expo '80 promotion in 50 U.S. cities, and Apple's Expo-81 four-city tour.

Local organizations abound to serve the needs of the personal computer enthusiasts. Such clubs are either organized along brand-name lines or serve the common interest of owners of diverse equipment. An example of an especially active club is the California-based Orange County TRS-80 Users group with a mailing list exceeding 1000 names. Other clubs are the Chicago Area Computer Hobbyist's Exchange, the Amateur Computer Group of New Jersey, and the Delaware Valley Computer Society.

Some partisan groups include the CP/M Users Group, organized around Digital Research, Inc.'s CP/M operating system, and Apple computer enthusiasts rallying around clubs such as Apple-Holics in Alaska, Apple Core in California, and Apple Pie in Illinois.

In addition, users have also begun to organize themselves as a national force seeking independent status through the creation of an association, the Personal Computing Society.

A highly professional publication industry serves the microprocessor users. These journals are serious contributions, despite occasionally outlandish names. They are all aimed at the personal computer marketplace. Heading the list are magazines such as *Dr. Dobb's Journal of Computer Calisthenics and Orthodontia*, *Byte*, *Creative Computing*, *Kilobaud Microcomputing*, *OnComputing*, *Interface Age*, *Personal Computing*, and the weekly newspaper *InfoWorld*.

Journals such as these generate thousands of readable pages each month containing newsy articles, promotional ads, and most importantly, a rich source of published code—almost exclusively written in BASIC—making available free application software for the public domain. A recent sample of such programs includes:

Investment analysis alternatives for maximizing returns.

Amortization table generation under varying hypotheses.

Calendar and appointment scheduling.

Trip planner.

Sales analysis and trend forecast.

Personal name and phone directory.

Income and expense logs.

Check entry and balancing system.

Home budgeting and planning system.

Beverage recipes and recommendations.

These programs are serious efforts, some consisting of 1000 to 2000 program statements, designed to perform a rather complete job.

Microcomputer owners are flooded by advertising, promotional leaflets, and informative newsletters. All of this material serves to sell accessories consisting of hardware, software, and computer-related paraphernalia to the personal computer user. Most of the materials start as giveaways, though some eventually obtain subscription status.

An example of such productions can be gleaned from the single market serving the TRS-80 computers where a variety of publications are produced. The list is headed by Radio Shack's own newsletter, the *TRS-80 Microcomputer News*, followed by independently published periodicals such as *T-Pal*, *Softside: S-80 Edition*, *PROG-80*, *The S-Eighty*, *TRS-80 Users Journal*, *80 Microcomputing*, *The Alternate Source*, and *Computronics*. The Apple computer community, on the other hand, is served by *Softalk*, and other comparable publications.

Newsletters have also sprung up in support of other elements of this burgeoning new industry. For example, *LIFELINES* is a publication solely devoted to those interested in software compatible with the popular and almost de facto standard of the microcomputer community, the CP/M operating system. In yet another direction, *S-100 Microsystems* is a periodical devoted to a hardware aspect, the S-100 based microcomputers and related software issues.

The interest in the micro has even extended vertically to an industry orientation. For example, *The Physicians Microcomputer Report* serves the medical professional in hardware selection and application guidance. Another example is *The Computing Teacher*, a journal oriented to the pre-college teaching professional and covering material related to teaching about computers and to teaching computer use, as well.

Now there has emerged a national organization, VisiGroup, which is an information exchange for owners, users, and others "who are enthusiastic about VisiCalc, the Visible Calculator." Membership provides a subscription to *SPREADSHEET*, devoted to the effective use of VisiCalc, or other similar products. VisiCalc is the popular personal-computer-based software product that automates many of the functions of spreadsheet operations on very small microprocessor computers.

All of these examples give some indication of the proliferation of special interest publications oriented to specific CPUs, to specific communications architecture, to operating systems, to vertical end-user markets, and to specialized software. In addition to the journals, a host of soft- and hard-covered books are available, ranging from very simple introductions to computers, computing, and programming to more sophisticated publications which expose the small computer user to the hardware and software aspects of microprocessing. The retail computer store displays these publications in open racks so that the consumer can browse and make a selection.

Software offered at low prices requires a large marketplace and low-cost distribution. Accordingly, most software for the small systems are sold as commodities, off the rack in the retail stores and through mass merchandising techniques such as mail order catalogs. These catalogs make available commercial software for a variety of hardware and operating environments. They are produced by individuals as well as specialized software companies. Examples of such software catalogs are the *Sensational Software Catalogue*, *Computronics Software Catalogue* and *Ye Compleate Computer Catalogue*. Specific software listings are also available from the individual hardware vendors and for certain special environments as, for example, the CP/M Users Group catalog of available software for execution under the CP/M Operating System. Radio Shack itself has instituted a catalog of available software for the TRS-80 line, the *Sourcebook*, but limits entries to application programs only.

Computer stores are individually owned, organized through a franchising network, or are part of a chain. Outlets for certain popular hardware, such as the Apple and TRS-80 computers, can range from fewer than 1000 to more than 7000 stores.

In a new and burgeoning industry, represented by vendors who market primarily by mail or through third parties, questionable practices and product quality issues must be expected. Indeed, some near-fraudulent business dealings have already occurred. To monitor the industry, and to further the interest of suppliers, the Microcomputer Industry Trade Association (MITA), with representation in Washington, D.C., has been formed. Local organizations also have formed as, for example, the Southern California Computer Dealers Association and a national trade association, The National Association of Computer Stores (NACS).

Not to anyone's surprise, personal computing could not contain itself and now has access to a variety of networking alternatives. In one approach a number of individual microcomputers can resource-share storage and printer devices through hookups to a common bus or other form of multiplexing. Such systems also allow for intercomputer communications.

A second approach opens up the whole world of commercial systems via conventional modems. Thus, for example, one can access public data bases or time-sharing systems via personal computers.

At least two time-sharing vendors have specifically oriented their system to client service of the growing number of microcomputer users. One of these, MicroNET, a service of CompuServe, now makes available its networks at almost 200 U.S. locations to provide downloading of software as well as data bank access and electronic mail to the personal computer enthusiast.

Another network service to the individual comes from Dun and Bradstreet, permitting access to computer financial data via microcomputer hookup through normal telephone lines.

The growth of microcomputers in what is essentially a consumer marketplace has also led to the growth of ancillary businesses that provide supporting systems. These entrepreneurs offer imaginative, even unique, combinations of hardware and software technology, often pacing the advances associated with the larger computers.

The Apple computer community is a good example of the growth of an industrial/business complex arising from the spread of consumer interest in the microcomputer. With a user base presently estimated at nearly one-half million, it is not hard to understand why the Apple hardware has brought into being a substantial subindustry in its support. It is bewildering to note the advances derived from interfacing such a variety of peripheral devices. The resulting capability often challenges the functionality present in today's big-machine environments.

The cooperative relationship between Apple Computer Company and these supportive businesses is unique for the industry. Indeed, Apple has encouraged and furthered these endeavors by providing ease of access to the back plane of the computer.

First there is the variety of fast-access storage devices ranging from the ubiquitous floppy diskette systems (5.25- and 8-inch size; single, double, and even quadruple densities; and single- or double-sided) to the 8- and 14-inch hard disk systems and the 5.25- and 8-inch Winchester-type storage units. Storage capacities now easily range from one-half megabyte to 20 megabytes—and, in combination, easily to 100 megabytes, all accessible from a single computer. But most attractive are the prices, which can be less than $5000 for a 20-megabyte capacity.

Printers are the second large category of peripherals tremendously influenced by the widespread use of the low-end personal computer. Included here are versatile matrix and full character printers suitable for bulk production, word processing, and graphics output.

Even more amazing is the versatility of the interface engineering which permits so many peripherals to adapt conveniently to a variety of CPU offerings through the use of low-cost interface cards. One can readily obtain multifunction communication cards, special key entry devices, and bar code word readers.

Both software and hardware adaptations have now been demonstrated showing how quick and relatively easy it is to modify or augment a computer. By adding a logic card, which in itself may be a computer, the entire host system can be modified. The Softcard produced by Microsoft, for example, will convert the Apple's 6502 chip-based performance to a Z80/8080 chip environment, which can then execute the rich software body existing for these latter chips under the widely used CP/M operating system.

A more avant-garde offering is the VET/2 voice entry terminal from Scott Instruments. For less than $1000, a microphone and attachable unit can be hooked to the Apple or TRS-80 to replace keyboard entries with voice. Sets of 40-word vocabularies can be dynamically generated and subsequently used, in a voice-driven mode, during execution of programs normally requiring input through the terminal's keyboard. The vocabulary must be associated with a particular voice, whose signature or template is established by repeating each desired word four successive times to the VET/2 preprocessor. Once the word patterns are "learned" by the system, the user can speak to the computer, employing this vocabulary whenever external keyboard prompts or commands are solicited. The technology works, and the system is a beautiful example of bringing together digital computer software and hardware in solving a difficult and intriguing analog problem. Now, one only needs the proper application in order to exploit this facility.

Another significant hardware advance in the area of communications is Nestar Systems Incorporated of Palo Alto, California, which offers the Cluster/One network. Cluster/One allows as many as 65 connected devices to talk to each other, be they computers or peripherals. The architectural approach of this networking system is termed "Ethernetlike," where local serial loops can be combined with daisy-chain branches. This ensures that no single device failure can bring down the entire system, as would be the case with star-type configurations or shared resource systems that multiplex use of a single CPU or commonly accessed storage facilities.

Pure software offerings are also available, ranging from languages to accounting applications to microprocessor-sized data management systems that can compete with offerings on mainframes (see Section 7.4).

The software is distinguished for its user-friendly attributes as well as its interactive, screen-driven form. In this sense, software for the microprocessor is far advanced over software now available for the mainframe and many minicomputers.

The mushrooming invasion of the microcomputer into the business and professional world is effecting such rapid changes and astonishing innovations in all of computing that the area of change is properly called a new frontier. Hardware technology has created the frontier, but to exploit the potential fully, the challenge lies with software.

8.2. THE CHALLENGE OF INCREASING COMPUTER LITERACY

The youngest generation is growing up surrounded by computer technology. Games are chip-driven. Video tubes tied to computers are available even to students at primary level. Children are using hand-held calculators and related devices, such as spelling and translation units. This new breed will emerge well aware of, and knowledgeable about, what can be expected from computers. They will possess the appropriate vocabulary and understanding of DP concepts and they will appreciate the computer's capabilities. In short, they will drive the market of the future, rather than be led.

Before the chip-oriented consumer environment reached its present stage of development, many terms in common use among computer professionals sounded mysterious to the public at large. Take, for example, the term *default value*. The idea denoted by this word has always been one of the harder concepts for the noncomputer person to grasp.

Defaults are standard or built-in values for given parameters of a computerized system. These values are usually invoked during execution of the application, unless overridden and modified by the user prior to initiation of the processing. Thus default values are the preset values assigned to parameters in order to protect the user and the system from operating with deficient or insufficient data. One other purpose is also fulfilled; input demand on the user is minimized. This advantage is accomplished through avoiding extra keystrokes and possible mistakes in entering data, at least for the parametric settings, which may remain invariant most of the time anyway.

This notion of default values, formerly so difficult to explain to a novice, is readily understood by any youngster familiar with one of the widely available electronic games. As he plays the game, noting the options provided, he learns that he can operate the game in its natural, or default, mode, or override certain preset conditions to modify the play.

From switch "on," today's youths are exposed to all the fundamental notions involved in operating a computer, and they absorb them with remarkable ease because these concepts are introduced as fun. There is the display unit which may be the ubiquitous video screen or simply a one-dimensional register. There are likely to be a keyboard and switch settings. Imagine the impact on the child who notes the various options or alternatives available by switch selection. Certainly the "function key" concept will readily emerge.

But switches and keys are not the limit for input. The toy may also have analog devices for controlling the play action or may even be able to detect and respond to the pressure or contact of a finger. The notion of recognizing screen location or position through a cursor will easily develop.

Every game player gets into a jam once in awhile and is led into a blind corner or bewildering situation. But all is not lost, and one is trained to return to the initial or neutral state by pushing the reset button. Can one more dramatically teach the restart and recovery function?

Of course, wrong actions may be selected or bad data entered. The beep has become an internationally recognized signal alerting the user/player that something has gone amiss, or at least that the device wishes to communicate some message to its operator. Indeed, voice synthesizers have found early common use in these low-cost devices, long before such use was comtemplated for the larger computer systems.

Two-player games usually can be modified by having one player compete with the game board itself. This is an illustration of a human being playing with or against a computer. Through this operation, the human player begins to understand the nature of preestablished (i.e., programmed) scenarios as well as dynamic responses to randomly entered prompts. What a way to teach and appreciate aspects of artificial intelligence!

The varying behavior of the computer during game performance as a function of player prompts must arouse the curiosity of the young. The observation of these unpredictable responses will surely lead to an early understanding and appreciation of the random number concept as well as its utilization. Unlike their seniors, members of this new generation will casually employ as tools sophisticated mathematical theories of probability. Early familiarity with this kind of thinking will lead to later understanding of statistical analysis and business applications, such as economic planning and forecasting.

Computer-related lingo may, of course, be more technically oriented, but even that does not seem too difficult for the consumer marketplace. The following caption on an attractive box indicates the degree of understanding already developed in the young:

It's a calculator, has 6 digits, 4 functions and floating decimal . . . for four years old and up. . . .

Another reads:

Two-digit operation, three-digit number.

Then there's the anthropomorphic approach:

I'm programmed to beat you.

Just imagine the difficulty of teaching such concepts in the classroom!

While **PEEK** and **POKE** may not yet have entered the lexicon of the younger set, other computer terms have certainly been introduced. Terms like memory, console keys, readout, field display, overlays, clear and enter buttons and error messages have all become commonplace.

The concept of system capacity is also understood. Young people realize that a game that is acquired with a limited set of options may be enriched, or enhanced, with the purchase of additional options affecting the number of plays, number of players, skill levels, and other variants.

Finally games can be modified by changing skill levels or operating modes, and altering the logic process. Although some of these changes are effected by switch setting, others may be a result of replacing plug-in modules. Whichever is applicable, the idea of being able to change the environment through a changed program becomes apparent. Storage options, too, become familiar through the various packagings of cassettes, cartridges, and disk-ettes.

In addition to the toys, a new summer experience is provided by computer camps. At least two of these, one on each coast, have announced programs for "the world of computers," mixed with outdoor activity for youngsters aged 10 and older.

The electronic toys of today are serving to expand and heighten the level of computer literacy among the young. They are providing the springboard for a new generation that will swim easily in the waters of a society where the computer will seem as common and friendly a device as waterwings. As these younger people mature and enter the industrial/technological complex, they will create a swell of interest and demand for computer utilization which only a few years ago would have been unimaginable.

8.3.   SERIOUS SOFTWARE FOR MICROCOMPUTERS

Although BASIC, the programming language, started out as the "beginner's all-purpose symbolic instruction code," BASIC is no longer necessarily limited to the neophyte. Still simple and easy to learn, BASIC has dramatically increased in breadth and depth since its introduction in the mid-sixties as a programming tool for the noncomputer professional in the university time-sharing environment.

Rather than being a true innovation, BASIC was more like a return to an initial subset of FORTRAN, defined and contained in an IBM document issued in the middle fifties called the "FORTRAN Primer." BASIC was distinguished not so much by the development of the formal language and syntax as by its introduction for operation in the emerging conversational and interactive time-sharing environment. Its "simplicity" was chiefly the convenience of entering a line-at-a-time statement under the power of an on-line edit program and the subsequent execution of that code in an interpretative environment. BASIC was fun and easy to use because its convenient and simple language facility operated in a substantially improved and friendlier user environment.

Although BASIC has evolved into many more complex forms and capabilities, these fundamental attributes are still present. That is why it became the obvious first choice in programming facility for the microcomputers entering the personal computing marketplace. BASIC has kept up with the times. Its associated language statements, functions, and commands not only encompass conventional data processing needs but also provide capability to control and execute processing related to graphics, color presentation, and sound. These latter features are a contribution from the microprocessing industry to the entire computing world.

How simple and elegant BASIC can be! Allowing for arithmetic and Boolean operations on both numeric and character strings, a good slice of typical computing can be accomplished with only seven statement types, namely, CLEAR, LET, INPUT, IF . . . , THEN . . . , FOR . . . NEXT, and despite the prejudices of today, the GOTO. What more can the beginner need and want? The rest of the process can all be automatically provided with easy-to-use keyboards and screen that facilitate:

1. Syntax checking.
2. Edit functions.
3. Statement sequencing.
4. Program execution.

The spread of BASIC capability can be readily seen in one family of language offerings as, for example, the Radio Shack line for the TRS-80 computers. There are actually four BASIC programs offered by the manufacturer of the TRS-80, apart from competing compilers available from independent sources. These systems are named Level I and Level II for the Model I computers, an interpretative and compiler version for the Model II line, and an advanced system for the Model III.

Level I and II are resident in read only memory (ROM), as is the Model III BASIC. The system for Model II is random-access-memory (RAM)-based. Level I includes 26 statements plus a few variants, having the capability of video graphics, screen and cassette input/output, integer and floating point arithmetic, a single numeric array operation, and two string-variable representations. The system has very primitive edit capability.

On the other hand, Level II BASIC operates much faster and with additional input/output facilities to communicate with printers and disks. Level II includes more than 75 commands, statements, and functions with some variants, as well as a richer capability in error detection, double precision arithmetic, longer string length, a good file edit capability, and more flexibility in labeling both numeric and string variables, files, and arrays. In a diskette environment, Level II is extendable to a RAM-based Disk BASIC with commands suitable for operating with random or sequential files and some other, additional facilities.

Model II and Model III BASICs are further extensions of the Level II language and provide maximum upward compatibility from the Model I systems. The Model II capability adds over a dozen new commands and is an ongoing, supported system because it is RAM- and not ROM-based. The expanding progression of BASIC capability for the TRS-80 family of computers is effected by increasing the complexity of the environment and, hence, the system. The language extends to encompass these enhancements.

The large market of the TRS-80 has invited competition from independent sources who bring improved BASICs to that line. One vendor provides a compiler version with the attributes of faster execution speeds and optimized and relocatable object code. This compiler has the disadvantage of not being interactive in the program development phase, but offers the benefit of being able to distribute object code rather than source programs, thereby affording more proprietary protection.

BASIC has been criticized because of its slow operation as an interpretative system, the paucity of business-oriented data processing language capability, its lack of file handling and poor string manipulation, absence of a screen orientation, and, strangely enough, the ease of understanding the source code, which invites loss of code protection. Now that the more complex versions of BASIC are coming to the marketplace, there are good counter responses to all of these points.

There seems to be no end to the increasing power of BASIC. For example, a new advanced BASIC boasts:

1. Six data types.
2. Local and global variables, functions, and procedures.
3. Complete compiler, relocatable code, and automatic linking to libraries.
4. Enhanced language statements supportive of nestable, structured programming.
5. Recursively used functions and procedures.
6. Dynamic inclusion of files and library source modules at compile time.
7. Formatted printing.
8. Sequential and random files.
9. Efficient execution capability.
10. Debugging and documentation aids.

BASIC compiler building has become a big business. One vendor, Microsoft, boasts the use of its BASIC on nearly one million microcomputers, performing in a host of operating system environments. This BASIC is available in the interpreter mode as well as in compiler form for generating optimized and compact object code. The system also embraces programming features identified with big system compilers such as the WHILE conditional, CHAINING of programs with COMMON variable length records in random files, PRINT USING, and tracing.

The popularity and ubiquity of the BASIC language is reflected not only in the large number of executable programs, but also in the proliferation of a vast literature. Titles such as *My Computer Likes Me When I Speak In BASIC* and *Computer Programming For The Complete IDIOT* indicate the impact of this language.

BASIC has been popularized through catalogs such as *The BASIC Cookbook* by Ken Tractor and *The BASIC Handbook* by David Lien. The book by Lien is further described as an encyclopedia of the BASIC computer language covering 250 variations of statements, functions, operations, and commands found in hundreds of dialects or versions of BASIC existing today. Serious texts such as *Problem Solving and Structured Programming in BASIC* by Koffman and Friedman and *Foundations of Programming Through BASIC* by Moulton are also available.

It is possible to get lost in the alphabet soup of various BASIC implementations. The proliferation of everyman's BASIC is reflected in such offerings as BASIC-80, S-BASIC, extended BASIC, Business BASIC, BASIC-Plus, minimal BASIC, UBASIC, MBASIC, CBASIC, Power BASIC, Tiny BASIC, INFINITE BASIC and on and on . . .

One thing is clear. BASIC is now an important part of the computer scene. Most of the application software for microcomputers is developed in this language, as are the technical innovations associated with special devices such as color video, voice synthesizers, and analog controls. BASIC source language has become the de facto standard for program publishing and exchange in the personal computer marketplace.

Additional Readings

The material in this chapter can be further developed by referring to the following articles in the Bibliography at the end of the book: Crespi-Reghizzi et al., 1980; Gutz, 1981; and Raskin, 1981.

NINE

Acquiring Software

Having examined the various facets of software, we now come to the serious business of making an acquisition decision. Shall it be make or buy? In Section 9.1 we present some general views regarding the software purchasing advice offered to users through popular articles in the trade press. In Section 9.2, a model is presented that can be applied in the economic decision-making for software acquisition.

The apprehensions that haunt the typical software buyer are touched upon in Section 9.3. Finally, in Section 9.4, sources are identified that provide catalogs of available software.

9.1. ADVICE TO THE SOFTWARE BUYER

When it comes to the acquisition of software, there are many experts eager to provide advice to the end user. These experts range from legally oriented practitioners and contract administrators to marketing organizations and individual consultants. Sometimes the advice comes from the experienced end user himself.

Though offered with the best of intentions, such advice often breeds doubts. A typical user might well question the practicality and safety of buying commercial software when greeted by articles of advice with titles such as the following:

"Contract Ploys Suggested for Users"

"Perils of the Vendor-User Relationship"

"100 Things You Need to Know Before Buying Software"

"Software Licenses Fraught with Danger"

"License Pact Unfolded from Users' View Point"

One wonders how users react to articles by attorneys attempting to "help" the user-client, where we find statements such as "licensing a software product from a vendor is a terrible responsibility." Another advises that it is best to "create a disparity of knowledge in starting negotiations for a systems purchase."

Users are admonished by these well-wishers to adopt a *caveat emptor* attitude. One might be led to conclude that the software sector of the computer industry is made up of charlatans and exploiters. While good advice is not to be despised, some of the advice offered to the prospective software customer, however well-meant, is confusing and even dangerous. The end result for the user may be devastating. Here are some examples.

In purchasing a major software program, the purchaser is urged to include in the resulting sales contract a detailed software specification. This advice is given to insure that the software delivered to the end user will meet his expectations and fulfill his needs.

The advice, as applied to software products, is unsound. The commercial software that is delivered must rely for compliance on its own reference manual. It is not dependent on a user's specification. To the extent that the user's requirements come close to being fulfilled by the functionality contained in the reference manual, the user will be satisfied. If the user expects to obtain a perfect fit with his requirements, he misunderstands the entire concept of off-the-shelf, standard software. Indeed, if a client requires software exactly suited to his specifications, then he must buy customized software and pay the associated price.

Another warning from expert advisers unfavorably compares software companies to their hardware counterparts. It is often asserted that the software company is typically weak and short-lived. One recent article describes the software industry as a "revolving door environment." Furthermore, the author goes on to say that "only a relatively small number of software companies will mature into financially stable businesses." The facts, of course, belie the assertion.

Most software suppliers are members of the Association of Data Processing Service Organizations, Inc. (ADAPSO), the computer service industry association that fosters high ethical and performance standards. Furthermore, many software suppliers have been in business for almost a decade, and some even twice that long. Most important, many leading suppliers have recently become publicly owned companies and their operations are open to complete disclosure (see Section 10.3.).

Allegations that software companies are peculiarly impermanent are unfounded in fact, and they arouse unwarranted fear in the buyer. If indeed the prospective buyer is apprehensive about dealing with software companies, should he not be equally concerned about hardware firms? The issue really has nothing to do with size, or capitalization, or offering. Former users of computers manufactured by RCA, General Electric, and Xerox (née SDS) could well testify to the instability even among giants, whether hardware- or software-oriented.

Users are also often warned that delivered software may contain errors. One article asserted that a software purchase, once installed, should be expected to perform error-free. To protect the user from the possibility of errors in software, counselors sometimes suggest that such errors should be subject to liquidated damages. Such advice is misguided, and such well-meaning advisers simply do not understand the situation. Better advice is, of course, that delivered software *will* contain errors because no piece of software is ever 100 percent perfect. Up front we must all recognize that software is fragile and the user does indeed take a risk. He takes this risk whether he buys software from the outside or develops it in-house under his own absolute control.

Then there is the issue of the contract itself. Isn't it strange that highly qualified people will advise end users to be wary of standardized, printed contracts for commercial software? Why, in the case of software, is the user encouraged to insist on modification of the contract when, in other areas of business, standardizations are considered normal? Take, for example, the small print in a hotel laundry request sheet, which reads:

1. No claims of replacement can be made due to delayed delivery.
2. No guarantee can be assured for alteration in colors.
3. Liability is limited to five times the cost of cleaning in case of lost or damaged articles.

Does the hotel guest refrain from using the service because of these conditions?

How often is the end user given the opportunity to tamper with the printed contract terms of the hardware manufacturer? Is it possible to negotiate with IBM over their terms of agreement? Let us note, for example, what the typical IBM software contract agreement provides or, better, denies:

1. Lease and not purchase.
2. At most 6 months future support and maintenance.
3. No guarantee to fix defects.

Certainly, by any standard, the independent software industry far exceeds these limits.

The advice is not all negative. There are also many checklists and cookbook guides providing assistance in purchasing software products. These efforts usually include the obvious control items common to any acquisition of a product, whether hardware or software. Typically, they include checkpoints relating to the specific software characteristics, supplier background, purchase or lease options, contract terms, available training and support, and the prospects for future maintenance. The number of line items that are enumerated can easily range from 100 to 200. At times, however, the recommendations go beyond reason as, for example, the suggestion that the buyer obtain "rights to future enhancements" or subsequent price protection. When such "good" advice includes vendor-supplied free trials, no cost for on-site training, and subsequent support "at no additional cost," objections must be raised. In all such cases, the author of such advice should stipulate that any option or any right will have an associated price.

With software, as with everything else, there is no free lunch. One way or another, the customer must pay for what he receives. Rather than complicate the pricing and contracting situation by suggesting that all deliverable elements be subsumed under a single amount, the customer is better advised to have the vendor identify the component tasks and functions and establish a fair price for each such item.

The software product industry has come of age. Hundreds of firms provide quality and supported products. Many of these products have been offered for over a decade, demonstrating a viability tested both by numbers of installations and by the total sales dollar. In fact, the independent producers of commercial software will generate about one billion dollars of sales in 1981, and these sales are growing at about 30 percent per annum. Users can expect the same loyalty and commitment from the software vendor as they receive from the hardware manufacturer.

9.2. SOFTWARE MAKE OR BUY ECONOMICS

The goal of satisfying the data processing user is sometimes confused with the popular notion that the customer is always right. But an open-door or overly responsive policy with regard to computer users can be the perfect invitation to disaster in building software.

Certainly, we do not advocate placing restrictions on the user in specifying functional requirements for application software. However, throughout the definition stage of the software implementation process, the DP professional can make substantial contributions by always keeping in balance the cost/benefit equation. Scope of solution should always be matched to practicality of implementation.

The classical 80/20 trade-off is as operative in software implementation as it is in many other situations. Frequently, it is the last 20 percent of what users want that may well take 80 percent of the effort or create 80 percent of the ultimate difficulties. The user's needs and wants should be considered, but the consequent cost and risk should also be made clear. To avoid catastrophic or run-away costs, the user may prefer to reduce his expectations.

The cost of software depends on how it is acquired and how costs are calculated. Software development expenditures include the following cost components:

1. Requirements study.
2. Feasibility analysis.
3. Functional design.
4. System specifications.
5. Programming.
6. Testing.
7. Acceptance.
8. Documentation.
9. Training.
10. Conversion.
11. Operation.
12. Maintenance.

Not only is each of these activities a labor-intensive process, and therefore expensive, but the steps also take substantial time to complete.

There are additional costs seldom identified at the outset of a software project, such as:

1. Time and opportunity loss by not obtaining an immediate solution.
2. Poor estimates leading to project overruns.
3. Incompatibility of users' real requirements with what is actually delivered.
4. Change of the initial environment and requirements by the time the project is completed.
5. Ultimate and ongoing maintenance problems.

Internal manpower costs and displaced profits of an organization must also be considered when the best "people resources" are allocated to conceiving, defining, and architecturally designing the external characteristics of a given computer application solution.

User satisfaction and the price ultimately paid for a piece of software are a function of that software's timely availability as well as its performance against stated objectives.

At the outset, the user is really in a dilemma. He stands before the proverbial candy counter, not knowing which, or how many, pieces to select. We show this stressfull situation in Figure 9.1, where our "shopper" fills up the cart with everything in sight.

At this point the following issues must be confronted:

1. Is the requirement truly unique to the user?
2. Does the user really need report formats customized to certain unique specifications?

Figure 9.1. Software must satisfy the user.

3. Is every requested functional feature of equal priority or value?
4. Is time of the essence?

Some users do not know how to address these issues. Given a choice, they may well opt for anything that is available and ask for a custom solution, too. That is the point of this discussion. It is important for new users, as well as for veterans in developing applications, to differentiate among choices with all the economic alternatives clearly in mind.

Despite the present trend toward giving the user exactly what he wants, DP professionals should endeavor to follow these guidelines:

1. Provide the user with a candidate solution to be used as a checkpoint, or benchmark, rather than present an open invitation to include anything and everything the user ever wanted.

2. Lead the user to existing solutions (i.e., packaged software). These may be general-purpose and not necessarily an exact fit to the way the user is currently conducting his business or wants to conduct his business.

3. Wherever applicable, provide the user with a make-or-buy trade-off exercise.

With respect to the last point, the presentations of Figures 9.2 and 9.3 may help in analyzing the issues. Clearly a cost analysis such as suggested in

	MAKE	OR	**BUY**
ESTIMATED DEVELOPMENT COST	$250,000		$35,000
EVALUATION COST	N/A		15,000
DEVELOPMENT TIME	15 MONTHS		3 MONTHS
CONVERSION COST	$50,000		$50,000
CONVERSION TIME	3 MONTHS		3 MONTHS
EXPECTED ANNUAL SAVINGS	$100,000		$100,000
PAYBACK STARTS	18 MONTHS		6 MONTHS
INVESTMENT RECAPTURED	54 MONTHS		18 MONTHS

Figure 9.2. The make or buy economics.

Figure 9.2 is of paramount importance in reaching an early decision point. Following this, the risk versus leverage argument can be pursued to understand what is realized under the "make" option and what is achievable through the "buy." If a piece of software is available on the commercial marketplace and if it fits one's requirements, or even *nearly* fits, then current marketplace software prices are a bargain that the user cannot ignore.

In contemplating procurement of any software program, the economics almost always favors the low-risk, high-leverage solution of purchasing existing products. In make-or-buy trade-offs, paybacks from a purchase usually occur in one-third the time, while investment costs are also recaptured in one-third the time. The development time is reduced to one-fifth, and development costs to as little as one-seventh.

To the extent that users can make modest accommodations to standardized software and accept whatever that standardized software does, they will benefit economically. On the other hand, if the user continues to demand the kind of customization from software that he often does, the price of software will be driven up accordingly.

Standardized software is produced commercially for a large population and, by definition, has to be the sum total of requirements for that population. The circumstance of that software meeting across-the-board functional requirements for so many users, increases the likelihood that it will satisfy the needs of still other users. Knowing this to be true, a user wishing to make an economic breakthrough should strive to accommodate himself to existing commercial software.

Not only can the purchaser of commercially available proprietary software buy the operating code, but he also gets documentation, training, and continual maintenance. He is therefore able to shortcut many of the tasks identified at the outset of this section and avoid the accompanying pitfalls in implementing software.

Even if the software product is not the ultimate solution, its lower cost makes it attractive as a benchmark or strawman to use in identifying more specific, customized needs. The cost of the interactive process between the in-house user and DP staff, conducting their analysis (the first three components of cost) over many months, would more often than not equal the purchase price of the off-the-shelf software from outside sources.

In fact, the price of available software can often be justified solely on the basis of the associated documentation. This documentation can be the starting point for a subsequent internal development if it is deemed that the off-the-shelf software code in itself is not applicable or is insufficient. In other words, one can purchase the package, use the documentation and throw away the code—that's how inexpensive many packages really are.

There is an even more valuable—although frequently overlooked—tangible benefit. By associating oneself in the marketplace with other users of the same software product, one becomes a participant in a community of interest. The collective needs of such a varied client base will push the software

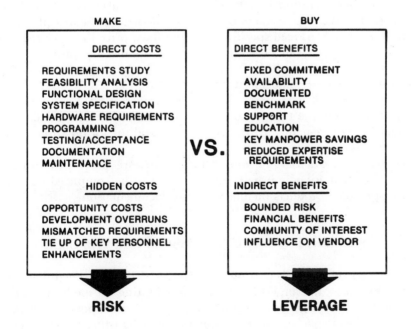

MAKE		BUY
DIRECT COSTS		**DIRECT BENEFITS**
REQUIREMENTS STUDY		FIXED COMMITMENT
FEASIBILITY ANALYSIS		AVAILABILITY
FUNCTIONAL DESIGN		DOCUMENTED
SYSTEM SPECIFICATION		BENCHMARK
HARDWARE REQUIREMENTS		SUPPORT
PROGRAMMING		EDUCATION
TESTING/ACCEPTANCE	**VS.**	KEY MANPOWER SAVINGS
DOCUMENTATION		REDUCED EXPERTISE
MAINTENANCE		REQUIREMENTS
HIDDEN COSTS		**INDIRECT BENEFITS**
OPPORTUNITY COSTS		BOUNDED RISK
DEVELOPMENT OVERRUNS		FINANCIAL BENEFITS
MISMATCHED REQUIREMENTS		COMMUNITY OF INTEREST
TIE UP OF KEY PERSONNEL		INFLUENCE ON VENDOR
ENHANCEMENTS		
RISK		**LEVERAGE**

Figure 9.3. Software acquisition.

product vendor into a continued enhancement program. If there is a substantial number of users, this situation will lead to a continually improved and responsive software product.

Membership in a software user group can also alleviate some of the problems of application software maintenance, which has now become a sizable (60 percent) portion of the programming staff's duties. This troublesome ongoing expense can, to a large extent, be displaced and the cost shared with many users.

Finally, purchased software can mitigate, if not avoid, the downside risks already identified as hidden additional costs of custom implementation, where time for completion and the end performance remain in doubt for too long. As an additional advantage for the financially concerned, purchased software can either be treated as a capital investment to help the statement of income, or it can often be leased, to help the cash flow.

In summary, the direct benefit of purchasing commercial software is the avoidance of the classical in-house cost components, including a requirements study, feasibility analysis, functional design, system specification, hardware requirements, programming, testing, documentation, and maintenance.

The significant indirect returns result from:

1. *Opportunity costs.* The ready availability of a purchased product permits earlier operation and, therefore, the earlier start of the payback period, as well as the improvement of operation desired in the first place.

2. *Lower risk.* Fixed specifications and fixed price limit the risk associated with any software developmental activity—meeting project completion schedules, staying within cost forecasts, and achieving operational goals set forth in the functional specifications.

3. *Key manpower savings.* A smaller number of key personnel, from both the user and the DP environments, is involved in reviews and evaluation of the requirements, feasibility analysis, and the formulation of functional specifications.

4. *Up-front documentation.* Unlike software developed in-house, where documentation is usually the last item to be completed (if at all), vendor-provided products include up-front documentation.

9.3. SOFTWARE BUYING ISSUES FOR THE USER

In its EDP Industry Report of February 28, 1978, IDC stated that "staff-related expenses, the largest budget item accounting for more than 44 percent of the 1978 budget, are dropping steadily . . . quite possibly the popularity of software packages may be a major factor assisting the DP manager in holding personnel costs to less than 50 percent of his budget." As seen in Figure 1.2, this forecast has been sustained.

With such a persuasive view of the value of software products, it is surprising that user budgets support outside purchases with less than 5 percent of their total DP expenditure. No doubt certain in-house issues still hold back users from what seems to be an obvious economic choice.

In the early sixties a senior officer in the Department of Defense presented the first argument this author ever heard against the purchase of proprietary software. This manager said that the in-house technical staff would be offended by having to work with programming designed by someone else; equally important, he said, was that such a purchase would preclude his staff from the technically challenging task of building the software. Quite obviously, this argument ignored fundamental economic issues. It also displayed confusion concerning the reason for the existence of a data processing facility and staff. Needless to say, the enterprise exists to solve problems for users, not to create jobs for programmers and analysts. The "not-invented-here" syndrome indicates a belief that each organization has problems and problem-solving capability unique to itself.

Another argument against proprietary software, and this is a better one, is that the acquisition of an outside software product may necessitate new training for personnel. This situation certainly arises when a product is implemented in a language unfamiliar to the client or inconsistent with his standards. Thus, PL/I- or Assembler-coded software are not usually welcomed in a COBOL shop. This argument may be given too much weight, however, since not all packaged software is delivered in source code anyway.

The language issue is usually raised in anticipation of the organization wishing to change the code. The temptation to tinker with purchased software, however, should be discouraged. Any alteration in the direction of specialization defeats a major purpose for the buyer of a standardized system, and may invalidate the maintenance support provided by the vendor.

There is always the issue of price. The in-house staff will often claim that the outside purchase of software can be matched by in-house development. These financial arguments are often incomplete and deficient because:

They ignore total costs, that is, the personnel overhead and computer costs incurred by the development team.

They overlook the cost of the definition and design phase, as well as the maintenance phase.

In other words, only the programming implementation expense is identified with the product purchase price.

A last point of resistance is the argument that the off-the-shelf software cannot possibly meet the often inflexible in-house requirements for function and capability. Little does the user realize that the last 20 percent of self-imposed needs may often lead to an 80 percent overrun on the project—a project that may never be completed or may be a year late. The user may be willing to adjust his "absolute" requirements if he is given the alternative of having immediate capability at a substantial cost reduction.

Even if all of these arguments against purchasing software have some merit, it is still true that first-time users can best be served by relying on existing, commercially available software. Such a user benefits directly from the documentation, procedures, training, and support which have evolved over a broad and experienced user base. With such a beginning, a user can, at a later optional point, redesign or restructure his application in a more customized direction—a direction based on a meaningful first experience.

For this purpose, many application software products provide user-accessible "hooks" that are strategically located to enable customized enhancements to be added through conventional procedural languages (e.g., COBOL, PL/I, etc.). Indeed, this is a means of following Kendall's advice (see Section 2.2) to install now and program later.

A much more interesting phenomenon, however, is on the horizon with respect to application software production. Veteran users are now facing insurmountable constraints with some of their bread-and-butter applications that have been running for 10 to 20 years. Such applications have seen the likes of the IBM 1410, the IBM 360, and the IBM 370. Shades of emulation may still be underlying the code!

When the time comes to replace the old payroll, the old general ledger, and the old personnel system, could any modern DP manager possibly commit his user organization to a redevelopment of projects entailing investments of hundreds of thousands of dollars when such applications can now be purchased off-the-shelf for less than one man-year of cost?

Before touching the pencil to the coding pad, users must look outside. The DP organization that does not budget a continued level of effort in "software watching," for both systems and applications, has not recognized the obvious and cannot claim to be a modern, cost-conscious business entity.

As noted, users who feel it necessary to "do their own thing" have traditionally placed obstacles in the way of purchasing proprietary software. Such users probably did not begin their computer education in the early days of the Computer Age and, therefore, do not know that many organizations once built their own hardware for the same reasons that users today advance for creating their own software. This early need for localized hardware innovation passed rapidly, even in the universities, where research and development are a recognized part of the activity, rather than a parochial indulgence. The fast pace of technology prevented each user from keeping up with the hardware evolution and, combined with the substantial capital needed for development, finally led to the commercialization of hardware. After 1960, no user allowed himself the luxury of building his own hardware, unless it was funded by the U.S. government on a cost reimbursement contract.

In those early days, users also tended to obtain hardware that was somewhat customized in order to accommodate a particular need. This practice became unacceptable as both manufacturer and user began to realize the benefits to be derived from standardization. The same economic principles that led to widely used and standardized hardware are operating now with respect to software. Yet in the software domain, users and suppliers have still to reach an accommodation that sufficiently recognizes the financial benefits accruing from the exploitation of the software product.

9.4. HOW TO FIND SOFTWARE

Software is available today in a wide variety of forms, from many sources, and under various terms. It is possible to acquire ready-made software for almost every conceivable computing function, including implementation aids (languages, debuggers); utilities (library handlers, sorts); environmental systems (teleprocessing, data base management systems); operational tools (measurement, scheduling); support systems (training, testing); application programs (payroll, general ledger); and industry systems (insurance administration, production control). Furthermore, software can be purchased to operate on large computers as well as on small ones. For example, the language compiler BASIC is available for operation on a mainframe, minicomputer, or microcomputer.

With such overwhelming ranges of offerings, one can obtain simple applications (e.g., recipe conversions on microprocessors) for $4.95, or sophisticated total systems (such as a life insurance administration system) for $500,000, reflecting an incredible price difference of five decimal orders of magnitude.

Software is available from either the hardware manufacturer or from independent organizations. Sales are made directly to users as well as to turnkey suppliers on an OEM basis. There are software middlemen who broker the products of others, as well as individual software entrepreneurs who may operate a mail-order business.

Industry subsectors have been established in which organizations make a living from the software products industry by providing catalogs of available software, consulting to users on how to buy software, and now, even advising individuals and businesses on how to package and market their own software.

Software can be purchased or leased. It can be obtained in source code or restricted to object code. It may be available through the mail, on a trial basis, acquired on the basis of benchmarks, or purchased on standard cassettes. Software is even available in publication form through program listings printed in popular computer hobby magazines or in the form of algorithms in several Association for Computing Machinery periodicals including the *ACM Transactions of Mathematical Software* and the *Collected Algorithms from ACM*.

In the early 1960s, software was openly disseminated at no cost, but nowadays this is no longer true. In return for a price, the seller provides a property well worth purchasing. The price will reflect a range of possible terms—

from a product sold "as is and unsupported" to a guaranteed and maintained product with appropriate documentation, training, and continued product evolution.

But how does the user find the software applicable to his requirements? For this objective one can turn to commercial sources.

The premier compendia of computer program listings are published by International Computer Programs, Inc. (ICP), which counts more than 2400 company suppliers and more than 10,000 products listed in the four volume ICP Software Directory:

Systems Software

Cross Industry Applications

Industry Specific Applications

Software Product and Service Suppliers

The *Software Product and Service Suppliers* compendium links company profiles to indexes that guide one to products by market specialty, industry orientation, or geographic area served. Also, a statistical summary is included for the top 100 U.S. companies providing information products and services.

ICP also produces *Interface*, a series of six quarterly magazines aimed at the specific interests of the following user sectors:

Data Processing Management

Manufacturing and Engineering

Insurance Industry

Banking Industry

Administration and Accounting

Small Business Management

Each issue contains articles pertinent to software topics for the particular sector as well as listings of available software products serving that sector.

Other commercial catalogs of software are available. One such source is Datapro's Directory of Software, a listing of offerings similar to the ICP catalog. This directory comes in two volumes and includes about 6000 listings showing offerings of manufacturers as well as independent suppliers. A convenient guide is available indicating programs available by machine and by manufacturers, of which there are over 100 identified. This directory also includes the "Annual User Ratings of Proprietary Software." This evaluation of software-in-practice can be a useful measure of a vendor's offerings as perceived by the user community.

Another alternative is the two-volume book, *Auerbach Computer Technology Reports*, from Auerbach Publishers Inc. Divided by applications and systems software, the information is grouped by major subject matter so that appropriate tutorials and available software alternative solutions are readily assembled and focused on behalf of the user.

A fourth reference book for available commercial software is the *International Directory of Software* published by CUYB Publications Inc., of Potsdam, Pennsylvania, and England. This British organization in its 1980–81 edition lists more than 3200 systems and application software with a special emphasis on worldwide origin. The compendium is organized into 107 categories and 24 industry groups, by product names as well as suppliers. Other foreign-based sources are the *Guide European des Products Logiciels* of the Centre d'eXperimentation de Progiciels in France, and the *ISIS Software Report* from the West German organization, Infratest Information Services.

An entirely new area of software availability is served by yet another publication, the International Microcomputer Software Directory, issued by Imprint Software of Fort Collins, Colorado, and London, England. This compendium lists over 5000 programs, fully indexed and cross-referenced by applications, machine, operating system, vendor, and name. This organization has also introduced a special code, the International Standard Program Number (ISPN) to identify each program.

The move to recognize the newly emerging microcomputer marketplace is encouraging others to provide valuable program source information. Datapro has announced the *Directory of Microcomputer Software* including over 2000 entries of programs for computers costing under $40,000. The products are indexed by application, name, vendor, and computer system.

There are also the software catalogs offered by the hardware vendors in support of their own equipment. Many times these reflect solely their own offerings, but sometimes such catalogs provide information regarding available third-party software. An example of the latter is the *Business Systems Software Directory* of Hewlett-Packard which cites application software produced by independent organizations for operation on the HP3000 series. Another example is the *Honeywell Software Catalogue* of Honeywell Information Systems, Inc.

IBM is, of course, the key software supplier among the manufacturers. The most noteworthy publication is the *Data Processing Division Software Directory; Keyword Index and Program Information*. This catalog is published annually and provides listings of over 1000 IBM offerings including System Control Programming, Program Products, Field Developed Programs, Installed User Programs, and Programming Requests for Pricing Quotations (RPQ). These program types are further organized for look-up by a keyword index, program order number, and product cluster.

The IBM product cluster index organizes the available programs by 7 major and 44 secondary topic areas. The major topics include two application areas, the cross industry and the industry orientation, with 22 further breakdowns. The remaining five categories of software are all systems-oriented, including data base/data communication systems, interactive systems, systems control for host systems, distributed systems, and subsystems control.

Price and product availability are, of course, dynamic. Hence periodic information is provided by IBM announcements of new offerings as well as changes. This information is made available through direct information mailers as, for example, the *Monthly DPD Support Bulletin*. There are often 10 to 20 such product announcements per month.

The most useful publication of IBM is, however, the *Systems and Products Guide*, published for the data processing executive and issued for the first time in 1981. In one compendium, a brief but encompassing overview is supplied of data processing concepts and systems. Key data processing functions are defined and pointers are provided to the software with which to implement or support the area. Of even greater significance are the software roadmap and family relationships that are provided for major systems. Finally, individual products are described indicating purpose, key functions, benefits, prerequisite, and product dependencies.

A specialized version of this publication is the August 1981 *Application Development Systems Catalog* which is a tutorial presentation of the key development environment software of IBM. Described therein are the component offerings in support of Data Systems, Development Center, and Information Center as defined by IBM.

The IBM document *Applications and Abstracts* serves yet another purpose. In it is provided a comprehensive listing of available applications software as seen through a cross-industry view, a scientific view, and 16 industry views. For each of these 18 major areas further categories and subcategories are defined including references to abstracts of available software that satisfy the identified function or requirements. Companion publications are now also becoming available from IBM which list application software available from non-IBM sources. Two such catalogs have recently been issued: *Engineering and Scientific Application Programs* (October 1981), and *Insurance Application Programs* (April 1981). Presumably more such catalogs are on the way.

The manufacturers of microcomputers are also promoting software. In this connection, we cite the *Applications Software Sourcebook* of Radio Shack which lists thousands of independently supplied programs available for purchase for the TRS-80 line of personal computers. Contrast this with the *80 Software Directory* of independent publisher Personal Micro Computers, Inc., of Mt. View, California, which aims for the same marketplace, listing 600 suppliers and over 7000 programs for the TRS-80 computer line. As expected, these catalogs can be obtained at a cost substantially lower than comparable software directories aimed at the user of large computers.

Major software vendors for microcomputers are also anxious to show what is available and compatible with their offerings. Thus, for example, Digital Research, Inc., issues the *CP/M Compatible Software Catalog*. This document lists the names and associated product offerings for over 100 independent software suppliers whose programs function within the standards of the CP/M operating system. The listing includes categories of software in languages, utilities, word processing, accounting, and for specialized vertical markets.

Finally, we cite the role of the U.S. government in recognizing software as a public asset. Two major sources of publicly developed software have emerged. One is the Technology Utilization Office of the National Aeronautics and Space Administration (NASA), which distributes more than 1500 programs through its Computer Software Management and Information Center (COSMIC), operated by the University of Georgia. A complete catalog on microfiche or printable magnetic tape can be purchased, having keyword and subject indexes as well as program descriptions. Prices range from several hundred dollars to several thousand dollars per program.

A second source is the Department of Commerce's National Technical Information Service (NTIS), which makes available government-developed software at prices ranging from $100 to $1000. A very complete information list is available from NTIS's Office of Data Base Services. Publications of NTIS relating to software include:

Directory of Computerized Data Files and Related Technical Reports. This includes more than 400 data banks and software programs covering more than 45 subject catalogs.

Directory of Federal Statistical Data Files. This publication identifies significant data files of statistical data accumulated and published by the Federal Government.

Directory of Computer Software and Related Technical Reports. This comprises a list of over 350 programs and related reports covering 27 subject categories.

Catalog of Directories of Computer Software Applications. Descriptions of available documentation and/or source programs for more than 25 subject areas.

Computer Control and Information Theory. This bulletin service lists abstracts of recently available software- and hardware-related reports and devices.

Additional Readings

The material in this chapter can be further developed by referring to the following articles in the Bibliography at the end of the book: Cottrell, 1978; Datamation, 1981; EDP Analyzer, 1977; Electronic Design, 1981; Keet, 1978; Pantages, 1978; and Snyders, 1979.

TEN

The Software Industry

An important influence on software direction and productivity is the commercial software product industry. In Chapter 10 the review of this industry is begun by a discussion of commercial software in Section 10.1, followed by an analysis of software prices in Section 10.2.

The industry sector is reviewed in Section 10.3 by identifying the participants and their economic influence on the marketplace. In Sections 10.4 and 10.5 detailed economic models are examined, which reflects the financial factors influencing the construction and distribution of software. Finally, in Section 10.6 is discussed the marketplace size for software and statistics are cited relating to sales successes.

10.1. COMMERCIAL SOFTWARE

As we have pointed out in earlier chapters, commercial software—that is, off-the-shelf packages—may be the only realistic way of improving productivity to match hardware's increasing economic benefits. The 1970s saw a continual drop in the unit price of hardware and a corresponding rise in its cost-effectiveness. During that decade, more and more hardware was acquired for additional applications and with deeper penetration into organizational entities. This process continues today, and users are struggling with the disparity in the cost of the labor-intensive software effort with respect to hardware.

The full impact of software in the 1980s can be appreciated only after examining trends and expectations in the economy as a whole. Considering aspects of the business environment as well as certain organizational factors clarifies what will be the fallout on DP in general and on software in particular.

Inflationary factors will continue to make labor more expensive. As a result, any modest productivity gains presently achieved in software will be nullified. There will be no net effect on the performance of application implementors.

The heightened tempo of the accelerating industrial world requires fast, correct responses to the demands of all who are served. Information needs are broadening, and reporting and record-keeping requirements are increasing, especially with the demands made by state and federal governments. Coping with such information needs can be met only by additional use of the computer, thereby increasing the demand for software. The labor force itself is becoming increasingly committed to a service role rather than being almost exclusively oriented toward production/manufacturing. This leads to further people-intensiveness, placing even greater dependency on the computer for support systems.

Finally, organizations are finding themselves in one of two positions:

1. The veteran DP user has practically exhausted the exploitation of his old application software, which may date back to IBM 1401 and 360 days; these programs, such as the patch-up payroll and general ledger, are ready for replacement with new software.
2. The new DP user, entering the fray with low-cost hardware, is confronted with wide-ranging software needs.

In both cases, the make-or-buy decision looms in the presence of the dramatic new economics which relates software to less expensive and more widely used hardware. To achieve productivity improvements, the business world and government have little alternative but to exploit the cost-effectiveness of commercial software.

Commercial software will get a boost from yet another direction. The business organization is now maturing in a DP sense, and the 1960s and 1970s will soon look like time spent in mere dabbling with computers. This change will come about from pressure applied simultaneously at the top and at the bottom.

The 1980s and 1990s will see managers experienced in DP promoted to executive positions. This change at the top will influence the impact and role of computers in the organization in the following ways:

1. Computing will be placed on a cost-justifying basis.
2. DP will be organized by applying techniques of "management by objectives."
3. Rationalization of computer usage will be required.

This new breed of executives will be able to ask the right questions and will not be baffled by DP jargon. Data processing will be placed in an atmosphere in which alternatives must continually be studied and justified.

The techniques of "management by objectives" can now be introduced into the DP organization because management knows what to ask for and what to measure. For example, it will be commonplace for the DP manager to have goals and objectives that measure such criteria and performance as:

1. *Financial*
   Budget components as percent of total.
   Year-to-year total expenditure.
   Total expenditure as percent of sales.
   Cost per unit of output.
2. *Operational*
   Percent computer availability.
   Percent nonproductive computer operation.
   Units of output per computer resources.
3. *User Satisfaction*
   Percent late reports.
   Budget adherence.
   On-schedule development.

A key notion affecting software production decision-making is the opportunity benefits derived from commercial software versus custom-developed solutions.

The executive who is sophisticated in the DP arena will know that customization has a price. The general-purpose product offering will typically satisfy the highest common functional needs of most organizations. When requirements perceived by a user are beyond a good product's capability, they will be suspect—not because they are less desirable, but because such add-ons may well be the most costly and will be deemed discretionary. As already noted in Section 9.2, the famous 80/20 rule is operating here: Conventional software goes a clear 80 percent of the way toward filling any one user's needs in a specific application area. The last 20 percent of what a user may require in a system will cause 80 percent of his cost or schedule overruns. A DP-knowledgeable executive will understand this fundamental point.

The second pressure on the business firm of the eighties and nineties will come from the entry-level cadre. Almost all current graduates of colleges, and even some high schools, have had an introduction to computers. As already discussed in Chapter 8, most citizens will shortly have such contact via the newer electronic toys, calculators, and computer offerings in retail outlets, including even department stores such as Sears and Montgomery Ward. This educational process will make the lowest level of personnel aware, receptive, and even demanding of electronic assistance in performing their jobs. This will become an invitation for vast commercialization of new software offerings at the microprocessor and workstation level.

These observations suggest an obvious target for improving DP productivity. The potential benefit of utilizing commercially available software will not go unnoticed by the astute managers of the 1980s and will lead to further support of this developing industry.

What is commercial software? It is all software sold as a product or service. This encompasses the conventional software product, an application service offered on a time-sharing system and the turnkey system. Commercial software has a somewhat broader meaning than that connoted by the software product alone. It reflects the totality of what can be purchased for solving a problem—and that which can be leveraged because more than one user is served.

The varied offerings for exploitation with commercial software in the 1980s will emphasize the high-payoff common need interests in the following major areas:

Accounting and financial systems.

Order entry and inventory control systems.

Regulatory and compliance reporting systems.

Administrative and personnel systems.

Word processing and related office applications.

Development tools and support systems.

Data management systems.

The first five categories are applications-oriented. They will be increasingly marketed on an industry basis, with emphasis on hardware and software offerings. The last two items include systems-oriented software to facilitate the implementation of applications by both professional programmers and end users. Expanded use of transaction processors and data management systems will occur.

The heavy emphasis on transaction processing systems operating in screen-dependent, interactive environments will lead to new implementation procedures. At first programmers, and then users, will be provided with automatic screen generators and dialogue builders. The ultimate offerings that will become prevalent in the mid-1980s will fulfill the dream of the "user's workbench." Inexpensive microprocessor-based workstations will provide the tools and techniques necessary to design and program applications.

What, then, will be the marketing environment of the 1980s in which commercial software will find itself? First of all, the economics for an expanding market are present. Users can make long-term commitments to a software investment and enjoy the resulting benefits. For example, the life span of computers compatible with the IBM 370 line seems certain to cover the next decade. Since 1980 it has been possible to obtain hardware capacity compatible with an IBM 370/158 which permits a compounded increase of the work load at the rate of 25 percent per annum for the next 10 years. Indeed, the capability can be obtained at a price/performance advantage better than the IBM 370/158 computer by a factor of four to five. In this favorable environment, the user can make an investment in currently available software and continue to exploit it for at least a decade.

Such users have a lot of room to maneuver and make gains. Today, only 4 percent of the existing and operating software (more than $200 billion) is made up of commercial software products. Users budget less than 5 percent for outside software product purchases. The conditions for the software boom of the 1980s are right.

The following additional factors will affect commercial software:

1. *Wide choice.* Software products will be available in four price categories, with accompanying limitations reflected in those prices. Take, for example, a general ledger program. One can acquire such a system for as little as $100 for operation on a microcomputer, $1500 on a small business system, $15,000 on a large minicomputer, or $30,000 on a mainframe. The user must know what his ultimate needs are and into which category he falls. He must then be prepared to spend accordingly.

2. *Price independence.* The fact that hardware cost-effectiveness leads to decreasing prices does not necessarily explain how software should behave. It is misleading to view the situation as one in which software costs are increasing relative to hardware. The truth is that the unit price of hardware is becoming less expensive and software is standing still, or possibly increasing slightly, but in an inflationary economy.

3. *Increased cost effectiveness.* Despite impressions to the contrary, software as well as hardware will be able to boast substantial increases in cost effectiveness. A number of software vendors have now been in business for more than a decade; they can make comparisons of product performance over a series of releases and enhancements. In Section 6.2 we have already seen how Informatics' MARK IV system showed an increase in performance by a factor of 10 or more. Such benefits in software will multiply during the next decade.

4. *More appreciation.* The leveraging aspect of software over hardware will be better appreciated, as discussed in Section 1.3.

5. *Increased maintenance cost.* Software maintenance charges will increase substantially from the current annual 8 to 10 percent of product value to 15 percent. The following argument is offered in defense of this increase. Software maintenance is typically two to three times the cost of the initial development of an application. If a user can economically justify paying a fraction of the cost of developing a particular software product in the first place, then it would appear that this same user should expect to share proportionally in the subsequent upkeep and maintenance of that product. Assuming that the software life cycle is as long as 10 years, an annual maintenance charge of 15 percent of initial product value is required if the vendor attempts to recoup his costs.

6. *Hardwiring.* Hardwired software will be introduced in the early 1980s. This form of delivering software has the associated benefit of providing automatic protection from unauthorized reproduction and use.

7. *Proprietary interests.* With the increasing importance of software, its potential value, and widespread use, vendors' problems of protecting proprietary interest will increase. Accordingly, new techniques will emerge to control software usage. This protection will be achieved by hardware-imposed devices as well as by software processes which permit operation as a function of the physical CPU, the calendar date, or numbers of transactions. Perhaps there will be created an American Society of Computer Analysts and Programmers operating in the world of software just as the American Society of Composers, Authors and Publishers monitors and protects the interests of artists and authors for records and films.

8. *IBM.* IBM will become an ever increasing participant as a commercial software vendor. It is, of course, already a substantial producer of commercial software, renting software for a value of over $1 billion a year on the international scene, or nearly 50 percent of the total commercial software market serving IBM users.

If IBM continues to emphasize and nurture its software business component, two effects will result:

The market will be increasingly blessed and will expand even more.

Software pricing umbrellas will appear for the independent software vendor.

9. *New entries.* The Japanese will surely enter the hardware and software markets of the West. At present, there is complacency about Japanese software, especially in the applications area. Nevertheless, Japan is possibly more automated in certain sectors than is the United States. A Japanese impact on software in the late 1980s can be expected.

10. *Consolidations.* Business consolidations in the computer industry will continue, with software becoming a more dominant factor. Accordingly, software companies will be acquiring hardware entities in their efforts to provide total solutions for users.

Commercial software in the 1980s will become an increasing portion of every DP budget. Prospects are encouraging for the suppliers, headed by IBM, and for the independents, such as Informatics, Applied Data Research, Cullinane, and Management Science America. At the heels of these mainframe suppliers are the new breed of software producers, including such firms as Microsoft, Digital Research, and VisiCorp, which serve the entry-level microcomputer community.

10.2. COMMERCIAL SOFTWARE VALUES

The free marketplace dictates values. Buyers and sellers determine the point of equilibrium between cost of delivering a product and benefit received. Thus price is determined. Is this fundamental economic principle operating in the commercial software arena? Is software a commodity that allows these marketplace factors to function'

For many years, and especially with respect to software for the larger computers, the answer was no. On the other hand, in the case of low-end microcomputers, the market is operating beautifully and elastically. Why the difference?

Consider a typical example. The general ledger, representing application software, is a good case in point. It is available for as little as $500 for operation on a $12,000 small business system, for $10,000 in conjunction with a $200,000 minicomputer, and for $30,000 for a large-scale $1 million dollar mainframe. The smaller systems will most often be unsupported and available off-the-shelf, on an "as is" basis, while the more expensive product will be offered with ongoing support and maintenance at an annual price of approximately 10 to 15 percent of its original purchase value.

We ignore for the moment the difference in function between products that are so widely separated in price. Obviously, one must be buying something of greater worth for $30,000, plus maintenance, than for $500 on an "as is" basis. In fact, this spread, measured over a five-year application life cycle, is really $60,000 to $500, assuming a 15 percent annual maintenance fee for the higher priced system. For the purpose of making the comparison, we do not question whether an organization can tolerate unchanged software for five years. Note that the ratios of the software purchase amount (and maintenance price, where applicable) to the value of the three identified hardware systems are 4, 5, and 6 percent, respectively.

The apparent software value obtainable with small systems comes primarily from producers who observe the marketing rule of standardization. They avoid custom changes and therefore gain the economic benefits of mass production. Most large-scale users do not, however, accept these restrictions and therefore must pay proportionately more for their desired flexibility.

What then is the marketplace situation that supports such discrepancies in values and pricing? There are a number of factors:

1. Software packages for small computers are often products of cottage workers and therefore do not command the same price as those produced by larger vendors. Often the private label versus name brand phenomenon also comes into play.

2. The distribution costs, nearly 50 percent of sales price in the large system marketplace, are substantially lower for the microcomputer when offered through retail stores and catalog sales.

3. Ongoing warranties and support available with software for large systems is not usually available for software produced for small systems.

4. Historically, software was always expected to be substantially less expensive than the associated hardware. Therefore, low-priced hardware led to lower-priced software.

5. Applications built for microprocessors and minicomputers typically operate in one environment. Big system software must be available for operation in a variety of circumstances and conditions, so this adds to its development and maintenance cost.

6. For small systems, development costs can be amortized over more users, by an order of magnitude, than is the case for the more limited market size of the large system.

The overwhelming factor affecting price of software is the last point. Consider this example: The average one-time price for cataloged software for the Radio Shack TRS-80 entry-level system advertised to sell for $499 is $16 per package. For the basic business system selling for $3300 the average software package retails for $55. Meaningful business-oriented software for the latter configuration is priced, on the average, at $150 per copy. There are now more than 400,000 family members of the TRS-80 in the hands of users.

We contrast this situation with a successfully marketed big software system offered at the average sales price of $50,000 per unit and having a sales penetration of 10 percent in a potential market of 20,000 medium- to large-scale installations. The larger software system purveyor, under this hypothesis, would have generated $100 million of revenue and, with a reasonable 10 percent profit rate, would have generated income of $10 million.

Applying these big system figures to the larger market of the TRS-80, assuming only half the penetration, and if our profit motive of $10 million were still operative, the product could be sold for $5000. Since distribution costs in a mass marketing situation would have dropped significantly, one could expect a 10-percentage-point reduction in sales cost and a consequent doubling of the profit rate to $20 million. If one wished only to generate the same profit margin as before, one could now reduce the price to $4500. To achieve a $5000 product price in the large computer arena, under a similar hypothesis, would require a 100-percent market penetration, which, even in the case of an IBM, is not realizable.

The software entrepreneur can, of course, play the game of the big manufacturers and price the product to reach a maximum return. Market elasticity can be tested under varying assumptions, all based on potential market penetration as a function of price and associated sales cost.

Returning to the small computer marketplace, it is now easy to see how the unit price of the "expensive" software can range from a conservative $5000 to an almost absurd $500. We have assumed for the latter case a 40-percent market penetration and an associated 10-percentage-point reduction in distribution cost, such that the same $10 million profit objective is retained. At $500, the price in a heavily penetrated and large microcomputer market would be two orders of magnitude less than the $50,000 established for the mainframe market.

If we consider 50 equal payments to be a reasonable conversion of sales price to monthly rental fees, then the software monthly fee would drop from

$1000 to $100 to $10 per month for each of the foregoing three pricing models. This analysis goes a long way toward explaining the sometimes seemingly low IBM software prices for products that can only be leased, and not purchased, and are distributed to a wide market.

We see, therefore, that software unit prices can provide much the same cost benefit to users as hardware, as long as such software can be amortized over a large number of users. The problem is, of course, that the actual big-user market is not large enough to allow such low pricing, nor are such big users as willing as small users to standardize their purchases.

This point deserves more emphasis since there is much confusion in relating hardware to software prices. It is not uncommon to be informed that "hardware prices are going down, software prices are going up." But statements such as this refer to the ratio of hardware to software costs as, for example, with the IBM 4300 series, and not necessarily to relative cost-effectiveness. What is closer to the truth is that software prices stand still as the unit price of hardware goes down.

Even that does not really fully explain the spending patterns for hardware and software. Decreasing unit prices of hardware cause more hardware to be utilized and therefore more money to be spent for hardware. Availability of more commercially developed software at attractive prices leads to a higher expenditure for software. In both cases the user responds to perceived values which must be independently assessed. The fact that commercial software is highly leveragable and cost-effective, and therefore leads to larger expenditures, is not in itself bad, regardless of what is spent on hardware.

But what about the economic benefits for the conceiver of software sold for $16 per unit? The same principles operate. This author is typically an individual who is playing the monopoly game of business life by working to achieve a "hit," in the same way a song writer will slave away hoping for a gold record. For indeed, the rewards can be gratifying, even at $16, but the risks are great, since there will be only a small number of successes. Think what could accrue to the author of a program that sold 100,000 copies at a 25-percent royalty. One hit a year for several years would quickly make a millionaire.

10.3. THE SOFTWARE PRODUCT INDUSTRY

The software product industry is a subsector of the computer services industry which also includes professional services and data services. This industry accounts for approximately 20 percent of the total DP expenditures in the United States today. The software products subsector is comprised of two major vendor groups, software from the hardware manufacturer and software from independents.

Independent companies in this industry subsector are typically small- (80 percent with sales of less than $5 million per annum and with fewer than 100

Table 10.1. Commercial Software Sales Activity[a,b]

Type of Sales	1981	1986[c]	Percentage Growth
Hardware manufacturers			
Systems	$1,155	$4,530	32
Utility	805	3,435	34
Applications	235	610	21
Subtotal	2,195	8,575	31
Independents			
Systems	$ 140	$ 300	16
Utility	465	1960	33
Applications	665	2,725	33
Subtotal	$1,270	4,985	31
Total	$3,465	$13,560	31

[a] Sales figures are given here in $million.
[b] Data from IDC.
[c] Projected.

employees) to medium-sized ($5 million to $15 million). Only a few companies report their software product sales at $50 million or more as, for example, Management Science America, Inc., and Informatics General Corporation. Generally the smaller organizations offer one or two major products, whereas the larger companies market an integrated offering of families of products.

Market forecasts by International Data Corporation (IDC) estimated the business of U.S. software product vendors at nearly $4 billion in 1981, and forecast this business to grow by almost 30 percent per annum for the five-year period to 1986. A detailed forecast from IDC is presented in Table 10.1, showing the role of both of the major software sources as well as the expected growth performance for three types of commercially available software. While not so designated, most of the hardware manufacturer's sales are due to IBM. Estimates for worldwide software sales of IBM are often quoted at almost one billion dollars for the year 1980, or about 30 percent of the overall market.

Another statistic is derived from Datapro Research Corporation's annual survey in which users rate proprietary software. The December 1981 report tabulated results from nearly 4000 reporting units, rating more than 6000 packages. The average and median individual unit spending for purchased software was:

	1980	1981	1982
Average	$117,831	$98,568	$130,157
Median	20,000	20,000	25,000

where 1980 data is actual and the two later years are estimated. The trend is up, despite the unusual dip for 1981. However, the absolute amount spent for purchased software is still small relative to the total budget of typical **DP** shops. In fact, when compared with total **EDP** expenditures, the product purchases represent less than 5 percent of the budget.

Data Decisions of Cherry Hill, New Jersey, also conducts surveys of software usage. For the 1981 survey, more than 7000 users of 107 systems software packages at 5900 sites were contacted, yielding a 38-percent validated response. This survey verified the very positive satisfaction users obtain from packaged software. Users of IBM and compatible equipment comprised 84 percent of the responders, showing how influential and important that marketplace is to software vendors. Other hardware vendors participated at no more than 5 percent of the reporting sample of software packages.

While the amount spent for off-the-shelf software may not be terribly impressive with respect to total expenditures, the growth rate and influence of proprietary software is on a much grander scale. As an example, the IBM users organization, GUIDE, surveys its member installations yearly to identify utilization of "non-IBM generalized teleprocessing systems, program development systems, and/or simulation systems." Response to this survey for the past several years is summarized in Figure 10.1.

The data shows increasing influence of purchased software with certain products making significant market penetration. In this regard, of particular note are the performances of Pansophic's Panvalet, the Librarian of Applied Data Research, the Fast Dump Restore of Innovation Data Processing, Sync-

INSTALLED NON-IBM SOFTWARE PRODUCTS					
	1977	1978	1979	1980	1981
Number of reporting installations	1013	1020	1119	1313	1079
Total number products identified	32	53	58	73	83
Total number products in use	3110	4350	5469	7901	7562
Average number products per installation	3.1	4.3	4.9	6.0	7.0
Average number installations per product	97	82	94	108	91
Number of products in over 200 installations	4	5	6	10	10
Product with highest installation count	415	407	499	642	507

Figure 10.1   Guide installation survey results, GBP-8, 1981.

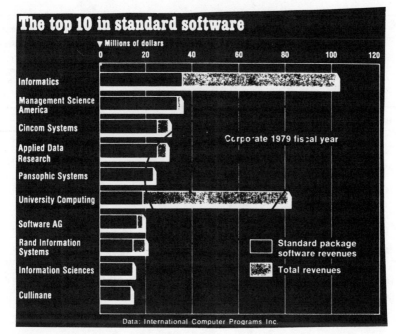

Figure 10.2. Key software suppliers. (Reprinted from *Business Week*, September 1, 1980.)

sort of Syncsort Inc., and UCC ONE of University Computing Company, each of which has a penetration of over 30 percent with respect to the sampled companies.

The viability and growth of the software product industry sector is reflected in the success of the companies participating in this marketplace. These companies and their activity were heralded in a September 1980 cover story in *Business Week* (*Business Week* 1980a and 1980b). Major participants are identified in Figure 10.2.

It is interesting to compare the financial performance of software producers with other related computer industry participants. We present relevant financial highlights in Figures 10.3 and 10.4.

In Figure 10.3 we first show the performance of hardware and computer services companies. Representing hardware is giant IBM and medium-sized Data General. Automatic Data Processing (ADP) and Tymshare represent the larger suppliers of information processing services. We observe that, except for IBM, the cost of goods sold and marketing costs for these companies are remarkably similar. In the hardware area, however, the cost of the R&D effort is significantly higher. Profit performance is comparable, except, again, for IBM, whose enormous size makes comparisons inappropriate.

The recent public stock offerings of a number of leading software product companies make it possible to study the financial makeup of this homo-

	IBM		DATA GENERAL CORP.		AUTOMATIC DATA PROCESSING INC.		TYMESHARE INC.	
	(12/80)		(9/80)		(6/81)		(12/80)	
	$	%	$	%	$	%	$	%
Revenue	26,213	100	654	100	558	100	236	100
Cost of revenue	10,149	39	329	50	298	54	122	52
Selling/G&A	8,804	33	152	24	146	26	64	27
Development	1,520	6	66	10	18	3	12	5
Profit before tax & interest	5,740	22	107	16	96	17	37	16
Net earnings	3,562	14	55	8	49	9	19	8

Figure 10.3. Financial statements of hardware and computer service companies (In millions of dollars).

geneous grouping of organizations. The data shown in Figure 10.4, because it is derived from different reporting schemes, is uneven and inconclusive with respect to the marketing and cost of goods portions. There are, however, enough clues to suggest that the marketing costs for software products as a percent of revenue are 50 to 75 percent higher than comparable costs for hardware and processing services sales. It is clear, however, that R&D for software product companies is a much more important factor than for any of the other computer industry sectors. Profit performance is on a par with the results of the representative companies shown in Figure 10.3.

Critical for the software product vendor are the high marketing costs and the need to sustain an ongoing, high-level R&D program. Both of these factors are affected by the need to educate users to understand software and by the continuous pressure to develop changes in order to keep software operable and up-to-date. Successful software selling ultimately depends on a proper understanding of the unending requirement for continuing maintenance, enhancements and improvements, and on the adequacy of pricing for these services.

Some purchasers believe that software prices should be less. Such purchasers may have a marginal costing viewpoint that ignores sunken costs. They may view software manufacturing costs as nil and they may forget about some of the hidden costs. It is, therefore, important to point out the costs confronting the software vendor above and beyond his direct marketing and support costs.

First, there is the matter of product quality. Because of the vendor/supplier relationship and the need to provide service to a wide variety of users,

	Applied Data Research, Inc. (12/80)		Cullinane Database Systems, Inc. (4/81)		Management Science America, Inc. (12/80)		Panasophic Systems, Inc. (4/81)		Software AG International, Inc. (5/81)	
	$	%	$	%	$	%	$	%	$	%
Revenue	37.1	100	29.4	100	51.7	100	30.2	100	18.9	100
Cost of revenue	30.8	83	19.3	66	11.8	23	1.6	5	12.4	66
Selling/G & A	—	—	—	—	22.0	43	20.1	67	—	—
Development	4.3	12	3.6	12	12.0	23	2.7	9	1.8	10
Profit before tax & interest	2.0	5	6.5	22	5.9	11	5.8	19	4.6	24
Net earnings	.9	2	4.6	16	3.2	6	2.6	9	2.3	12

Figure 10.4. Performance of publicly reporting software product companies (In millions of dollars).

software product quality must be substantially above that of software obtainable through other means, including in-house development and contract programming. Commercial software suppliers tend to produce a higher quality product, if only to minimize their own subsequent maintenance. Thus, software produced as a product is often three to five times more complex and expensive to engineer than comparable software produced on a custom basis for a single user. The end user, therefore, cannot properly compare his expected expenditure for a personalized system to that proposed for the general marketplace.

Next we note the need to support manifold environments. Because of the proliferation of various hardware/operating systems environments, it has become necessary for software products to fulfill quite a number of needs hardly imagined years ago when software first became commercially available. For the IBM line in particular, a product may need to operate in any one of the following environments: OS, DOS, CP, VM, TSS, MFT, MVT, VS, MVS, VS1, SVS, Hasp, ASP, JES2, JES3, CMS, TSO, CRJE, Call/OS, VSPC, ATS, and ATMS.

There is also the aspect of product dynamics. If there is one factor that needs emphasis, it is that software products are dynamic and constantly changing. During the early years of developing software products, it was believed that once a program was created, it could sit on the shelf and be available for sale by simply replicating a master tape. It was quickly seen, however, that software must be continuously maintained and enhanced. It must evolve with the changes in hardware and in operating system environments. It must also respond to the increasing performance demand of the application, and the constant maturing of user needs.

There is also an economic factor which relates to the lengthening life cycle of hardware families. Software has often been viewed as a one-time sale, with the user expecting the product to be continuously available and operable, at least for the lifetime of his computer. The life cycle of software has now been extended to successive machine generations largely because of the exploitation of compatible hardware. Under these circumstances, software can live almost forever. Now the situation becomes a question of cost/benefit for the software product vendor. He must revise his prices upward to reflect this new economics of a much longer support period.

Products are also taking longer to develop and reach the marketplace. From initial conception through prototype development, subsequent engineering, and achieving reasonable market acceptance, the product gestation period may last for as long as five years.

Then there are certain marketplace expectations that seem to be ignored as vendor costs when price is under consideration. These items include the following:

1. *Demonstrations.* There is sometimes a belief that users are entitled to demonstrations without any obligation.

2. *Free trial.* Associated with the free demonstration idea is the free trial which users have come to expect as part of the inducement-to-buy process. This has become so accepted that users were recently advised that "there should be no cost to the user if the package proves totally unacceptable after a reasonable period of time."

3. *Warranties.* Unqualified and unlimited warranties of performance against specifications at the time of sales and continued operation against unknown future environments seem to be expected. Vendors cannot be placed in the position of having to accept business conditions that are not possible to fulfill at any reasonable price.

4. *User groups.* Provision for and support of user groups is another benefit expected from product vendors. In some cases, the costs are partly absorbed by the participants. Nevertheless, if the activities of such organizations are subsidized by the vendor, then they become part of the cost structure.

5. *Protection.* Because of the lack of useful measures for protecting the proprietary rights of software product owners, the additional cost of securing and policing ownership becomes a necessary element of the business.

6. *Source code.* Providing source code to users creates several problems for the software vendor, including that of protecting proprietary interests. It also opens the door to user-generated changes that will subsequently affect the maintainability of the software.

The recitation of these items is not made to suggest their elimination or curtailment. The list is simply provided to emphasize the point that software vendors have been asked to undertake enormous obligations as part of a product sale. Every one of these line items ultimately translates into a cost that can be borne only by the user himself.

10.4. THE SOFTWARE PRODUCT ECONOMIC MODEL

In order to understand the economics operating in the construction and marketing of software, it is necessary to delve into the process in detail. A model for the software product vendor's structure can be developed in much the same way that Phister developed the life cycle model for the hardware manufacturer (Phister 1976). The model is based on the overall assumption of a 15-year software product life cycle with its associated revenues and expense periods. We assume an initial two-year development activity. This is followed by a seven-year marketing effort and thirteen years of software maintenance operation during years three through fifteen. This span is diagrammed in Figure 10.5.

The software is merchandised on an all-sold basis, ignoring the possibility of leasing. This is not an unreasonable assumption, since most independent software is sold on a front-end license basis or according to monthly payments for a fixed period.

For example, in a software sellers' survey conducted by International Computer Programs, Inc., 43 percent of the respondents indicated their software

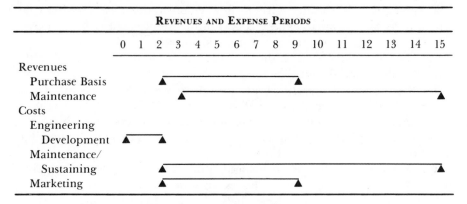

Figure 10.5. Software life cycle.

is made available on a single-payment basis, whereas only 7 percent said they offer their products just for rent. The remaining sample of the survey apparently provides either alternative. Furthermore, 62 percent of the respondents indicated that fewer than 5 percent of current contracts were rental, as opposed to single payment. Finally, nearly all software leases were ultimately either canceled or converted to purchase.

A standard industry practice with respect to maintenance is to offer a warranty period for the first year as part of the one-time product payment. Subsequent maintenance is typically available under a yearly contract. This arrangement generates revenues that begin one year after the first sales are made and continue through the remaining period of the life cycle.

Following Phister's hardware model, costs are identified to include development, maintenance, sustaining effort, and marketing. The first three elements are collectively called "engineering."

With software we are unable to identify separately a sustaining effort, as Phister did with hardware. Hence, it is included in the definition of maintenance. It is known that certain post-development activities take place which could be called sustaining, but are typically wrapped up in the maintenance effort.

Left out of this model are activities that might be termed enhancements of the product. Such efforts must be separately justified on a profit-and-loss basis and have their own independent life cycle model. In other words, the base product, as shown in its 15-year life cycle of Figure 10.5, must stand on its own. Each enhancement in turn would require cost justification in order to support itself.

This economic model differs in approach from the one developed by Phister which is related strictly to hardware. It does not apportion any of the development costs of the main product to enhancements or optional features. For this reason, such additional facilities can have substantial leverage, not requiring the absorption of any of the costs which were incurred in developing the basic product. Accordingly, special features or optional capability offered by the vendor on a separately priced basis can be much more profitable (on a marginal basis) than the basic product itself.

We next make assumptions concerning our idealized product. As noted from Figure 10.5, the product involves a two-year development cycle. We assume that the cost of this development, on a fully burdened basis, is $750,000—representing some 15 man-years of development, together with its associated use of computer time.

We further assume certain basic marketing parameters. Our product will be sold for an average of $30,000 per installation. This average price gives consideration to the fact that customer revenue will include the following price components:

Base product.

Educational services.

Special supplies.

Multisite discounts.

We again note the fact that optional features are not included in this analysis and maintenance is separately priced.

The product price of $30,000 is reasonable and in line with the already cited ICP survey results, showing that 41 percent of the vendor respondents offered products whose prices were less than $10,000; 66 percent, less than $25,000; and 85 percent, less than $50,000.

A key assumption is the expected sales level generated by an experienced salesperson. Often this is characterized in terms of describing such an individual as a "quota salesperson." There is remarkable agreement in the software products industry regarding quota levels for sales personnel. This number typically ranges between $300,000 and $400,000 per annum. For the purposes of this investigation, we assume a conservative $300,000, which represents about 10 sales per quota salesperson per year.

The sales for the model are depicted in Figure 10.6, where the number of units sold, the associated product value revenue, and maintenance revenue are shown for years three through fifteen of the product cycle.

For the purposes of this analysis, sales will also be recorded revenue, since we make the basic assumption that all products will be sold for a one-time purchase price.

The maintenance revenue assumes that the first year of support is bundled into the initial price of the product and that in subsequent years 10 percent of the prior year's maintenance subscriber base is lost.

The maintenance charge is assumed to be 8 percent of the product value per annum, or $2400. This amount is realistic, based on the ICP survey of vendors; the survey found 18 percent of the respondents have maintenance fees in the range of 0 to 4 percent, 15 percent in the 5 to 8 percent range, 31 percent in the range of 9 to 12 percent, and 7 percent indicated an annual

	3	4	5	6	7	8	9	10	11	12	13	14	15	Total
Number of Units Sold	50	80	120	150	120	80	50							650
Product Value Revenue[a]	1.5	2.4	3.6	4.5	3.6	2.4	1.5	1.0	.9	.8	.8	.7	.6	19.5
Maintenance Revenue[a]		.1	.3	.5	.8	1.0	1.0	1.0	.9	.8	.8	.7	.6	8.5
Total Revenue[a]	1.5	2.5	3.9	5.0	4.4	3.4	2.5							28.0
Number of Quota Salespersons	5	8	12	15	12	8	5							

[a] Revenue in millions of dollars.

Figure 10.6. Sales/revenue summary.

maintenance charge of more than 12 percent. The composite average was 6.9 percent.

Finally, Figure 10.6 shows the number of quota salespersons needed to produce the indicated revenue during years three through nine of the product cycle. We observe that 65 quota salesperson years are needed over a seven-year sales activity to generate the indicated $19.5 million revenue.

Since the quota salesperson is the basis upon which we expect to build our cost model, two additional factors must be incorporated to provide realism. Quota salespersons require initial training, during which time they are not necessarily producing sales, and turnover among sales personnel is substantial. We therefore make an adjustment to the indicated quota person years by 25 percent, calling for 81 quota salesperson years during the seven-year sales period.

Now we turn to the life cycle cost model. The elements of cost are attributable to the engineering and marketing efforts, comprised of the following components:

ENGINEERING	MARKETING
Management	Management
Development	Planning
Quality assurance	Promotion
Maintenance	Salespersons
Product support	Sales support
Administration	Trainers
	Administration

The total manpower requirements to support the product for the 15-year life cycle are estimated at 100 man-years of engineering and 275 man-years of marketing and sales support. Assuming that the annual cost per person in these two activities is $40,000 and $50,000 respectively, and assuming a G&A rate of 10 percent, the statement of operation for the products can be derived as shown in Figure 10.7.

This composite profit-and-loss statement for the 15-year period is (coincidentally) equal to the maintenance fees. While this relationship is noncausal, it does underline the significance of the maintenance revenues, as we shall see presently. From this cash flow, and ignoring other investment capital needs, the internal rate of return is calculated to be 29 percent.

A more detailed analysis of year-by-year performance is shown in Figure 10.8. All the calculations are done and shown in 1980 dollars, not taking into account inflation or the cost of money.

Since software is so labor-intensive, the correction for inflation can be directly embedded in pricing, and therefore the overall structure as given in this analysis does not alter from the point of view of the percentages.

	MILLIONS OF DOLLARS	PERCENTAGES
Revenues		
Product Sales	19.5	70.0
Maintenance	8.5	30.0
Total	28.0	100.0
Expenses		
Engineering	4.0	14.0
Marketing	13.7	49.0
Total	17.7	63.0
G&A (10%)	1.8	6.3
Gross Profit	8.5	30.7

Figure 10.7. Profit/loss product cycle recap.

Moreover, the statement of operations (if we assume a 60-day collection period on receivables) is so close to cash flow that Figure 10.8 can be the basis of a return-on-investment calculation.

Additionally, we take note of the following:

The first three years of the 15-year product cycle operate at a loss (a $2.7 million risk before positive cash flow).

The payback point occurs between years five and six.

The yearly statement of operations displays erratic behavior, fluctuating from a significant negative position to a positive peak of $2.2 million and then trailing off—a swing of $3.4 million.

The latter point, of course, exhibits the frustration of software product vendors who, at this time, are limited by a Financial Accounting Standards Board ruling that discourages the capitalization of software development and its amortization over the period of related revenues.

We restate Figure 10.8 in Figure 10.9, where we capitalize $1.8 million of development and marketing start-up and write off the investment at $3000 per unit sold for the first 600 product sales. The erratic effect of the earlier model is dampened, and the swing on the bottom line is reduced by $1 million.

We reach the following conclusions:

1. The idealized product under consideration here provides a good profit margin at 30 percent.

	Cycle Year														
	1	2	3	4	5	6	7	8	9	10	11	12	13	14	15
Yearly Revenue			1.5	2.5	3.9	5.0	4.4	3.4	2.5	1.0	.9	.8	.8	.7	.6
Cumulative Revenue			1.5	4.0	7.9	12.9	17.3	20.7	23.2	24.2	25.1	25.9	26.7	27.4	28.0
Yearly Cost	.6	1.2	2.1	2.4	2.8	2.8	2.7	2.0	1.4	.3	.3	.3	.2	.2	.2
Cumulative Cost	.6	1.8	3.9	6.3	9.1	11.9	14.6	16.6	18.0	18.3	18.6	18.9	19.1	19.3	19.5
Yearly Profit/Cash Flow	(.6)	(1.2)	(.6)	.1	1.1	2.2	1.7	1.4	1.1	.7	.6	.5	.6	.5	.4
Cumulative Return	(.6)	(1.8)	(2.4)	(2.3)	(1.2)	1.0	2.7	4.1	5.2	5.9	6.5	7.0	7.6	8.1	8.5

Figure 10.8. Product life cycle financial performance (In millions of dollars).

	Cycle Years														
	1	2	3	4	5	6	7	8	9	10	11	12	13	14	15
Revenue			1.5	2.5	3.9	5.0	4.4	3.4	2.5	1.0	.9	.8	.8	.7	.6
Cost Net of Amortization			2.2	2.6	3.1	3.3	3.1	2.3	1.4	.3	.3	.3	.2	.2	.2
Gross Profit			(.7)	(.1)	.8	1.7	1.3	1.1	1.1	.7	.6	.5	.6	.5	.4

Figure 10.9. Product life cycle financial performance/capitalized model (In millions of dollars).

2. This gross profit rate is very dependent on the unit price, maintenance fee, and salesperson productivity rate.

3. The internal rate of return at 29 percent and payback over five years is a very respectable and acceptable indication of a good—but certainly risky—investment.

4. The cash flow requirements for a product are significant, necessitating an amount that may range between 10 and 12 percent of the total expected product value revenues and between two and three times the initial development cost.

5. The opportunity to properly capitalize the development cost leads to a more realistic display of performance which, if appropriately phased with other product cycles, can result in a steady picture of company growth and profit performance.

Needless to say, we have shown here the profile of a product life cycle with very satisfactory financial parameters. Not all efforts by an organization, however, necessarily lead to success in every way. Hence, the composite situation, measuring a number of ongoing product activities, will not be as acceptable.

Based on a number of different organizations' experience, the composite model of the software product firm is as follows:

REVENUE	100%
EXPENSES	
Engineering	
Development	10%
Maintenance	15%
Marketing/sales	45%
G&A	10%
Total Costs	80%
GROSS PROFIT	20%

where development includes the initial product construction and maintenance supports the ongoing product installations.

The programming maintenance function, in the case of software, is substantially more encompassing than the physical maintenance function associated with hardware. We have already seen the tremendous effort users put forth in software maintenance: 40 to 60 percent of the total programming staff could well be occupied with this task.

Some observers have indicated, as Phister did, that "the number of programmers assigned to maintenance on a permanent basis often exceeds the number originally assigned to develop programs."

There are many reasons why this effort is ongoing as well as difficult. The ongoing aspect relates to the continual need for upgrades, new features, improvements, and corrections of defects. Not only does the application environment change, but so does the hardware and associated operating system of that environment.

It should not be a surprise to learn that software companies have notoriously underpriced maintenance when charging 5 to 8 percent of product value. In the long run, this can only hurt the user.

The maintenance effort is, as many assert, three to five times as costly as the original development costs. Surely a user should be willing to pay 15 percent of product value per annum for such maintenance, an amount which, over a five-year period, would be no more than the original price of the product.

10.5. THE ECONOMICS OF SOFTWARE DISTRIBUTION FOR MICROCOMPUTERS

The proliferation of hundreds of thousands of microcomputers in the form of desktop and personal computer offerings has generated a substantial new retail software market. Until recently, software-for-sale was primarily a sophisticated offering to mainframe and mini computer installations—more than 80 percent to IBM configurations and look-alikes. Now the hardware consists of a variety of systems from different manufacturers where the underlying bond, if present, may be a common CPU chip, a portable operating system or a standard programming language.

Other dramatic changes in this marketplace are in the software product price and the conditions of sale. Contrasting with the five figure prices of upper end products that are usually available on a fully supported basis, software for entry-level systems is typically priced in only three figures and offered on an "as is" basis.

The sheer scope of the marketing for low-priced software is a clear indication that the software business is changing dramatically. As shown in Section 10.4, successful larger system software product sales are typically measured in several hundred units sold per year. Individual salesmen, with quotas of $400,000 or so, are expected to sell one or two units a month. At this rate, a successful product should generate $5 million per annum and yield a 20 percent pre-tax income, or $1 million.

To obtain a similar result for low-priced software, it would be necessary to sell one hundred times as many systems, or approximately 20,000 units per year. With the 2,000 or more computer retail stores, and not counting the more than 7,000 Radio Shack outlets, it can readily be seen that this sales level will be achieved if each retailer sells only ten packages per annum, or less than one per month. This is certainly a feasible objective.

How does one organize to get that much sales drive behind a specific product? How does a product get recognized and promoted? Is there a viable economic model? The answer to the last question, as we shall see, is a resounding yes.

The burgeoning software market for microprocessors is fueled by a true cottage industry of innovators and contributors. Anyone who has developed a programming skill can readily attempt to author software. Creative programmers are lured by the same vision that often inspires writers, painters, and composers—the hope of a smash success. However, as in any market promising riches, two things emerge:

1. A large number of clamorous participants with only a small number of real successes.
2. A substantial infrastructure that comes into being to facilitate the evolution of the idea into a commercial success.

Hence the genesis of the agent, the publisher, the distributor, the racker, the mail order house, and the dealer—all the participants that usually drive the base cost of a product up by a factor of five or more, before it reaches the end user or consumer.

Software distribution channels are peopled by the author, publisher, distributor, dealer, and the retail purchaser. The structure of this network underlies the financial model which is presented here to aid in grasping the economics of software distribution. In terms of each participant's share of the retail sales price, the typical financial model looks like this:

Participants	Portion of Retail Price
Authors	10
Publishers	35
Distributors	20
Dealers	35
Retail Price	100

Each participant would like to make 20 percent pre-tax income (PTI) on its "piece of the action." This is impossible, however, for everyone except, perhaps, the author and the publisher. As one gets closer to the retail level, marketing concessions are usually made. The practice of volume purchasing and discounting may allow the distributor and dealer to achieve only 20 points of profit between them. The following represents the nominal available expense and profit levels for each participant, assuming that retail list prices are maintained:

	Sales $	Expenses	PTI	% PTI
Author	10	8	2	20
Publisher	45	26	9	20
Distributor	65	13	7	11
Dealer	100	20	15	15
TOTAL		67	33	

Now to appreciate the leverage of success, let us look at the results for each participant for several models based on the author's costs for development of the software at $50,000 and $100,000, respectively. The annual sales volume is represented first as 6,250 and then as 12,500 copies at $200 each, yielding $1.25 million and $2.5 million total sales, respectively.

The author would therefore receive 10 percent of the sales dollars, or $125,000 and $250,000, respectively. The author's benefit is as follows:

Cost of Development	Author's Pre-Tax Income	
	6,250 Sold	12,500 Sold
$50,000	$75,000	$200,000
100,000	25,000	150,000

While the model dictates a 20 percent pre-tax income, the author's actual profit percentage is highly leveraged as a function of sales because of the fixed cost base assumed for development. At $100,000 of development cost, and a sales level of 6,250 units, the profit before tax is indeed 20 percent, but for sales of 12,500 units, there is a dramatic pre-tax income of 60 percent.

Now consider the publisher. The publishing organization has a mixture of fixed costs and variable costs. This fact also leads to unusual leverage. Consider, for example, the impact on the cost structure of two products, one priced at $200 and the second at $400. The packaging (i.e., manufacturing) and the advertising costs per unit are essentially the same, regardless of price. The consequences can be seen from the following calculations for the publisher, assuming sales volume of about 500 units or more per month:

		Retail Price	
	Model	$200	$400
Net Revenue @45%		$ 90	$180
Expenses			
Royalty	(10% of Retail)	$ 20	$ 40
Manufacturing	($15 per unit)	15	15
Advertising	($15 per unit)	15	15
Marketing/Sales	(15% of revenue)	13	27
Administration	(10% of revenue)	9	18
Pre-tax Profit		18	65
% PTI/Revenue		20%	36%

The pre-tax income presented by the model rises from the nominal 20 percent for the $200 package to 36 percent for the higher-priced software.

The remaining constituents of the marketing process, the distributor and dealer, have a tough time since they face the reality of a competitive marketplace with no particular leveraging aspect. Hence, their costs and profits must be covered by approximately 55 points of the retail sales price, probably split between them at a ratio of 60 to 40, respectively.

Another important dimension in marketing is the selection of a pricing strategy to generate optimal returns to the various participants in the marketplace. A sensitivity analysis based on varying product prices can provide the analytical basis for making such marketing decisions.

If we postulate a software product with a retail price of either $200 or $400; and assume a four-to-one reduction in sales volume resulting from doubling the price, we obtain projected sales of 25,000 and 6,250 units, respectively. This produces the following comparison, given the indicated participant's share of the retail sales price:

	$200	$400
Product price	$200	$400
Units sold	25,000	6250
Total retail sales	$5M	$2.5M
Author's net at 10%	$ 500K	$250K
Publisher's net at 35%	$1750K	$875K
Distributor's net at 20%	$1000K	$500K
Dealer's net at 35%	$1750K	$875K

The pre-tax profit for each participant can be derived through the following process:

1. Assume the author's cost of development is $100K. The net profit for each example would then be $400K, and $150K, respectively. Clearly, the higher volume produces greater benefit.

2. The publisher has a fixed cost of $30 for each unit of software sold to cover packaging and advertising. The remaining costs of marketing and administration are variable and comprise 25 percent of the net sales.

Thus:

Product price	$ 200	$ 400
Publisher's net sales	1750K	875K
Fixed costs	750K	187K
Variable costs	562K	281K
Pre-tax income	$ 438K	$ 407K

Obviously, the publisher has little to gain from this price differential if the evaluation is based only upon net income received.

3. The distributor and dealer essentially share their combined overall profit, estimated at 20 percent of the retail price. For the two cases at hand, this amounts to a significant absolute differential—one million versus a half-million dollars, respectively.

Assuming that the unit sales volume increases by more than the ratio of the decrease in price, we conclude that the author and distributor/dealer are likely to derive significant benefit from low unit prices.

Quite apart from arithmetic calculations, lower prices render an additional benefit if they result in higher sales volume. It achieves market penetration. This in itself is a positive factor in establishing the product. Market share begets more sales on its own account, and once the product is well established, there is always the prospect of raising the price to obtain further advantages.

Now we examine yet another factor, the impact of the hardware sale which may accompany the sale of software. Traditionally, hardware sales have led to software purchases. To attract the buyer, the computer store dealer offers heavily discounted hardware, hoping that ancillary purchases of peripherals and software at more favorable margins will enhance profitability.

Today the trend is toward identifying desirable software first, and then purchasing the hardware necessary for its operation. How will this change the pricing and buying factors in microcomputer retailing?

We postulate a model reflecting the sale of a microcomputer system with list price of $4000 with an accompanying purchase of $500 worth of software. This software purchase at 12.5 percent of the hardware value reflects present marketplace experience with first-time buyers.

Table 10.2 breaks down the price and cost structure showing the participation of retailer, distributor, manufacturer/publisher, and developer/author for both hardware and software. For both, the list price, cost of goods, gross margin, cost of sales and profits are displayed. The assumptions underlying the cost of goods as a percent of unit list price for each participant in the sales cycle are as follows:

	Hardware	Software
Retailer	70%	65%
Distributor	50%	45%
Manufacturer/Publisher	20%	10%

while the cost of sales as a percent of unit list price assumes:

	Hardware	Software
Retailer	20%	20%
Distributor	10%	13%
Manufacturer/Publisher	15%	26%

The above analysis leads to the conclusion that the before-tax profit rates for the hardware and software would be 30 percent for the hardware manufacturer and 20 percent for the software publisher, after deduction of the

Table 10.2. Software/Hardware Economics[a]

	Price		Cost of Goods		Gross Margin		Cost of Sales		Hardware Unit Profit		Software Unit Profit		Total Profit[b]	
	H	S	H	S	H	S	H	S	H	S	H	S	H	S
Retailer	4000	500	2800	325	1200	175	800	100	400	10	75	15	20	3.75
Distributor	2600	325	2000	225	600	100	400	65	200	8	35	11	10	1.75
Manufacturer/publisher	2000	225	800	50	1200	175	600	130	600	30	45	20	30	2.25
Developer/author	800	50												

[a] H = hardware; S = software.
[b] Assume sale of 50,000 units; Figures are in millions of dollars.

author's royalties. The profits generated by the retailer and distributor, however, may have to be compromised by the extent of competitive discounting and large purchase deals that are popularly made.

Of course, the astounding conclusion is the difference in absolute value of the total profits generated from hardware and software. The model shows that profits from hardware are almost a decimal order of magnitude greater than those generated from software. Shouldn't this drive the software company into the hardware business to get a share of this largess?

10.6. SOFTWARE SALES AWARDS: THE MAJOR AND THE MINOR LEAGUES

For the past 10 years International Computer Programs, Inc. (ICP), has annually sponsored the Million Dollar Awards Ceremony and Executive Conference in order to recognize the performance of the independent software industry. Software in this context refers to computer programs that are sold commercially as off-the-shelf products.

The activities of the conference include identifying the aggregate sales levels achieved by software product lines as well as the companies and the sales personnel who are responsible. Seven award categories are recognized. They include the one, five, ten, twenty, thirty, fifty, and 100 million-dollar sales achievement level for individual software products measured from their time of introduction into the marketplace.

In the spring of 1982 the results for 1981 were disclosed (ICP 1982). Approximately 800 products had generated close to $4 billion cumulative sales with about 5 percent of those products at the $1 million-plus level, 20 percent at the $5 million level, 10 percent at $10 million, and the remaining 5 percent scattered between $20 and $250 million categories. Noteworthy are the ten products receiving the $50 million award, and one product, TOTAL of CINCOM Systems, Inc., capturing the $250 million award category.

Almost all of this software is designed for and sold to the large mainframe marketplace. The growth of this market is evident from the year-to-year progress of the ICP awards. In the four-year period 1978–1981 the number of identified products doubled and the aggregate sales represented by these products was up by 150 percent.

This growth supports the various forecasts currently popular which predict annual commercial software-for-sale levels to reach the $8 billion mark by 1985. This number, of course, includes all software for sale, from the manufacturers as well as from the independents, and also includes software for microprocessors.

The software package market for microcomputers is currently estimated by Interactive Resource Development, Inc., at $600 million and is forecast to grow at a 27 percent compound rate to $2 billion by 1985. Further, it was estimated that there will be more than one million product unit sales in

PRICE RANGE	NUMBER OF PROGRAMS REPORTED	AVERAGE PRICE IN RANGE
Less than $100	17	$ 53
$100 to $499	73	246
$500 to $999	25	671
$1000 to $1999	20	1272
Over $2000	7	3356
Total	142	$ 605

Figure 10.10.   Microcomputer software by price range.

1981, growing to 10 million packages sold in 1985. The participants in the low end of the computer marketplace, however, are unheralded. There has been no ceremony to give credit to a rising industry that may not yet be able to speak of gigantic sales volume, but has surpassed the distribution levels of large computer software by a significant measure.

In late 1981 we conducted a survey to measure the activity of this new and growing marketplace. More than 50 letters were sent to producers of microcomputer software asking for identification of their top five products and requesting the average retail price and the number of units sold.

The cooperation from the vendors was astounding. Thirty-eight software suppliers responded, identifying 142 products with an average price of $605 per product.

The prices for these programs ranged from $12 to $5000 and varied from system software to applications software, as is shown in Figures 10.10 and 10.11, respectively. The price data of Figure 10.10 show that more than 60 percent of the reported programs can be purchased for less than $500. The bulk of the programs, in fact, can be purchased for much less. The average for each range is also presented.

CATEGORY	NUMBER OF PROGRAMS REPORTED	$ PRICE CHARACTERISTICS (MIN/AVE/MAX)
Application (A)	59	70/1066/5000
General Function (F)	46	50/ 313/ 995
Utilities (U)	10	25/ 121/ 399
Language (L)	12	100/ 297/ 750
Systems (S)	6	150/ 283/ 595
Games (G)	6	12/ 29/ 50
Education (E)	3	40/ 50/ 70
Total	142	12/ 605/5000

Figure 10.11.   Microcomputer software by category.

In Figure 10.11 we note the preponderance of software in the Applications and the General Function categories. For purposes of definition we have designated an application to be a program which performs a very specific job—either industry or cross-industry in nature. On the other hand, the General Function label collects those programs that perform a task which is not specific. The general function program is more of a tool that is employed to solve a particular problem. For example, word processing is placed in this category, as is a data management system, since they are capabilities that can be brought to bear on a number of different applications.

In Figure 10.11 we show for each of the seven categories the minimum, average, and maximum price. Clearly the Educational and Game software category commands the lowest amount. Applications, at an average price of $1066 and median of $1000, are typically sold at three times the price asked for the software in the General Functions, Language, and Systems categories. Utilities are available at somewhat over $100 a unit.

The large number of programs recorded for the Application and the General Function categories deserve further breakdown as is shown in Figure 10.12. Standing out from this table are the accounting and data management packages, which seem to be the most popular.

Six reporting companies gave no sales information regarding their product offerings. Other companies declined sales information for certain new products. Therefore, in Figure 10.13, we have information on sales and number of units sold for 32 companies and for 106 of their associated products.

In the case of software sales for microcomputers we have a problem in estimating the volume as well as the realizable revenue amount for a particular product because of the following reasons:

1. There are multilevels of distribution, each obtaining some mark-up, including one or more of the following: the author, the distributor, the OEM, and the retailer.

APPLICATION PROGRAMS		GENERAL FUNCTION PROGRAMS	
TYPE	NUMBER	TYPE	NUMBER
Accounting	28	Data Management	31
Order Entry/Inventory	8	Word Processing	7
Billing	7	Spreadsheet	3
Investment Analysis	8	Graphics	2
Miscellaneous	8	Statistics	2
		Project Management	1
Total	59	Total	46

Figure 10.12. Breakdown of two categories of reported software.

	ALL PRODUCTS	EXCLUDING TOP PERFORMERS
Number of Companies	32	29
Number of Products	106	103
Average Price	$647	$659
Total Units Sold	1,278,778	278,778
Total Sales	—	$74,753,265
Average Units Sold/Product	12,064	2,706
Average Sales/Product	—	$725,760
Maximum Units Sold/Product	700,000	20,000
Maximum Sales/Product	—	$9 Million
Number of Sales over $1M	20	17

Figure 10.13. Summaries of all products revealing sales. Sales figures represent end user, retail value.

2. A number of sales are a result of a one-time, front-end payment permitting unlimited subsequent distribution with little or no further royalties.

In Figure 10.13 we have not shown the computable equivalent retail value of the 106 surveyed software products because of the enormous distortion such figures would yield. Instead, we include a second column which excludes from the statistics the top three performers whose sales volumes are in the hundreds of thousands.

Even with this caveat the reader is further cautioned in interpreting the sales dollar volume. Since equivalent retail values are presented herein, no conclusion is warranted with respect to estimating revenue levels for software authors, distributors, or retailers. In fact, we believe that the overall realized sales in dollar amounts by the microcomputer software producing industry may well have been one-fourth or less of the so-called composite sales based on retail or list price.

The first column of Figure 10.13 shows the total number of units sold as 1,278,778. The average number of units sold per product is therefore over 12,000; this number is heavily influenced by the most widely distributed product, which is said to be installed 700,000 times. There were only 20 products that generated more than $1 million sales, so that the sample is heavily skewed to the low end in revenue production. Indeed, the median revenue level is $247,500.

Removing the three top performers from the sample of 106, we note the results in Figure 10.13. The average price per unit rises from $647 to $659, and the number of units sold becomes 278,778 with an associated sales level of about $75 million. The average number of units sold per product becomes 2706 and the average sales level per product is almost three-quarter million dollars.

Table 10.3. Number Units Sold by Category

NUMBER SOLD	TOTAL NUMBER	A	F	U	L	S	G & E
		BY CATEGORY					
Not disclosed	36	13	13	1	5	1	3
Less than 500	38	26	11	1	—	—	—
500 to 999	24	14	9	—	—	—	1
1000 to 4999	23	5	7	5	3	3	—
5000 to 9999	8	1	3	2	—	—	2
10,000 to 20,000	10	—	2	1	3	1	3
Over 20,000	3	—	1	—	1	1	—
Total	142	59	46	10	12	6	9

In Tables 10.3 and 10.4 we summarize the reported number of products for ranges of units sold and sales levels by category. We see that the high-range sellers are in the General Function, Language, and Systems software area as well as in Games and Education. In contrast, Applications tend to be more conservatively clustered at the lower ranges.

Turning now to the sales volume results of Table 10.4, the high revenue generators are in all categories except Games and Education with General Functions and Languages taking the lead.

Of course, this survey is limited in scope. Based on the survey figures cited earlier about microcomputer software, the reporting sample may represent 75 percent of the marketplace value. Fortunately, the data is reasonably mixed in representation, including three of the leading software products now on the microcomputer marketplace.

What is astounding, of course, is the very large number of software packages that have been sold in the microcomputer marketplace. In a recent advertisement Microsoft claimed more than 700,000 installations for its family of BASIC interpreters and compilers. This would certainly place Microsoft at the head of the hit parade for microcomputer software unit sales volume.

Table 10.4. Revenue Generated by Category

REVENUE AMOUNT ($K)	TOTAL NUMBER	A	F	U	L	S	G & E
		BY CATEGORY					
Not disclosed	36	13	13	1	5	1	3
Less than $100	25	14	7	2	—	—	2
$100 to $499	48	21	17	3	1	2	4
$500 to $999	13	8	3	1	—	1	—
$1000 to $10,000	17	3	5	3	5	1	—
Over $10,000	3	—	1	—	1	1	—
Total	142	59	46	10	12	6	9

Turning once more to the large computer area, we note that there may be only one or two products whose unit sales levels exceed 5000. To the best of our knowledge we give this leadership role to Syncsort, Inc., whose Syncsort product has registered worldwide sales of 6200.

But one cannot end a review of microprocessor software without citing the most widely known and visible product of all. This is VisiCalc, the automated spreadsheet composer, offered by VisiCorp. The literature cites over 100,000 unit sales for this product which operates on equipment from Apple, Tandy, Atari, Commodore, Hewlett-Packard, and IBM. It is said that VisiCalc grossed over $1 million sales in its first six months and some $15 million in the first two years of availability.

VisiCalc has also stimulated a submarket. For example, there are now several competitive products vying for the marketplace, such as SuperCalc from Sorcim Inc. There is also an independently organized user group called Visigroup[*] with a membership reaching 1000.

VisiCalc, sold originally for $99, then $150, and now $200, is undoubtedly a classical example of how software moves the hardware. If, for example, as some say, 20 percent of this product's sales led directly to hardware purchases, then we have the incredible story of software's true leverage—$3 million sales of software yielding sales of some $60 million in hardware.

This factor, greater than 20, reveals an important economic reality. Relative to hardware, software is severely underpriced. A correction will surely come about.

Additional Readings

The material in the chapter can be further developed by referring to the following articles in the Bibliography at the end of the book: Business Week, 1980a, b; Data Decisions, 1980; Datamation, 1981; Datapro, 1980; Horowitz and Hollies, 1981; ICP, 1978; ICP, 1982; IDC, 1979; Interface, 1981; Myers, 1978; and Phister, 1976.

---

*VisiGroup now known as Intercalc.

ELEVEN

Software as Seen through Terminology

Since the beginning of the computer era it has been popular to generate new terminology to reflect data processing innovations. Thus, we had UNCOL, IAL, and Automatic Programming. These examples of DP jargon dominated the vocabularies of technical conferences and trade literature in the early sixties. Today they are no more.

There are also terms that lasted, like *time-sharing* and *data management*. Other DP terms, such as *interface* and *input* have actually entered the English language as part of our everyday speech.

In creating new words to describe computer technology, we have also created some problems. In Section 11.1 we discuss some use and misuse of words by the DP community. This is followed in Sections 11.2 and 11.3 by a review of DP terminology past and present, an evaluation of the status of the concept or function and a forecast of the future.

11.1. THE COMPUTER INDUSTRY JARGON

Computer professionals sometimes employ a strange jargon. A layman or newcomer to the industry could well be confused by this unfamiliar terminology or by familiar terms used in a new setting. As an example, and on a historical note, consider the term *time-sharing*. In the early sixties, when the term was first introduced, it was often confused with competing expressions such as *parallel processing* and *multi-processing*. In any event, the operation described by the term *time-sharing* was certainly not the sharing of time, but rather, the sharing of space. Typically only one computer function for one user can be operable in any one segment of time, at least as it relates to the central processing unit.

Today we are not bothered by this anomaly. *Time-sharing* is a well-known expression, understood to represent the simultaneous cooperative use of a computer by a number of on-line users who alternately share the resources of a data processing system. The term has lost its intrinsic meaning and now represents a type of service whose quality and characteristics are generally understood. This observation leads us to look at other contemporary terminology and to comment on some current use, or misuse, of the English language as applied to data processing.

Consider first the popular designation, OEM, which is an acronym standing for Original Equipment Manufacturer. Why do we designate as an OEM a company that serves as a distributor for a manufacturer? If anything, such a company operates on behalf of an "original equipment manufacturer," but certainly is not *the* OEM itself. Yet the term has grown to mean exactly the opposite of what the words seem to convey.

Yet another acronym, RAM, deserves a challenge. This is a ubiquitous term for a ubiquitous device, and is usually explained as meaning "random access memory." RAM is actually the designator of that portion of computer memory that has the property of read/write facility as opposed to ROM, which correctly means "read only memory." Now, all computer memory, whether RAM or ROM, is random access. Hence the RAM designation seems not only inappropriate but also misleading. It might better be known as RWM (read/write memory), but how would you pronounce this?

Two very popular terms in today's computer vocabulary are *virtual* and *transparent*. How do you interpret the following sentence? "The virtual system is transparent to the user." Does this mean that an informally acknowledged system can be seen through? Let's examine each of these terms independently.

The term *virtual*, when used in conjunction with *memory system*, describes a computer system that has the capacity of an expanded memory manifested in some form of high-speed storage. The virtual aspect of this memory is a technical feature. This allows automatic sequential addressing to be handled by the system regardless of whether the information is located in "real" memory or in the extended memory contained on some storage device external to the CPU memory. It is this extended memory capability that is given the label of virtual memory system.

But what does the dictionary tell us about the word *virtual*? It is defined as "being such in essence or effect though not formally recognized or admitted— a virtual dictator, a virtual promise." Indeed, storage that has the appearance of memory fulfills the definition. But we have allowed ourselves to take liberties with the meaning, as shown in the following contemporary sentence extracted from a trade journal, "IMS ran in expensive real core memory . . . rather than in virtual storage." Storage is, of course, as real as is memory—it is their combination that can produce a virtual memory system.

This brings us to the term *transparent*, which has several nuances of meaning defined by the dictionary as follows:

having the property of transmitting light without appreciable scattering so that bodies lying beyond are entirely visible: pellucid.

easily detected or seen through: obvious.

readily understood: clear.

But how do we use the term *transparent* when we speak computerese? We say that the physical structure of the data is transparent to the user, or that the way the computer solves a particular problem is transparent to the terminal user's communication dialogue. In both of these cases, we do not intend the dictionary meaning of "being visible" nor of "easy detection" nor "readily understood." Instead, we imply that the designated process is hidden or unnecessary for comprehension. An exact semantic opposite!

The word that gets the grand prize for use and misuse is *syntax*. The advocate of a particular computer language will necessarily claim that "its syntax is the best," or, "the syntax is user-friendly," or, "the syntax is nonprocedural," and so on. The word *syntax*, in this context, is used to make claims for language form, structure, grammar, meaning, semantics, vocabulary, and anything else that can describe language. The language purist will, of course, wish to limit the applicability of the term *syntax* to "sentence structure," which, with respect to languages, means the form taken by the medium of expression, as exhibited through sentence diagramming.

Let us take an example. Consider the following four typical and equivalent operations directed to a personnel file:

1. List the name if the age is greater than 50.
2. If the age is greater than 50, list the name.
3. IF AGE > 50 THEN PRINT NAME
4.
200	LD	A	Load accumulator with Age (=A)
	SU	B	Subtract 50 (=B)
	JP	300	Transfer to 300 if Accumulator is positive
	J	100	Transfer to 100 for next record
300	SB	N	Subroutine to Print Name (=N)
	J	100	Transfer to 100 for next record

These four examples illustrate two variations of Englishlike query statements, a formulation that reflects a statement from a BASIC language program, and a piece of assembler code showing a snapshot of algorithmic logic.

Many people in the computer field would categorize each of these alternatives with a different syntax. The first two, for example, although sharing the same basic structure, reverse the position of the conditional clause. The third approach is a coded shorthand and the last entry is an ordered presentation where position is everything.

Actually, the syntax of the first three statements is equivalent, since all three can be diagrammed in the same manner. The fourth approach is not only a different syntax, but also a different language. Strangely enough, since all four formulations direct the computer to do the same thing, we can conclude that their meanings are identical. Putting it into linguistic terms, they possess equivalent semantics, although on the level of ordinary human perception they vary considerably. The use of the terms *syntax* and *semantics* as applied to computer languages has been our concern in Sections 6.4 and 6.5 where we adopted the popular usage of the terms.

This brings us to the most current of hot buzzwords in the vocabulary of the computer culture. This is *personal computer*. Approximately five years ago, the term *personal computer* emerged along with related terminology such as *hobby computer* and *home computer*. Today the adjective "personal" has survived and has gained substantial acceptance, even dignified by its use when IBM gave that appellation to its most recently announced new computer product at the lowest end of its line.

What can be personal about a computer? Can a computer have any greater affinity for an individual than, say, a typewriter does for a clerk or a secretary? Indeed, the very meaning of the term suggests that the item should be limited in use and availability to a specific individual. This is surely not a notion most organizations would wish to associate with any of their assets.

The term *personal computer* will not survive. Can you imagine a doctor, lawyer, or plumber wishing to acquire a small business system inquiring about the purchase of a "personal" computer? More than likely, a name such as *desktop computer* or even a new term, such as *professional computer*, will eventually supplant the less appropriate phrase now in use.

While borrowed terms may suffer some distortion in adjusting to a DP environment, there are others whose DP meaning has been added to our everyday language. The wide use of the words *input* and *interface* is one evidence of the way computerese is beginning to affect the language of the general public. The increasing importance of computers in our society will surely accelerate further transfer of terminology from computer professionals to common speech. From an industry that specializes in precision, one ought reasonably to expect a comparable discipline in communication. The computer industry can do a better job than it is doing now in improving and formalizing its jargon.

11.2. STATUS OF THE OLD TERMINOLOGY

In Figure 11.1 we list the popular EDP terminology of the past 30 years and evaluate the prospects for each term. The terms are organized by three classifications:

1. Software development.
2. Systems/organization.
3. Applications.

CLASSIFICATION	CATEGORY		
	A	B	C
	Insignificant impact, unproven, has practically disappeared	Low profile, not yet significant, may still have something to offer	Prospects look good, has not yet attained full acceptance or respectability
Software Development	Higher Order Language Automatic Programming Universal Computer Oriented Language Implicit Programming International Algebraic Language Software Transportability	Problem Oriented Language Decision Tables Flow Chart Program Generator	Modular Programming On-Line Programming Non-Procedural Languages Software Products
Systems/Organizations	Automated Display Systems Associative Memory Content Addressable Memory Hierarchical Storage Polymorphic Systems Self Organizing Systems Graceful Degradation Integrated Data Base PERT/CPM	Multi-Computers Automated Resource Allocation Self Diagnostic Systems Parallel Computing Firmware Facility Management	Value Added Network Packet Switching
Application	Management Information Systems Language Translation	Automatic Abstracting Computer Assisted Instruction Pattern Recognition Automated Factory Artificial Intelligence Medical Diagnosis	Source Data Entry Word Processing

Figure 11.1. Current status of old terminology.

The terms are also assigned to one of three categories indicating their respective degree of importance and impact. These categories are as follows:

1. Category A—Insignificant impact, unproven; has practically disappeared.
2. Category B—Low profile, not yet significant; may still have something to offer.
3. Category C—Prospects look good; has not yet attained full acceptability or respectability.

For the most part, Figure 11.1 shows the more controversial terms and excludes those phrases and labels that have already achieved a clearcut place in the DP environment. Most of the "failures" in Software Development shown in Categories A and B of Figure 11.1 relate to programming languages. The search for better implementation tools once pursued so enthusiastically and suggested by

Higher-Order Languages

Problem-Oriented Languages

Automatic Programming

Universal Computer-Oriented Language

Implicitly Programmed Systems

International Algebraic Language

Decision Tables

has not really been rewarded. Furthermore, very little today suggests a possible breakthrough in these directions. We reluctantly put these ambitions to rest.

The *Higher-Order Languages* that have evolved are essentially COBOL and FORTRAN and their derivatives (PL/I, BASIC, etc.). No other language has developed a comparable acceptance, despite the vast efforts by research organizations and the commercial world. APL has made a run for it, but has not arrived. Pascal may claim current fancy and attraction, especially in the world of microprocessors, but the final returns are not yet in—and more important, Pascal is not really much "higher" than the higher-order languages of the past two decades.

While there have also been efforts to promote *Problem-Oriented Language*, only one clearly stands out as a success. This is APT, the language for implementing numerical control of machines and tools.

Automatic Programming fell into disuse in the sixties and is now an archaic term. Nothing really became "automatic" in the programming of computers. Despite the optimism concerning them, the *Universal Computer-Oriented Language* (UNCOL) and *Implicitly Programmed Systems* failed in rapid succession. For example, we note the short-lived enthusiasm of *Datamation*'s report in its January/February 1960 issue.

"Those who think of UNCOL as a pie-in-the-sky concept should be advised that an effort of considerable magnitude, in quality, if not quantity, is underway to make the Universal Computer Oriented Language a reality. Representatives of manufacturers and users from all parts of the country have met and are meeting to attempt to put UNCOL on paper."

Implicitly Programmed Systems was actually given a trial, and a death sentence as well, by a special U.S. Air Force committee. They decided the quest for an automatic application development system for the end user was a 1963 pipe dream.

A second attempt at universality was the promotion of the *International Algebraic Language* (IAL). In the race for an appropriate "algebraic" or scientific application-oriented programming language, independent computer communities in the United States and Europe were advocating the use of FORTRAN and ALGOL respectively. The IAL would have supplanted both of these had it been successful, but it failed.

Decision Tables also looked like a real nonprocedural language breakthrough in the late fifties and early sixties, but where can you find these techniques in use today?

With the failure of UNCOL and IAL, attention turned to more brute force methodology for achieving machine-to-machine *Software Transportability*. However, these efforts did not gather support or generate results.

The most surprising fall from popularity has been the sacred *Flow Chart*. In the sixties and early seventies, good programming demanded flow charts as the basis for design and documentation. Applied Data Research Inc. (ADR) is today one of the leading software product vendors because of its early success in the sale of over 2000 units of their proprietary automatic flow chart system, Autoflow. Now, flow charts have been replaced by other documentation techniques.

Other organizational techniques to increase code production included the *Program Generator, Modular Programming, On-Line Programming* and *Nonprocedural Languages*. The first of these concepts, the *Program Generator*, seems to have disappeared completely, unless it is now embodied in the new phrase *Application Generator*. The remaining terms are still popular and efforts continue in their promotion. But where are the results? There is today no convincing proof that *On-Line Programming* is more cost effective than more conventional approaches. Some experts even refuse to categorize nonprocedural, implementation systems such as RPG and the MARK IV System as "languages." These approaches, however, have great potential and we are now seeing more successful use and broader acceptance of them.

Of great significance is the promise of the Software Product. Users can achieve productivity gains in application development as well as obtain real economic leverage on a cost basis. However, software purchased as a product is still a mere 5 percent of the user budget. Plenty of room is left for the user community to embrace this economically beneficial opportunity.

The Systems and Organization classification in Figure 11.1 primarily deals with mixed hardware/software-oriented approaches. Among clear "failures" are *Automated Display Systems, Associative Memories, Content Addressable Memories, Hierarchical Storage, Polymorphic Systems,* and *Self-Organizing Systems.*

In the early sixties, there was some promotional fanfare surrounding fully automated displays. These systems would produce real-time, large screen, color displays from computer-generated information. It was thought that the military on one hand, and executive management on the other, would be receptive to such a medium for assisting them in decision making. While a lot of money was spent on systems such as *Iconorama* and *Eidiphor*, the technology was never well received. The usefulness of the technique seemed questionable and the CRT took over. Incidentally, color in displays is just beginning to become popular again today.

Associative Memory and *Content Addressable Memories* are also items of the past, although related research still goes on. Basically, software techniques have replaced the pursuit of improved hardware. The current interest in relational data bases is an example.

Hierarchical Storage was another technological dream. This concept envisioned the presence of at least three types of memory/storage devices—and the ability to move data automatically (the word was "trickling") from low speed, slow access to high speed, fast access as a function of need and as a function of frequency of use of the data. Where are these systems today?

The *Polymorphic System* was a multicomputer system of many parallel, nonhomogeneous CPUs and peripherals brought to bear on a problem and communicating between modules through electronic switching. The approach was an overkill first plunge into what today may be seen as the *Attached Processor* concept of IBM or the "nonstop" performance emphasis by Tandem Computers.

A related notion was the desire to achieve *Self-Organizing Systems*. Computer resources were to be automatically brought together and assigned to execute a specific problem. But since we ourselves didn't know how to organize, it was a bit presumptuous to expect the computer to organize for us.

Another very popular term in the early seventies was *Graceful Degradation*. The words were beautiful! We don't seem to talk in this way now, preferring terms such as *start-up* and *recovery procedures*. Possibly these techniques are not as graceful.

Integrated Data Base is included in Category A because of the conviction that the data base will not (and should not) be so tightly coupled that elimination of redundant information becomes the primary objective—as the integrationist would have us believe. Why don't we just use the term *data base*?

What has happened to *Project Evaluation and Review Techniques* (PERT) and *Critical Path Method* (CPM)? These project-planning and computer-monitoring systems were the rage of the sixties. Government procurement required their use in project management. PERT charts abounded in every proposal and subsequent operations report. Strangely, however, PERT and CPM charts soon degenerated to simple milestone schedules and Gantt charts. The use of more sophisticated planning by computers seems to have disappeared.

The above discussion of *Polymorphic Systems* and *Self-Organizing Systems* should not be taken to mean that the associated ideas have gone away. They have been replaced by the modern terms of *Multi-Computers* and *Automated Resource Allocation*. Though not yet in wide use, the concepts show sufficient promise to be placed in Category B. Similarly, *Self-Diagnostic Systems* is included, since we now have the ability to implant the microprocessor in a hardware complex to help in checking out its state of health.

The term *Parallel Computing* was quite popular in the early sixties and was often confused with multi-processing or multi-computing. The term also refers to *Parallel Computer*, which is yet another form of *multi-computer*, bringing to bear numbers of CPUs operating simultaneously on a particular problem in a parallel, rather than a sequential, manner. Although the word went almost out of style, the concept still underlies a good number of systems and is relegated to Category B.

A favorite term of the sixties, suggesting a new generation of software production and capacity, was *Firmware*. Today this word is an unpopular way of describing two hardware-related means of writing and executing computer code:

1. In the form of "microcoded" instructions executed in a controlled access memory.
2. As "locked up" code executed in ready only memories (ROM).

These techniques have led to higher performance systems, but no programming method breakthrough. In any event, Firmware, the word, is out. "Hardwired" or "burned-in" programs are in.

Another phrase looking for a home is *Facility Management*. This was an important, but short-lived, movement in the late sixties when it seemed that businesses would turn over their data processing facilities, personnel, and problems to a third party. How many new Facility Management contracts are now signed each year? The concept is virtually dead, although there is a possibility that it is a "sleeping giant."

Our sole survivors for Category C are in the communication area. Two major system concepts have dominated the seventies: *Value-Added Networks* and *Packet Switching*. Both have found commercial presence and it's only a matter of time for a wider dissemination to occur.

Finally we come to the Applications category which included one-time favorites for exploitation. Heading the list is the *Management Information System*. So prominent was this notion that titles of organizations, individuals, and even a society reflected the associated acronym MIS, if not the name itself. MIS was to be the strategic and decision-making aspect of DP support systems as contrasted with tactical or operationally oriented applications. But where has MIS gone?

In the June and October 1979 issues of *Infosystems*, a series by the Diebold Group on the information environment of the 1980s states that the concept of Management Information Systems is an outmoded notion because it concentrates on the *process* rather than the *results* of the process. Accordingly, a new catch phrase is introduced, *Information Resources Management* (IRM). A likely companion to IRM is the even newer term, *Decision Support Systems* (DSS). The idea behind DSS is to increase the effectiveness and productivity of decision making, or, in other words, another MIS, under a different acronym.

Another application very popular in the late fifties was *Natural Language Translation*. Highly motivated at that time by Federal Government political and intelligence needs, the idea was thought to be a natural for computer implementation. The technological breakthrough to make this process economical never came, and today there seems to be no commercial interest in language translation.

Very close to falling into disuse are three other applications from Category B: *Automatic Abstracting, Computer-Assisted Instruction* and *Pattern Recognition*.

Automatic Abstracting was pursued for its impact on indexing text for subsequent retrieval. Today commercial systems basically apply manual indexing schemes in categorizing text-oriented data bases.

Computer Assisted Instruction, or CAI, as it was known, was another pivotal application. Hopes were very high for new breakthroughs in leveraging teaching by instructors and increasing the productivity of students in the learning process. CAI struggles along today with little economic impact. This application also could be a sleeping giant, especially now, with the growing use of microprocessors.

Pattern Recognition as a discipline has not led to a specific product. If it exists at all, it is relegated to the research laboratory setting. Important derivatives have replaced the term, however, as for example, *Voice Recognition Systems, Signal Analysis*, and so on.

The remaining three examples in Category B are still kicking, but perhaps their labels have become archaic. Each of them is based on the idea of achieving more humanlike behavior or performance through automation. Automation in the factory was advanced to increase worker productivity. The *Automated Factory* however, while progressing nicely, is far from realizing the vision of the early sixties, when production facilities without human beings were predicted. A vast untapped potential is now becoming available as a result of the new microprocessor technology.

Artificial Intelligence was the most sought after accomplishment of the early days of computers. Achieving demonstrated intelligence with machines occupied many early pioneers—whether computer professionals or fiction writers. The most significant result of these efforts was the development of chess playing systems. More serious efforts, such as the Perceptron experiments in the mid-sixties have disappeared. Interest has swung to *robotics*, game playing, and conversation systems, the emphasis is no longer on true human understanding and decision making.

Artificial Intelligence has made progress and more is expected. Rather than achieving humanlike behavior and responses from machines, however, emphasis is on the production of specialized systems performing a specific job, giving a number of programmed choices which are activated through both audio and visual stimulation.

A sign of the times for both artificial intelligence and computer-assisted instruction is the article in *Psychology Today* (November, 1979) by J. Gardner entitled, "Toys With a Mind of Their Own." Gardner goes on to say this about electronic toys:

They can beat you at chess, play back melodies as soon as you compose them, stump you with historical trivia.
With their quick and challenging computer wits, the new electronic toys provide an alternative to the Skinnerian model of the mind. They may be the learning machine of the future.
I believe the learning machines, as I call them, come closer to imitating the style of human intelligence than the teaching machines of the past and may well represent the educational wave of the future.

The last entry for Category B is *Medical Diagnosis*. Early researchers certainly thought that today's medicine would be much more computer dependent in the diagnostic area. Actually very little, if any practical computer-based diagnosis takes place. This simply was an idea whose time had not come. Instead medicine has made unusual, and then unpredictable, advances in applying micro-electronics to instrumentation systems, such as patient monitoring devices.

Two applications—*Source Data Entry* and *Word Processing*—under Category C were highly touted applications during the recent decade and have now reached a level of acceptability and commercial viability.

Source Data Entry takes its rationale from the fundamental premise that data should be handled once and once only, preferably at its origin. Hence there is interest in developing entry devices serving various uses from the retailing counter employing electronic cash registers and associated specialized readers, to optical character-reading devices for capturing printed material, to specialized forms that are marked for subsequent sensing as, for example, the Universal Product Code. The introduction of micro-electronics and new, specialized, hand-held devices will increase the opportunity for such automated data capture. We are rapidly approaching a society where most data will be manually handled only once.

| | **CATEGORY** | | |
CLASSIFICATION	**A**	**B**	**C**
	Insignificant impact, unproven, has practically disappeared	Low profile, not yet significant, may still have something to offer	Prospects look good, has not yet attained full acceptance or respectability
Software Development	Advanced Languages Structured Programming	Design Technology User Development Systems Application Generator	Data Dictionary Implementation Systems Transaction Development System Programmer's Workbench
Systems/Organizations	Robustness, Forgiving User Oriented, Friendly Data as a Resource Data Base Administrator Personal Computer Compatible Systems	Software Engineering System Security Home Computer Voice Recognition Distributed Data Base	Distributed Processing Relational Data Bases User Workstation Transaction Processing
Applications	Electronic Files Paperless Office Office of the Future Total Information System	Automated Office Teleconferencing Electronic Funds Transfer Videotex Systems Robotics	Electronic Mail Query Systems

Figure 11.2. Future status of new terminology.

Word processing is, of course, a specialized aspect of source data entry. Soon no medium-sized office will be without at least one such computer-based text handling device. Assuredly, both source data entry schemes and word processing systems are here to stay.

It can be seen that a variety of computer-based concepts and functions have been advocated over the years. There is, however, no automatic acceptance of each of these ideas just because they may be associated with the computer. Rather, each innovation must prove itself on an economic and cost-effectiveness basis.

11.3. STATUS OF THE NEW TERMINOLOGY

Following the scheme of Section 11.2 concerning the status of old computer-oriented terminology, we present in Figure 11.2 a review of some of the current terms. We evaluate these expressions with respect to their prospects for the period 1985–1990.

In the years ahead, our strongest needs are going to be productivity enhancements in software development. Unfortunately, as seen from Figure 11.2, there is a paucity of ideas that show much promise for the future.

Some practitioners are still awaiting the *Advanced Languages*. The lack of success in prior decades in breaking through the COBOL and FORTRAN bind seems not to have lessened their enthusiasm and expectation for a language breakthrough. Application developers are desperately seeking a superior mode of expressing problems to computers in order to enhance the implementor's productivity.

The most current such effort is in the Department of Defense where a new language effort was undertaken through a series of recent procurements. A specific language system, Ada, has survived various experimental efforts and is under development as the generic language system for DOD. In another area, the microcomputer sector, a recent language entry, Pascal, has attracted enormous attention and appeal, especially for system implementors. We once more have language followers who believe that a new era is about to arrive in facilitating computer programming expression. However, there is insufficient progress in any present language endeavors to warrant much hope for a marked improvement in the production of software as a result of superior procedural languages. Advanced Languages is therefore relegated to Category A, unproven.

There are those who have recognized that procedural languages have limitations in terms of enhancing the production of software. A number of these individuals have turned their attention to enhancing productivity through organizational methods such as Structured Programming, Top Down Programming, Egoless Programming, and Chief Programmer Organization. Unfortunately, these efforts are temporary diversions from achieving long-term benefits. This phenomenon is similar to what was expected from the flow chart and modular programming which were thought to be aids in facilitating improvements of the programming process.

In Category B, three varying approaches are listed that are systems-oriented methodologies for improving the process of implementing a computer-based application. First there is *Design Technology*. This involves techniques and methodology for describing the nature of the application and its required functionality. The purpose of such a system is to better and more accurately achieve a functional design reflecting the user's requirements. A primary objective of such systems is to describe fully what needs to be implemented, with appropriate external and internal consistency checks, to avoid potential defects in the ultimate system. Design Technology meets the critical aspect of system implementation. This is the consequential point before errors or defects can be propagated and thereby minimizes the cost of maintenance during the life cycle of the system. There is every reason to hope that substantial improvements can be forthcoming in Design Technology although none seem to have taken hold.

A second direction in easier implementation of computer systems is through *User Development Systems* and *Application Generators*. These are typically nonprocedural approaches to express a user's application requirement. The objective is to employ a simple and comprehensive manner by which a computer program, typically a transaction-oriented system, can be generated automatically. Few, if any, such systems are available today. Examples in a more batch-oriented environment have been RPG and the Informatics MARK IV System. Likely new systems are emerging in this area. IBM, for example, has begun to emphasize such a capability by introducing the notion of "application enabling" systems.

At this point, these systems are geared to the professional programmer rather than the more casual user. Although the objective is a necessary and desirable one, it is probably not achievable for the "user" in the near future.

Under Software Development are four identified propositions that will probably have strong impact and ultimately become commonly available tools. The list is led by the fast-emerging *Data Dictionary* facility. This concept is now taking its place as an important architectural element alongside the data base management systems and teleprocessing monitors.

The remaining items are:

Implementation Systems—encompassing the expected growth of nonprocedural language systems.

Transaction Development System—combination of procedural and nonprocedural tools for generating interactive, screen dialogue-driven applications.

Programmer's Workbench—a computerized workstation consisting of a dedicated microcomputer, printer, and storage for assisting a programmer in performing his tasks.

Each of these entities is gathering a good technical basis and will surely make important contributions to future application development needs.

The Systems and Organization classification begins with some comments on three current terms which are placed in the category for which there is little hope. These terms are: *Robustness, Forgiving; User Oriented, Friendly;* and *Data-as-a-Resource*. In all three cases, imagery is generated that suggests more than the words actually say. For this reason alone the terms will probably fall into disuse. The first two of these concepts promote the idea that computer-based systems should favor the end user and lead to software that is convenient during operation of the system. This view is in opposition to the interests or convenience of the programmer who built the system in the first place. No doubt we will achieve these objectives in the 1980s but not because of these labels, rather because of the competitive offerings of different vendors who will vie for the same marketplaces.

Possession of data is of course important. Data in itself, however, is useless until it is transformed into information. Organizations will value data processing operations for the information which is supplied rather than for what data can be collected. The term *Data-as-a-Resource* will find an early grave.

A few other popular terms seem temporal in nature. These are *Data Base Administrator* and *Personal Computer*. In the case of the former, the suggestion that there is a single individual or even group that becomes the czar of all data for an organization seems a bit far-fetched and unrealizable in the scheme of large and complex organizations. The Personal Computer has already been discussed in Section 11.1. This term conjures a symbiosis which simply is not going to occur. A secretary's typewriter is surely not viewed as a personal item. Why should a computer be one? The term *personal computer* will go away, but the concept will remain under some other term already in the lexicon, such as "terminal," "workstation," or "desktop computer."

The last item mentioned in Category A is *Compatible Systems*. This subject is at the brink of present day concern because of the significant impact of the IBM plug-compatible mainframes. Compatible systems are in the limelight because of the continued extension of hardware life cycles and the presence of a vast body of software that can be exploited on more cost-effective hardware.

As software becomes an ever-increasing portion of the total computer system sale, the impact and economic benefit from "compatible" hardware itself becomes less significant. In the long run, compatible systems will disappear. We may ultimately be seeing compatible software systems. This reversal is already present in the microcomputer area.

Category B is a mixed bag of terms ranging from engineering capability to hardware disciplines. It begins with *Software Engineering*, a much-heralded label of the late 1970s. There is no doubt that the production of software requires an engineering foundation if we are ever to succeed in adequately predicting and fulfilling software project forecasts. Nevertheless, there is little basis today for an engineering discipline that can be imposed and measured so that programming can move from its current state as an art to a more scientific basis. No significant advance and promise is seen for the decade of the 1980s in software engineering and it is reluctantly placed in the category "may yet have something to offer."

System Security is another concept in search of realization. Aside from some hardware protection techniques and some software coding schemes, we are far from achieving what can be termed a "secure system." Nevertheless, in the next few years innovations will be forthcoming so that toward the end of the 1980s, some progress will be achieved.

While the Personal Computer is already debunked, the *Home Computer* idea is given a bit more hope. In fact, it is quite likely that there will be a computer in most *new* homes by the end of the 1980s. At that time one can envision that the basic construction and wiring of such homes will include computer-based control systems and interfaces to all electrical items as well as video and telephonic transmission. Current vintage homes will not have such built-in electronics and will move in a much slower fashion toward a wired facility. In any case it appears that computers will begin to find a place in many homes toward the end of the 1980s.

Voice Recognition will also take on increased application roles in the next decade. The initial applications will be in limited areas, primarily promotional and highly specialized. Wide utilization is at this time questionable, and therefore the term is relegated to Category B.

The next two terms are *Distributed Data Base* and *Distributed Processing*. Note that these related terms are split between Category B and Category C. At first glance, it might be concluded that one cannot exist without the other. However, there is a difference in distribution of computer power, application decoupling, and division of data among dispersed data processing units.

We do not envision dispersal of data. The issues of control and integrity are too encompassing. Rather we view dispersed computing as two modes of operation:

1. Decoupled functions for a specific application operating in a disjointed system.
2. Pre- and post-execution of portions of an application for which the data base is centralized and from which data subsets are derived as needed.

Relational Data Bases is another popular term in the limelight today. It appears that we are swinging emphasis from hierarchically structured data bases to those that are relational in nature. The trend is clearly in favor of relational, and it is expectd that this approach will dominate the data processing scene in the next decade.

The concept of the *User Workstation* has arrived. We have been driven to this notion as a result of the development of computer hierarchies. Processing capability has been moving in the direction of the user beginning with the minicomputer, accelerated by the microcomputer and brought home with the microprocessor itself. The User Workstation has been further accelerated by the development of electronic-based office systems that will assist the user to perform his daily tasks, whether oriented toward administration, production, or service.

If the User Workstation becomes the dominant tool for employing computers in the future, then *Transaction Processing* will be the dominant mode of utilizing the computer system. The User Workstation will be screen-oriented and all activity will be geared to the interactive dialogue between the human being and the formatted displays which will be presented and operated upon through keyboards and other notational devices. This does not mean that the batch system will go away. It will simply be interfaced through workstations and transactions-oriented processing systems.

The last classification for consideration is Applications. We are rather bold in pronouncing the prospects for *Electronic Files,* the *Paperless Office,* and the *Office of the Future.* These notions imply a radical change in office operation and management. Although we do not ignore the vast potential for improving the productivity of white collar service workers, we cannot accept that the radical notions suggested by these three terms will be readily and generally adopted, and we therefore relegate them to future disuse.

A death sentence is given to the term *Total Information System,* which seems to be a meaningless phrase, a catch-all for nothing.

Category B lists a number of potential applications that show promise, but still may fail to reach a level of acceptability during the next decade. These are the *Automated Office,* as distinct from the already cast-aside term, *Office of the Future.* Word processing will probably constitute the most real and significant change in the office of the 1980s. *Teleconferencing* is another office- and management-related concept that fosters the idea that face-to-face meetings between individuals can be eliminated, or at least minimized, with the advent of better communications and audio/visual hookups between people in remote locations. There is real potential for this capability, especially now that the cost of travel and lodgings is on the increase. Beyond these capabilities and the likelihood of electronic mail as discussed below, offices will probably not change very much in the next decade.

Electronic Funds Transfer is operating in limited areas today. It will continue to move into our business and personal lives in the next decade. We are cautious, however, in placing this term in Category B, since it may require another ten years before the majority of people will accept these notions.

Videotex Systems are making their appearance primarily on the European scene. They are also beginning to touch American society. However, it remains to be seen whether a large scale, viable business can develop along these lines, and therefore the term is reserved for this "wait and see" category.

Finally *Robotics* is cited, which is the current popularization of artificial intelligence. We certainly expect the beginning of developments in very simplified and specialized areas where a robot can perform a needed function. By the end of the 1980s we will be able to see whether wider prospects for robots can be realized.

Two entries are shown in Category C, *Electronic Mail* and *Query Systems*. The first of these will assuredly develop in the next decade to further communications, at least in the commercial and business area. The ability to capture text through word processing systems and subsequently transmit it throughout an organization by electronic means will advance rather substantially in the next few years. Electronic mail will become an economically viable alternative competing with normal communications to satisfy the increasing need for rapid delivery of information in keeping with the accelerated tempo of the business world.

The *Query System* consists of a variety of inquiry and interrogation systems played against existing data bases. The language or syntax of such systems varies from stylized English to structured, nonprocedural techniques. As data bases develop in the 1980s, containing more and more resident information, ready made Query Systems will become ever more useful to end users who need selective pieces of the data base or have ad hoc information requirements. The current existence of a number of such Query Systems makes clear that more and more of them will be available in the near future.

The prospects for current DP dreams and aspirations are not much different in scope and import than those of a few decades past. As we have seen in the first 30 years of the computer age, some will succeed and others will fall by the wayside. We have herein made our assessments for the future. Let us now wait and see.

TWELVE

The New Software Economics

During the last 30 years, hardware and systems software advances contributed continual quantum jumps in computer architectural and performance improvements. Users sought to maintain pace, and the application software began its chase after the hardware. Now, in the early years of the 1980s, the user community has entered a new era of computer economics. The prolongation of the software life cycle is the consequence, and it is now expected that hardware will chase after the software. This phenomenon is already occurring in the traditional, large-computer areas and, independently, in the nascent microcomputer marketplace.

Section 12.1 describes the scenario of the mainframe computer user, and Section 12.2 outlines the activity of the microcomputer user.

12.1. THE EVOLVING SOFTWARE ECONOMICS FOR LARGE COMPUTERS

During recent decades users were influenced primarily by the hardware implication of batch, on-line, data base, and now transaction environments. This transition is displayed in Figure 12.1, which shows an IBM-oriented trail reflecting a typical large computer user's movement from a 360/50 to a 360/65, then to a 370/155, next to a 370/158 configuration, and, finally, to an IBM 3033 system.

The user rode the crest of the wave throughout the sixties and seventies, embracing each of the innovations that became available. Initially, the user started in a batch environment operating under DOS, but soon found he required more sophisticated and complex operations. He advanced to OS, which required additional core memory.

The user outgrew his batch environment and entered the realm of teleprocessing by first incorporating data entry and inquiry capability with respect to certain limited business functions. These capabilities demanded random-access storage, terminals, and additional core. The user then required more sophisticated communications software and, therefore, a need for either BTAM or CICS. Of course, to achieve the desired response time, an upgrade to the next 360 model was in order.

In 1969, the user was attracted to the newly announced IBM 370 line and opted for a 370/155 mainframe, planning to move in the direction of data base. Now more of the applications would go on-line and, more important-ly, all of the files would become integrated under one system, the Informa-tion Management System (IMS) of IBM. In order to achieve the desired throughput and response, additional hardware was needed, involving more mass storage, additional I/O channels, more core memory, and the necessary controllers for remotely placed terminals and the associated communications network.

But in 1972, the user was dealt a blow when the virtual systems were announced and he found himself with a CPU that fell short of this technol-ogy. The user, however, was not necessarily outraged, if he was renting the

| | | SYSTEM IMPACT | |
COMPUTER	ENVIRONMENT	SOFTWARE	HARDWARE
IBM 360/50	Batch	DOS OS	128K-Byte Memory
IBM 360/65	On-Line	CICS/BTAM	Terminals 512K-Byte Memory Disks
IBM 370/155	Data Base	IMS	1M-Byte Memory Controllers Networks/Channels Mass Storage (DAT Box)
IBM 370/158	Transaction	VS	4M-Byte (Real) Memory Virtual System Front End RJE Stations Data Entry System Extension
IBM 30XX or PCM	Transaction Extended	MVS	8M-Byte (Real) Memory Bigger Virtual Memory Microcode Enhancement Cross Memory Services

Figure 12.1. Scenario of a user's mainframe data processing environment.

hardware and was not committed to a long-term purchase. For a modest monthly increase he was able to upgrade to the more modern IBM 370/158. This computer truly promised him the opportunity to enter the transaction-oriented world where virtual memories, as well as an entirely new operating system, VS, would become available. Naturally, he needed a better front end, remote job entry (RJE) stations, and more sophisticated data entry equipment. The virtual system became the "silent salesman."

Of course, if the user made an error in calculations and purchased his 370/155, the manufacturer did not forsake him. There was an opportunity to make a one-time purchase of the famous Dynamic Address Translation (DAT) box with which, for more than $300,000, he could field-upgrade the 155 to a virtual version of a 158.

Throughout the decade of the seventies, the manufacturer gave the user additional options that would make the hardware perform even more effectively. The user was able to increase his capacity and performance by continually upgrading to higher density and faster tapes, as well as disks, drums, and data cells.

All this technology and capability gave the typical user enormous new power and capacity at a price. It was not unreasonable, over any 10-year period, to move through three or four machine models, increase core by a factor of 10, add to auxiliary storage by two orders of magnitude, convert the operating system three or four times, and end with 50 to 100 terminals, both local and remote. The monthly cost for such additional capacity could well have increased by factors of 4 to 6 in that 10-year period.

Under this scenario, our hypothetical user operating a 360/50 computer in 1968 with 128K bytes of core moved to a 4M-byte 370/158 in an on-line, terminal-oriented environment, inclusive of several billion-byte capacity disks. The price/performance index comparing the two end points increased by a factor of 5. This user could well have spent $7 million in machine rental during the course of these 10 years and have ended by licensing software from IBM for a monthly fee of $5000.

But hardware advances did not stop. A new epoch began toward the end of the seventies when the IBM mainframe plug-compatible machines (PCM) began to proliferate. The advent of the IBM 30XX family at one end, and the IBM 43XX at the other, together with their look-alike compatible sisters, energized further hardware upgrades or additions in order to take advantage of lower memory and storage costs, as well as faster performance for the same dollar spent. Now the machine costs for the user could be more than $100,000, or $10,000 per month, depending upon which end of the spectrum the hardware fitted.

The situation with respect to software is now also a different matter. At the outset of this scenario, the software from IBM was "free," in that its availability was bundled with the machine rental. Also, there did not exist an independent commercial software market. Now, however, the monthly rental of IBM software could well be nearly $10,000 for the large computer, and

$5,000 for the smaller machine. Software acquired from the independents could easily add a monthly amount equivalent to another $5,000.

By all measures, the individual user obtained better unit performance as he escalated his hardware expenditure in the direction of more modern and more cost-effective equipment. In an advertising campaign of 1978, IBM correctly pointed out that a series of computations (really instruction executions) costing $1.26 when performed on a 1952 computer could be executed on 1978 computers for 0.7 of a penny, or a factor of 180 times less. Had the calculation been made using fixed dollars, it would have yielded an even more impressive improvement factor of 400. As pointed out in the following, however, the cost of *useful* business transactions may have been improved by far less—perhaps by a factor of only 5.

Users substantially upgraded the complexity of their applications consistent with the more sophisticated hardware and software environments that were made available to them. These more encompassing programs then required more hardware resources for their execution.

Over the course of the years, in keeping with the ever-increasing complexity of hardware, the operating system software also expanded. For example, compare the operating system of the IBM 650 machine in the mid-1950s to the operating systems of the 360 and 370 lines of the late 1960s and early 1970s. In this case, the number of lines of code for the operating and support system software increased by a factor of 10.

As the hardware manufacturer's operating system became more complex, the user bought more hardware in order to achieve or retain performance. The software product vendor, on the other hand, was obliged to stay in pace with the hardware manufacturer's environmental changes. The net effect was incrementally more hardware sold and greater costs thrust upon the software supplier, who was running on a treadmill.

There was an even more insidious factor involved while hardware was running the show. The producer of the more complicated operating environment (e.g., the hardware manufacturer offering a data base management system) benefited in three ways. First, this vendor typically charged for the unbundled portion of his operating environment software. Then, as already explained, he managed to sell more hardware to support the software.

The third factor is the machine efficiency issue with respect to operating the applications themselves. Over the last decade, the number of machine cycles utilized by the application programs has steadily decreased from approximately 80 to 85 percent in the 1960s, to current operations, where one obtains only 40 to 50 percent efficiency. In stating this, we recognize that the additional machine cycles taken by the more complex operating system are not necessarily lost to the user. Many features are now provided by the operating system itself that formerly had to be supplied by the application program or were completely ignored.

Nevertheless, this additional overhead requirement leads to yet further hardware acquisition. Typically, the choice is to add core or upgrade the model of the machine in order to achieve or retain throughput performance so that the application, in the more complex operating system environment, does not degrade in performance.

But manufacturers do not always make it easy for the user. Sometimes there was planned obsolescence to induce upgrading by the user. All one had to do was produce more modern peripherals and limit their operation to the latest CPU and/or operating system. This was the case, for example, in going from the IBM 2314 to 3330 storage devices, forcing a move from the 360 to the 370 family. Thus it was possible to replace a 360/65 by a 370/158, reduce the actual cost of auxiliary disk storage, and, in the process, enjoy more capacity and faster performance, but with the requirement of a system family and model change. Another technique was to limit the core size in one CPU model to force an upgrade to the next model level when more capacity was required.

There was also the trap of small numbers. How many users began to put up CICS and/or IMS environments as a result of experimenting and finding two terminals working exceedingly well? What was not appreciated was the occasional nonlinearity in hardware demand as a function of increasing the number of terminals. Hence, more terminals were added, more of the processor capacity was taxed, response time dropped—and the users complained.

A ready solution was the addition of more hardware to sustain the application performance, which by this time had reached the point of no return—the software had already been implemented. After all, the end user wants to be satisfied, and more hardware can usually solve performance problems in a rather transparent way.

These hardware vendor strategies led the user to fret and worry about what was around the corner. In such an environment, the user was prone to rent for fear of being locked into antiquated devices. He was also concerned that his software might become obsolete.

Times are now changing. With the prospect of long-term availability of higher performance and more cost-effective, compatible hardware, the user can focus on his cumulative investment in software. Extending the life cycle of developed software will realize economic benefits heretofore not readily available.

Two fundamental reasons for the change in the industry can be identified. They are attributable to technological and operational factors. In both the hardware and systems software areas we have arrived at a remarkably stable situation from the point of view of implementing applications. It is feasible to design application systems so that the ultimate software can operate in various environments.

For example, a generic terminal can be the input and/or output medium in a transaction-based order entry system. Only at runtime is it necessary to fix the mapping of this generic terminal onto a specific physical device. Similarly, this is the case in printing output when operating in a spooling mode.

There is also a significant stability in the systems software area. So many layers of protective systems and utility software now surround the application that the user can isolate his specific problem and have substantial flexibility in its implementation and ultimate maintenance.

Thus, not only can the user leave the problems of the basic executive and input/output control to the operating systems software, but applications can also be quite independent of such functions as:

Teleprocessing monitors

Data base manager

Data dictionary

Transaction processor

Security control

Restart/recovery

To achieve ultimate flexibility, one or both of the following tasks must still be done:

The selection of a few universal implementation languages and the standardization of the interfaces (i.e., hooks) to the various systems software entities.

The fixing of machine internals and the optimization of the hardware cost effectiveness ratio.

In such an environment, the focus can be on maximizing the application software, which becomes central to the various interests of the users. Interestingly enough, we are rapidly moving there. Certain operational situations themselves are encouraging a change in the economics.

First, consider the question of a common language. COBOL is by far the overwhelming choice. In the GUIDE annual survey cited in Section 9.5, COBOL was clearly the front-running application development language when measured against Assembler, FORTRAN, PL/I, BASIC, APL, RPG, and MARK IV.

The operational success of IBM itself makes the second of the above goals realizable. Indeed, it is the vast amount of software for the very large IBM user community that has stimulated the plug-compatible CPU manufacturers to standardize production of computer mainframes based on the IBM 370 family. And, to help matters, IBM has publicly stated that it expects to further its product line on an evolutionary, not revolutionary, philosophy.

Today's user, therefore, can stabilize his software investment over a substantial period of time. It is for this reason that users are advised to take the following steps in capitalizing on the new software economics:

Adopt major software utilities offered by the manufacturer and independent software product vendors.

Inventory the currently operating software and identify what is outmoded and/or requires undue maintenance.

Replace the outmoded software by software products if available and if feasible.

Survey current and expected needs and determine if solutions are available through purchasable software.

For needs not satisfied by purchasable software, consider commissioning a software product vendor, either alone or in the company of other interested parties.

In light of the foregoing, reassess the organization and budget of the DP activity and determine if there is a restructuring option (for example, reduction in further software maintenance costs).

This advice may not seem profound, but this new view of software relative to hardware may be the single most beneficial step users can take to achieve more cost-effective computing. And the software product has a timely role in contributing to this new economics.

Users may have considered purchasing software years ago and concluded that the software product vendors were young, immature, and not to be entrusted with their business, that the products looked primitive and unstable or that there were not many installations and therefore there was a question of acceptability. Sometimes the user really did not know what he wanted.

But all that has changed. It is time for a second look, and the timing could not be better, as users seek new approaches to riding the crest of the wave of the new software economics.

12.2. THE RAPID EVOLUTION OF SOFTWARE DOMINANCE FOR MICROCOMPUTERS

The mainframe computer scenario described in Section 12.1 covered a period of more than 20 years. Comparable progress took place in the microcomputer marketplace in less than five years. This history is discussed by highlighting a few examples of hardware and software offerings as shown in Figure 12.2. The progression of this table is ordered so that entries in each successive step embody the capability of previously listed offerings.

The first microprocessor-based computers appeared in the mid-seventies when several kits became available for constructing one's own computer. Shortly thereafter, an economically viable industry began when Tandy Corporation introduced its off-the-shelf TRS-80, Model I computer through the Radio Shack retail outlets. This device, priced at $599 in 1979, was aimed at the hobbyist. It provided an 8-bit processor, an auxiliary cassette storage unit, and a 4K-byte memory. Memory expansion up to 16K bytes was an option, as was several hundred thousand bytes of floppy disk storage. The initial software attraction consisted of a rudimentary, but excellent, ROM-based BASIC interpreter and some games. This introduction was a notable success. In three years, more than 100,000 such computers were sold, exceed-

| COMPUTER | ENVIRONMENT | SYSTEM IMPACT | |
		SOFTWARE	HARDWARE
TRS-80, Model I	Hobby	GAMES BASIC	8-bit processor 16K-byte memory 300K-byte floppy disk
Apple II	Business	FORTRAN COBOL VISICALC™	64K-byte memory Expansion slots
Xerox 820	Professional	CP/M™ WORDSTAR™	1M-byte floppy disk Communications standards Full screen
Altos ACS8000	Extended Business	MP/M II™ PEACHTREE	208K-byte memory Multi-terminal Hard disk
IBM Personal Computer	Super- Professional	IBM DOS CP/M-86™ PASCAL	16-bit processor, 8-bit bus 256K-byte memory Graphics, audio Expanded keyboard
Altos ACS8600	Complex Business	MP/M-86™ XENIX™	16-bit processor, 16-bit bus to 1M-byte memory to 80M-byte disk storage
Convergent Technologies IWS™/AWS™	Cluster	CTOS™	Multi-workstations Networking Expanded screen

Figure 12.2. Scenario of a user's evolving microcomputing environment.

ing the entire worldwide population of larger computers at the time. The commercial success of this endeavor did not go unnoticed, stimulating an industry that has since dramatically broadened in market scope and in technical depth.

Following close behind the TRS-80 was the introduction of the Apple II computer by Apple Computer Inc. Apple II moved hardware a step forward by allowing memory expansion to 64K bytes and facilitating the attachment of peripheral devices through easily accessible expansion slots. System software was broadened by making available some of the big system computer languages such as COBOL and FORTRAN. The focus of this machine shifted from games to business, helped immensely by the introduction of VisiCalc, a new piece of software that automated the calculations associated with accounting spreadsheets.

Both Tandy and Apple had chosen to stake their futures on proprietary operating systems. Language standards, however, began to emerge, mainly through the efforts of Microsoft's BASIC interpreters and compilers.

The overwhelming success of these top vendors attracted many competitors, such as Commodore, Ohio Scientific, Exidy, Cromenco, Durango, and others. Some of the early entries, however, have dropped out of the race, and some were absorbed by other entities.

The device on which this commercial activity depended, and which became known as the personal computer, moved another bold step forward in a short time. This resulted from a software endeavor of significant proportions, the CP/M™ operating system. This product was developed by Digital Research Inc., and became a de facto standard for all but a few of the largest suppliers. The economic rationale for standardization was clear. A good, long list of application software was developing under CP/M. Hence, new hardware systems could attract this software as long as CP/M became the host operating system.

Transportability of software, however, does not depend on operating systems alone. The implementation language is also a necessary factor. Thus, the coupling of the popular CP/M operating system with the widespread Microsoft BASIC (MBASIC) really became the vehicle that made it easy to accomplish software proliferation and exploitation.

The recognition of leverage from software through standardization was not restricted to hardware manufacturers producing new systems. Innovative peripheral suppliers noted the possibility and practicality of enhancing non-CP/M machines, such as the Apple and TRS-80, by attaching a modest hardware/software unit that turns the native machine into a CP/M host. Suddenly, software became the leader and, as in the case of the mainframe computers discussed in Section 12.1, the microcomputer hardware began its chase after software.

The impact of CP/M can be gauged by the fact that several hundred manufacturers, both domestic and foreign, adopted it. This policy is exemplified by Xerox, which delivers its 820 line with a standard CP/M system. Thus, on the first day of this offer, Wordstar™, a popular word processing system, became available on the most advanced 8-bit machine of the moment.

Xerox emphasized the professional aspect of the desktop or personal computer. The auxiliary storage was more varied including an eight-inch floppy disk arrangement with 1 million byte storage capacity. Another advanced feature is the provision of "full" screen capacity, allowing presentation of 24 lines by 80 characters, equivalent to that of big system terminals. Finally, Xerox emphasized standard communications facilities, recognizing the emergence of the workstation concept which will require links to other computers.

While the struggle for market positioning was going on in the $500 to $5000 price range, as exemplified by the offerings so far mentioned, a second tier of microcomputer-based vendors were emerging. These manufacturers aimed their product line toward the more extended business needs of the marketplace by meeting the need for a much larger storage capacity and for simultaneously operating terminals. Hence, the systems departed from a personal computer image to a true small business system. Good examples of such suppliers are Vector Graphic Inc., Altos Computer Systems, and Cado Systems Corporation.

This hardware advance is exemplified by the Altos ACS8000 offer of a 208K-byte memory system with hard disk capacity up to 40 megabytes, operating CP/M, and the multi-user version of CP/M, called MP/M™. Independently emerging was the micro-based business application software offered by Retail Sciences Inc. and dubbed Peachtree. The Peachtree line-up, now part of Management Science America, includes general ledger, accounts receivable, accounts payable, inventory management, order entry, payroll, and sales analysis. Naturally, this software is based on CP/M and MBASIC so that almost the entire world of micro-hardware can be embraced.

The break with 8-bit desktop computers came in 1981, when IBM offered its entry-level product based on the 16-bit processor, but retaining the 8-bit data transfer capability. This offering gave the appearance of a super-professional tool—promising a compromise between a new operating system (IBM-DOS) and the option of a CP/M variant, CP/M-86, suitable for 16-bit machines.

The memory of the IBM Personal Computer is now expandable to 256K bytes, and the keyboard is a more complex input and control device. A combination of software systems, such as Pascal, and hardware features for graphics and audio, enhanced the hardware's capability to provide a more complex and sophisticated workstation, including color at the screen. The popular Peachtree business systems became an official IBM offering, as did VisiCalc and the Easywriter™ word processing system. The key, revolutionary step taken by IBM was the application of the lessons already learned elsewhere—let the hardware fit the software. IBM turned to its own advantage the very technique used against it in the big computer marketplace, where competitors leveraged IBM-based software with their own compatible equipment.

A full 16-bit processor with a 16-bit data transfer bus is exemplified by the Altos ACS8600 line, an outgrowth of its comparable 8-bit ACS8000 offering. Now we see the transition of 8-bit software technology reflected by the multi-user operating system of Digital Research's MP/M-86II™ in a head-on clash with the emerging Xenix™ operating system of Microsoft. Xenix is a Bell Laboratories Unix™-derived system bringing the larger minicomputer technology down to the microcomputer.

Another advance reflected in the Altos system is the potential of extending the memory to 1 million bytes, with up to 80 million bytes of hard disk storage. This system, capable of supporting eight terminals in a multiprocessing, multitasking environment, lays the groundwork for solving complex business problems.

Finally, we reach current state of the art through the offering of the Convergent Technologies cluster configurations of workstations. This approach to modularity in intelligent workstations, shared peripherals and networking affords the user big computer sophistication and power at microcomputer prices. With a proprietary operating system, CTOS™, and the future availability of Xenix, we have the balance of capability providing environments for both transaction-based application execution and application software development. The networking and communication facility allows for integrating workstation functions with companion workstations as well as more remote mainframes or other clustered systems. The video capability and appearance is outstanding, providing a new level of achievement with a 34- by 132-character position display with each character formed from a 10 × 15 pixel raster.

The extremely fast pace of microcomputer evolution has been immensely assisted by the rapid achievement of de facto standards in both hardware and software. Underlying this progression was the initial widespread popularity of certain chips, such as the Intel 8080 and the Zilog Z80. Uniformity of interfaces was immeasurably helped by the standards set by certain bus structures, such as the S-100 and Intel's Multibus[R]. Communications were effectively standardized by the line conventions of the RS-232C serial connection and standards set by IEEE 488.

Software achievements were equal to the hardware advances in adopting standards for operating systems and languages. Even end-user products, such as VisiCalc, because of widespread marketplace presence, are leading to de facto standards such as file format conventions. This will make it easier for application software to bridge hardware physical gaps and software logical ones.

Conclusion

The computer has brought society to the brink of an intellectual revolution, an event with effects so far-reaching as to be presently incalculable. It will influence social behavior as well as economics. The resulting metamorphosis of our society will someday be compared to that following the industrial revolution of 200 years ago. Indeed, both movements owe their dramatic potential to similar breakthroughs: the discovery and applicability of fractional horsepower motors and the development of low-cost, powerful microprocessors.

Observers of the computer industry agree that computers in general, and microcomputers more specifically, will significantly pervade both business and the home. Professionals will augment their analysis and decision-making activity through workstation support, provided by desktop computers; individuals in the privacy of their homes will become increasingly dependent on information appliances driven by the computer. By 1990 it is expected that 80 percent of the labor force in the United States will interact with computers, and more than 50 percent will need some knowledge about using the computer.

The magnitude of the challenge can also be judged by market statistics that forecast a growth in microcomputer use from an installed base of less than one million in the early 1980s to as many as 30 million by 1990.

This enormous growth potential in exploiting the benefits of data processing may not be realized to the full unless comparable progress is made in producing and understanding software. This has been the topic and focus of this book. The discerning user must learn to understand the requirements of his job, know how to evaluate software and then bring this understanding to bear on the resolution of his problems through intelligent utilization of software.

The focus of data processing for the first 30 years of the computer era has been on hardware. This had led many to espouse the notion of *computer literacy* as a distinguishing mark of a developed society, placing emphasis on the means rather than the end. What is now required is a *software literacy*, because it is the software that ultimately leads to the solution of a user's problem. To create and disseminate this literacy is the challenge now before us.

APPENDIX A

Terms and Acronyms

The following is a list of acronyms and special terms used in the data processing and computer fields.

BASIC *Beginners All Purpose Instruction Code*, a computer language suitable for beginners

COBOL *Common Business Oriented Language*, a computer language oriented to business data processing computing

CP/M Control Program for Microcomputers, the name of a commercial operating system offered by Digital Research, Inc.

CPU Central Processing Unit

CRT Cathode ray tube, a video display device

DB/DC Data base, data communications

DBMS Data Base Management System

DMS Data Management System

DP Data Processing

EDITOR (Or Text Editor), a program facilitating the computer entry and manipulation of character strings of information, allowing operations on such strings for purposes of modifying, moving, deleting, and rearranging such information

EDP Electronic Data Processing

FMS File Management System

FORTRAN *Formula Translation*, a computer language oriented to scientific and engineering computing

IMS Information Management System, a software product of IBM

I/O Input/Output

IOCS Input/Output Control System

JCL Job Control Language

K Kilobyte, representing multiples of 1024 units when referring to computer memory or storage size

M	Megabyte, representing multiples of one million units when referring to computer memory or storage size
MIS	Management Information System
OS	Operating System
PASCAL	A computer language suitable for developing systems oriented programs
PCM	Plug Compatible Machine
RAM	Random Access Memory
ROM	Read Only Memory
TP	Teleprocessing
WP	Word Processing

APPENDIX B

Software Product Directories and Catalogs

1. Auerbach Publishers, Inc.
   Computer Technology Reports
   Software Reports
2. Centre D'Experimentation de Progiciels (France)
   Guide European des Products Logiciels
3. CUYB Publications, Inc. (England)
   International Directory of Software
4. Datapro Research Corporation
   Directory of Software
   Annual User Ratings of Proprietary Software
5. Honeywell Information System, Inc.
   Honeywell Software Catalogue
   Application Reference Index
6. IBM
   Keyword Index and Program Information
   Service for Consultants Manual
   Systems and Products Guide
   Applications and Abstracts
7. Imprint Software
   International Microcomputer Software Directory
8. Infratest Information Services (Germany)
   ISIS Software Report
9. International Computer Programs, Inc.
   Interface Series
   The ICP Software Directory

10. Management Information Corporation
    Packaged Software Buyer's Guide

11. U.S. Government, Department of Commerce, National Technical
    Information Service
    Directory of Computerized Data Files and Related Technical
      Reports
    Directory of Federal Statistical Data Files
    Directory of Computer Software and Related Reports
    Computer Control and Information Theory

12. U.S. Government, NASA, Technology Utilization Office
    Computer Software Management and Information Center
      (COSMIC), University of Georgia

13. UNIVAC
    Consultant's Handbook

APPENDIX C

Computer Organizations and Companies

The following is a list of organizations and companies identified in this text.

AFIPS
American Federation of Information Processing
  Societies, Inc.
1815 North Lynn Street
Arlington, VA 22209
(703) 558-3600

ACM
Association for Computing Machinery
1133 Avenue of the Americas
New York, New York 10036
(212) 265-6300

ADAPSO
Association of Data Processing Service Organizations
1300 North 17th Street
Suite 300
Arlington, Virginia 22209
(703) 522-5055

Auerbach
Auerbach Publishers, Inc.
6560 North Park Drive
Pennsauken, New Jersey 08109
(609) 662-2070

Datamation
Datamation
Technical Publishing Company
666 Fifth Avenue
New York, New York 10103
(212) 489-2200

Datapro   Datapro Research Corporation
                     1805 Underwood Boulevard
                     Delran, New Jersey 08075
                     (609) 764-0100

GUIDE   GUIDE
                     One Illinois Center
                     111 East Wacker Drive
                     Suite 600
                     Chicago, Illinois 60601
                     (213) 644-6610

ICP   International Computer Programs, Inc.
                     9000 Keystone Crossing
                     Indianapolis, Indiana 46240
                     (317) 844-7461

IDC   International Data Corporation
                     P.O. Box 955
                     5 Speen Street
                     Framingham, Massachusetts 01701
                     (617) 872-8200

IEEE   Institute of Electrical and Electronics Engineers, Inc.
                     345 East 47th Street
                     New York, New York 10017
                     (212) 644-7900

INPUT   INPUT
                     2471 East Bayshore, 600
                     Palo Alto, California 94303
                     (415) 493-1600

SHARE, Inc.   SHARE, Inc.
                     One Illinois Center
                     111 East Wacker Drive
                     Chicago, Illinois 60601
                     (312) 822-0932

Bibliography

Allen, F. E., "The History of Language Processor Technology in IBM," *IBM J. Res. Dev.*, **25**(5), 535–548 (September 1981).

Alloway, R. M., "User Managers' Systems Needs," Center for Information Systems Research, Massachusetts Institute of Technology, May 1980.

Astrahan, M. M., and D. D. Chamberlin, "Implementation of a Structured English Query Language," *Commun. ACM*, **18**(10), 580–588 (October 1975).

Auslander, M. A., D. C. Larkin, and A. L. Scherr, "The Evolution of the MVS Operating System," *IBM J. Res. Dev.*, **25**(5), 471–482 (September 1981).

Bernstein, M. I., "Hardware is Easy: It's Software That's Hard," *Datamation*, November 15, 1978.

Boehm, B. W., "Software Engineering," IEEE *Trans. Comput.*, December 1976a.

Boehm, B. W., *Software Engineering Economics*, Prentice-Hall, 1981.

Boehm, B. W. "Software and Its Impact: A Qualitative Assessment," *Datamation*, May 1973.

Boehm, B. W., "Structured Programming: Problems, Pitfalls, and Payoffs," *TRW Software Series*, July 1976b.

Braddock, Fred, "How to Stretch Your Software Lifecycle," *ICP Interface*, Spring 1980.

Brooks, F., *The Mythical Man-Month*, Addison Wesley, 1975.

Business Week, "Missing Computer Software," September 1, 1980a.

Business Week, "A Rush of New Companies to Mass-Produce Software," September 1, 1980b.

Caine, S. H., and E. K. Gordon, "PDL—A Tool for Software Design," *Proc. Am. Fed. Info. Process. Soc.*, 1975.

Cave, W. C., and A. B. Salisbury, "Controlling the Software Life Cycle—The Project Management Task," IEEE *Trans. Software Eng.*, **SE-4**(4), 326–334 (July 1978).

Champine, G. A., "Perspectives on Business Data Processing," *Computer*, November 1980.

Chen, Edward T., "Program Complexity and Programmer Productivity." IEEE *Trans. Software Eng.*, **SE-4**(3), 187–194 (May 1978).

Christensen, K., G. P. Fitsos, and C. P. Smith, "A Perspective on Software Science," *IBM Systems J.*, **20**(4), 1981.

Clapp, Judith A., "Designing Software for Maintainability," *Comput. Design*, September 1981.

Computer, IEEE *Comput. Soc.*, **14**(4), April 1981a (Issue devoted to Programming Environments).

Computer, IEEE *Comput. Soc.*, June 1981b (Issue devoted to Ada—Programming in the 80's).

Cornym, J. J., "Life Cycle Cost Models for Comparing Computer Family Architectures," *Proc. Nat. Comput. Conf.*, 1977.

Cottrell, S., "Applications Software Trends: Evolution or Revolution?" *Gov. Data Systems,* January/February 1978.

Crespi-Reghizzi, Stefano, Pierluigi Corti, and Alberto Dapra, "A Survey of Microprocessor Languages," *Computer,* January 1980.

Data Base, Assoc. Comput. Mach., 11(3), Winter-Spring 1980.

Data Decisions, "Software Users Survey," Cherry Hill, New Jersey, October 1980.

Datamation, August 1981 (Issue devoted to Software & Services).

Datapro, "Estimating Software Development Costs," Datapro Research Corp., October 1976.

Datapro, "User Ratings of Proprietary Software," December 1980, 70E-010-40a.

DeRoze, B. C., and T. H. Nyman, "The Software Life Cycle—A Management and Technological Challenge in the Department of Defense," IEEE *Trans. Software Eng.,* **SE-**4(4), 309–318 (July 1978).

Dolotta, T. A., M. I. Bernstein, R. S. Dickson, Jr., N. A. France, B. A. Rosenblatt, D. M. Smith and T. B. Steel, Jr., *Data Processing in 1980–1985,* Wiley, New York, 1976.

EDP Analyzer, "The Arrival of Common Systems", Canning Publ., Inc., 15(1), 1–12 (January 1977).

EDP Analyzer, "DBMS for Mini-Computers," Canning Publ., Inc., 19(3), 1–13 (March 1981a).

EDP Analyzer, " 'Programming' by End Users," Canning Publ., Inc., 19(5), 1–15 (May 1981b).

EDP Analyzer, "Supporting End User Programming," Canning Publ., Inc., 19(6), 1–15 (June 1981c).

EDP Analyzer, "A New View of Data Dictionaries," Canning Publ., Inc., 19(7), 1–15 (July 1981d).

EDP Analyzer, "Easing the Software Maintenance Burden," Canning Publ., Inc., 19(8), 1–12 (August 1981e).

EDP Analyzer, "Developing Systems by Prototyping," Canning Publ., Inc., 19(9), 1–14 (September 1981f).

EDP Analyzer, "Application System Design Aids," Canning Publ., Inc., 19(10), 1–17 (October 1981g).

EDP Analyzer, "Portable Software for Small Machines," Canning Publ., Inc., 19(12), 1–12 (December 1981h).

EDP Analyzer, "Programming Work-Stations," Canning Publ., Inc., 1–13, October 1979.

Electronic Design, "Systems & Software," Hayden Publ. Co., November 1981 (Issue devoted to Software Automation).

Enos, Judith C., and R. L. Van Tilburg, "Software Design," *Computer,* February 1981.

Eventoff, William, Gary Anderson, Ronald Price, and Irving Rabinowitz, "Ada: A Significant Software Engineering Tool," *Mini-Micro Systems,* 209–231 (1981).

Fagan, M. E., "Design and Code Inspections to Reduce Errors in Program Development," *IBM Systems J.,* 15(3), 182–211 (1976).

Fisher, D. A., *Automatic Data Processing Costs in the Defense Department,* Report P-1046, Inst. Defense Anal., October 1974.

Gutz, Steve, A. I. Wasserman, and M. J. Spier, "Personal Development Systems for the Professional Programmer," *Computer,* April 1981.

Hayes, Phil, E. Ball, and R. Reddy, "Breaking the Man-Machine Communication Barrier," *Computer,* March 1981.

Horowitz, Ellis and Robert Hollies, "A Study of the Computer Software Products Industry," Univ. So. Calif., 1981.

IBM, "Inspections in Application Development—Introduction and Implementation Guidelines," Report No GC20-2000-0, July 1977.

ICP Insider's Letter, "Software Pricing: Reflections on the Black Art," Intern. Comput. Progr., Inc., 5(12), (December 1977).

ICP Report No. S1, "ICP Software Sellers Business Practices Report," Intern. Comput. Progr., Inc., June 1978.

ICP "Eleventh Annual Million Dollar Awards Ceremony," Intern. Comput. Progr., Inc., April 1982.

IDC 1981 Computer Industry Briefing Session, Intern. Data Corp., March 1981a.

IDC's SASI Memorandum, "Marketing and Pricing Strategies of the Packaged Software Vendors," Intern. Data Corp., March 1981b.

IDC Report 1978, "The Independent Packaged Software Market," Intern. Data Corp., March 1979.

IEEE Transactions on Software Engineering, SE-4(4), July 1978 (Issue devoted to Software Management).

IEEE Transactions on Software Engineering, SE-7(5), September 1981 (Issue devoted to Programming Environments).

Interface, 1981 Special Edition, Intern. Comput. Progr., Inc., 156 pp. (Issue devoted to computing services industry).

Jackson, M. A. *Principles of Program Design*, Academic Press, New York, 1975.

Jensen, Randall W., "Structured Programming," *Computer*, March 1981.

Jones, T. C., "Measuring Programming Quality and Productivity," *IBM System J.,* 17(1), 39–63 (1978).

Jones, T. C., "Programing Productivity Issues for the Eighties," IEEE 1981, EH0186-7.

Joslin, P. H., "System Productivity Facility," *IBM Systems J.,* 20(4), 388–406(1981).

Keet, Ernest E., "Eliminating the Risks of Buying Software," *Infosystems*, Hitchcock Publ. Co., February 1978.

Kendall, R. C., Management Perspectives on Programs, Programming, and Productivity, *Proc. Guide 45*, Atlanta, Georgia, November 1977.

Lanergan, Robert G., and Denis K. Dugan, "Requirements for Implementing a Successful Reusable Code Productivity System," Raytheon Co. Missile Systems Div., 1980.

Lee, Edwin, "Debunking the Development System Myth," *Mini—Micro Systems*, Cahners Publ. Co., August 1980.

Lientz, Bennet P., and E. Burton Swanson, "Problems in Application Software Maintenance," *Commun. ACM,* 24(11), 763–769 (November 1981).

Ling, Robert F., "General Considerations on the Design of an Interactive System for Data Analysis," *Commun. ACM,* 23(3), 147–154 (March 1980).

Lucas, P., "Formal Semantics of Programming Languages: VDL," *IBM J. Research Dev.,* 25(5), 549–561 (September 1981).

McFadden, Fred R., and James D. Suver, "Costs and Benefits of a Data Base System," *Harvard Bus. Rev.,* January/February 1978.

McGee, W. C., "Data Base Technology," *IBM J. Research Dev.,* 25(5), 505–519 (September 1981).

Miller, L. A., "Natural Language Programming: Styles, Strategies, and Contrasts," *IBM Systems J.,* 20(2), 184–215 (1981).

Myers, E. D., "Should Software Be Copyrighted," *Datamation*, March 1978.

Myers, Ware, "A Statistical Approach to Scheduling Software Development," *Computer*, December 1978.

NBS Software Tools Database, ed. R. C. Houghton and K. A. Oakley, (U.S.) Nat. Bur. Standards, October 1980.

Nyborg, P. S., et al., *Information Processing in the United States*, AFIPS, 1977.

Pantages, A., "Software Packages Explode on World Market," *Datamation*, December 1978.

Phister, M., *Data Processing Technology and Economics*, Santa Monica Publ. Co., 1976.

Proceedings Application Development Symposium, Share Inc., and Guide Intern. Corp., 1979.

Putnam, Lawrence H., "A General Empirical Solution to the Macro Software Sizing and Estimating Problem," *IEEE Trans. Software Eng.*, SE-4(4), 345-361 (July 1978).

Raskin, Jef, and Tom Whitney, "Perspectives on Personal Computing," *Computer*, January 1981.

Rauscher, Tomlinson G., and Phillip M. Adams, "Microprogramming: A Tutorial and Survey of Recent Developments," *IEEE Trans. on Comput.*, January 1980.

Reisner, Phyllis, "Use of Psychological Experimentation as an Aid to Development of a Query Language," *IEEE Transactions on Software Engineering*, Institute of Electrical and Electronic Engineers, SE-3(3), 218-229 (May 1977).

Reisner, Phyllis, "Human Factors Studies of Database Query Languages: A Survey and Assessment," *Computing Surveys*, 13(1), 13-31 (March 1981).

Ross, D. T., and K. E. Schoman, Jr., "Standard Analysis for Requirements Definition," *IEEE Trans. Software Eng.*, SE-3(1), January 1977.

Sammet, Jean E., "History of IBM's Technical Contributions to High Level Programming Languages," *IBM J. Research Dev.*, 25(5), 520-534 (September 1981).

Shneiderman, Ben, "Human Factors Experiments in Designing Interactive Systems," *Computer*, December 1979.

Sisson, Roger L., "Solution Systems and MIS," *Proc. Twelfth Annu. Conf., Soc. Mgmt. Info. Systems*, September 1980.

Snyders, Jan, "Data Dictionary: The Manager in DBMS," *Computer Decisions*, October 1981.

Snyders, Jan, "How to Buy Packages," *Computer Decisions*, June 1979.

Snyders, Jan, "Slashing Software Maintenance Costs," *Computer Decisions*, July 1979.

Soltis, Frank G., "Design of a Small Business Data Processing System," *Computer*, September 1981.

Teitelbaum, Tim, and Thomas Reps, "The Cornell Program Synthesizer: A Syntax-Directed Programming Environment," *Commun. ACM*, 24(9), 563-573 (September 1981).

Waltz, Daniel L., "An English Language Question Answering System for a Large Relational Database," *Commun. ACM*, 21(7), 526-539 (July 1978).

Wasserman, A. I., and D. T. Shewmake, "Rapid Prototyping of Interactive Information Systems," Med. Info. Sci., Univ. Calif., San Francisco, 1981.

Wasserman, A. I., "Software Engineering: The Turning Point," *Computer*, September 1978.

Wasserman, A. I., "Software Tools and the User Software Engineering Project," in *Software Development Tools*, ed. W. E. Riddle and R. E. Fairley, Springer-Verlag, 1980a.

Wasserman, A. I., "Toward Integrated Software Development Environments," *Scientia*, Annus LXXIV, 115(9-10-11-12) 1980b.

Wasserman, A. I., "User Software Engineering and the Design of Interactive Systems," Proc. 5th Intern. Conf. Software Eng., San Diego, California, March 1981.

Wilks, Yorick, "An Intelligent Analyzer and Understander of English," *Commun. ACM*, 18(5), 264-274 (May 1975).

Wulf, William A., "Trends in the Design and Implementation of Programming Languages," *Computer*, January 1980.

Zelkowitz, M. V., "Perspectives on Software Engineering," *Comput. Surv.*, 10(2), 197-216 (June 1978).

Zloof, Moshe M., "QBE/OBE: A Language for Office and Business Automation," *Computer*, May 1981.

Subject Index

Supplier Index

Product Index